WOLF COUNTRY

WOLF
COUNTRY

ELEVEN YEARS TRACKING THE ALGONQUIN WOLVES

JOHN B. THEBERGE

with MARY T. THEBERGE

Illustrations by

MARY T. THEBERGE

M&S

Canadian Cataloguing in Publication Data

Theberge, John B., 1940-
Wolf country: eleven years tracking the Algonquin wolves

Includes bibliographical references and index.
ISBN 0-7710-8562-1

1. Wolves – Ontario – Algonquin Provincial Park.
I. Theberge, Mary T.   II. Title.

QL737.C22T43 1998   599.773'09713'147   C98-931230-5

To the extent that this book contributes to an ecological perspective about
wolves and their world, Mary and I should share the credit. How we selected
and strung the events of eleven years together into an accurate account has been
a joint effort. To the extent that our story disturbs people, we share the blame.

We acknowledge the financial support of the Government of Canada through
the Book Publishing Industry Development Program for our publishing activities. We further acknowledge the support of the Canada Council for the Arts
and the Ontario Arts Council for our publishing program.

Typeset in Bembo by M&S, Toronto
Cartography by Visutronx
Printed and bound in Canada

McClelland & Stewart Inc.
The Canadian Publishers
481 University Avenue
Toronto, Ontario
M5G 2E9

1 2 3 4 5   02 01 00 99 98

To the wolves of Algonquin, in hope that our research
and this book make their world a safer place

CONTENTS

LIST OF MAPS

Foreword by Monte Hummel

President, World Wildlife Fund Canada

It happened more by accident than design. Ontario's Algonquin Park, which was set aside over a hundred years ago for entirely different reasons, has become a last refuge for the southern-most viable population of wolves in North America. Now our challenge is to make sure the park continues to serve that purpose. And no one has furthered this goal more than John and Mary Theberge.

The Theberges come about as close as any two humans could to knowing the Algonquin landscape the way a wolf does – the den areas, rendezvous sites, deer yards, beaver lodges, moose browse, salt licks, travel routes, game trails, ridges, low spots, rivers, lakes, and the territory of an adjacent pack. They know where the kills are on frozen lakes, how many pups survived the summer in each family group, and when a strange wolf is moving *in*, not just moving through. But most important, John and Mary know what they don't know, as their research poses an endless stream of puzzles and surprises that leave us all scratching our heads trying to figure out "what's going on."

Based on this knowledge, these questions, and thousands of hours in the bush, the Theberges are clearly left deeply concerned about the future of Algonquin wolves. Consequently, this book sounds a note of disappointment and impatience with the pace at which steps are being taken to ensure the wolves' long-term survival. World Wildlife Fund shares this frustration. But we also recognize that we've come a long way since the 1950s when government employees were legally killing wolves in the park. That has stopped. There is no longer a bounty on wolves in Ontario.

Thanks to John and Mary's work, the provincial government has extended protection to Algonquin wolves outside the eastern boundary of the park when they follow deer there in late winter. I'm convinced that we will soon see wolves dignified with long-overdue bag limits and seasons in Ontario. Finally, a new multi-party initiative shows promise of extending protection outside Algonquin to all wolves that have 50 per cent or more of their range inside the park.

So the momentum is on the side of the wolf, as it should be. But this momentum hasn't come about by magic. It has been built by vigilance, pushing, and teamwork with kindred spirits both in and outside government. Its maintenance requires an active, adequately supported research presence in the field. Above all, it requires agreement that without healthy "wolf country," which is the crucible of evolution itself, there can be no wolves or anything else marked by wildness.

This book is testimony to ongoing work. Today, John's students continue his efforts. John was a student of Doug Pimlott, who left John his canoe when he died in 1978 and who in turn was a student of Aldo Leopold, who died fighting a fire in 1948. Their combined achievement is a reflection of great beginnings, deep traditions, and an important cause. It now remains for the rest of us to speak up and make sure none of this good work has been in vain.

Radio-Collared Wolf Packs Studied in
Algonquin Park and Adjacent Southeast Land, 1987-1998

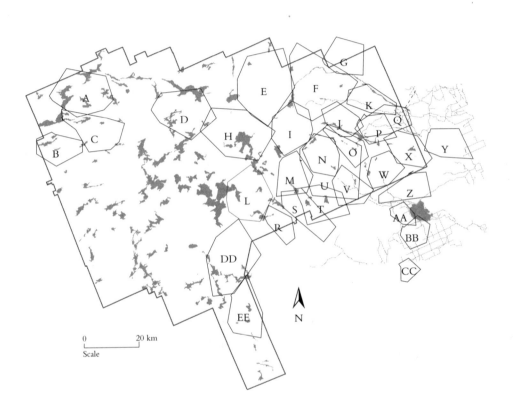

A Ratrap Lake	I Jack Pine	Q Hardwood Lake	Y Military
B Nahma Lake	J Grand Lake West	R Billy Lake	Z Acorn Lake
C Birchcliffe Lake	K Mathews Lake	S Ryan Lake	AA Cybulski
D Charles Creek	L Annie Bay	T Vireo Lake	BB Byers Creek
E Travers	M Redpole Lake	U Foys Lake	CC Wilno
F Pretty Lake	N Jocko Lake	V Basin Depot	DD East Gate
G Northeast	O McDonald Creek	W Zigzag Lake	EE Little Branch
H Lavieille	P Grand Lake East	X Sec Lake	

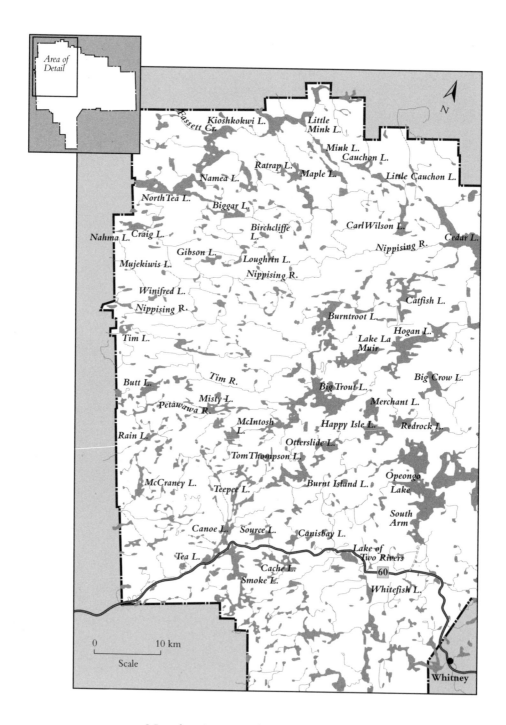

Northwestern Algonquin Park

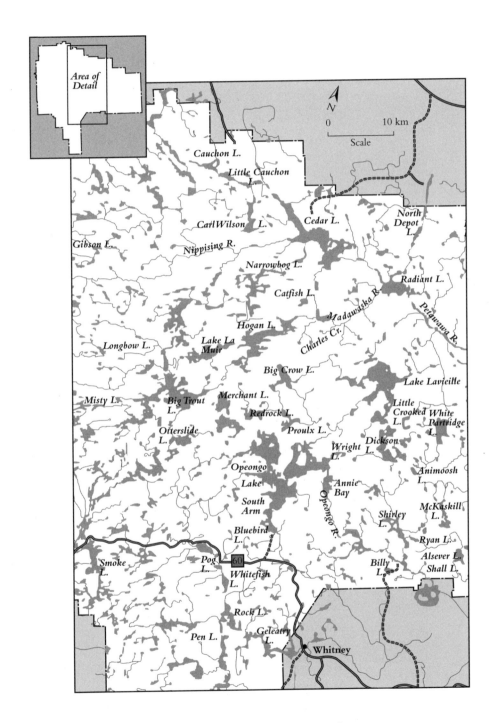

Central Algonquin Park

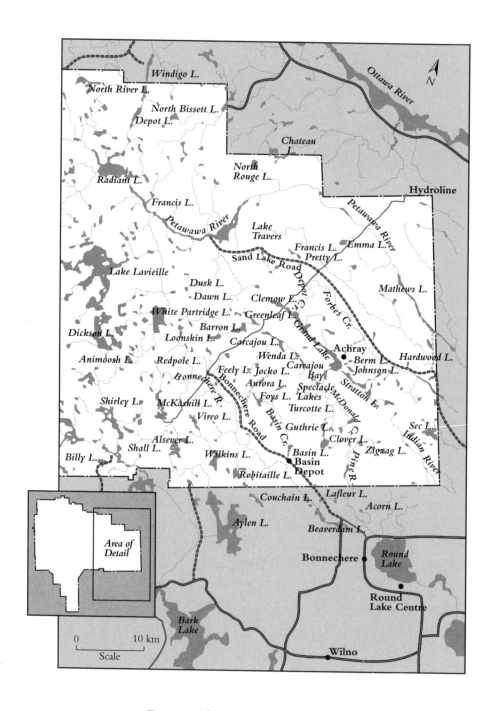

Eastern Algonquin Park

WOLF HORIZONS

This is the story of an ongoing research study – eleven years, 1987 to 1998, following the most loved and hated of North America mammals, learning what wolves contribute ecologically to wilderness, probing their alchemy that brings out both the best and the worst in us. It is a story of science, and conservation issues, and conflicts with government and segments of the public. Controversy swirls around almost every study of this species.

So our narrative goes beyond what wolves do on starlit nights at thirty below in the snow-draped Algonquin forests into what unfolded in boardrooms and appeared in newspapers and on television. Introduced will be the stock players in such a conflict with their varying attitudes and behaviour.

Myth, folklore, fable, and outright lies plague the wolf as no other species. No more controversial animal lives. None is so hated, none so misunderstood. Its mystical presence persists in our memories from childhood stories, Jack London's novels, werewolf horror films, western movies, and newspaper clippings about alleged wolf attacks. The wolf's secretive nature alone typecasts it as villain. For some people, it is a danger, a shadow on our perception of "up north."

At the same time, paradoxically, the wolf is a much beloved symbol of wilderness, its disappearance a measure of human meddling gone too far. In its howl is the distillate of wilderness. Just by being there, the wolf spices wild country with intrigue.

So, we who now control the destiny of most wild things come to the embarrassing question of what to do with the wolf. It has become our ward, a passive reflection of our varied, whimsical, and emotion-laden attitudes towards nature. Not an enviable fate for any species.

The only antidote to wolf mythology, for those with open minds, is knowledge gleaned from careful observation, sieved through the research process. Knowledge breeds wisdom – or makes it possible. Sometimes we succeeded in quelling hostile argument with the question: Whatever you think about wolves, don't you want to base your opinion on fact? Occasionally even that didn't work.

The questions we wanted to answer were broad ecological ones. What are the rules of both cooperation and competition that wolves live by, hunt by, and use to space themselves out across the land? How do they maintain their social order? Do they play a vital role in wilderness as some people claim? We asked an unorthodox question: Is there any room to believe in survival of the best-fit group? This proposition, except when applied to kin groups, has been generally discredited. It runs contrary to traditional Darwinian natural selection. We asked if the standard interpretation of territorial behaviour is really valid. We also constructed and attempted to test some narrower, bite-sized hypotheses – the essence of the scientific method – such as: Algonquin wolves are limiting the size of the white-tailed deer and moose populations, or the distribution of wolf packs depends primarily on the distribution of their prey. Then we predicted the field evidence necessary to support or reject these statements.

We asked conservation questions too. How large must a park be to protect a wolf population? What is the impact of logging on the predator-prey system? Are Algonquin wolves, living as they do on the southern edge of wolf range, in danger of gene swamping by coyotes?

As an underlying concern, through studying this persecuted species, we tried to find a fundamental, sustainable relationship between humans and things wild and free. If there is none – even with such a fellow social mammal, the progenitor of dogs that we invite into our homes – then how will all the other less empathy-inducing ecosystem parts that make a viable biosphere – slime moulds, ferns, salamanders, soil nematodes – survive?

We already knew, or suspected we knew, some of the answers based on studies conducted elsewhere. Nevertheless, species-wide generalizations need broad confirmation and, besides, we found the unexpected so often that we came to expect it. We realized early in the study that we were chasing an ever-retreating horizon of knowledge. While research will never allow us to fully, or even adequately, understand the wolf, we may understand both ourselves and it better.

"Haven't they been studied to death? They kill sheep. What more do you want to know?" In an auditorium full of sheep farmers one Saturday afternoon, a large, red-faced man in the third row obviously had not been impressed by my talk. I had explained the differences between wolves and coyotes that made coyotes more successful in farmlands like theirs. To his question I replied that one question in science inevitably leads to others, but he was not listening. As he took his seat he muttered, "The only good wolf is a dead one."

I sat down wondering why I had agreed to come, especially because the convenor had warned me there would not be much pro-wolf sentiment in the room. Then the farmer sitting beside me leaned over and whispered, "Good talk. A voice of reason in a room full of rednecks. You can fence out the critters and still have them around. I like 'em. So do a few others, but they won't admit it."

Across central Canada, east of Alberta, in an abrupt northwest-southeast line, the edge of the Canadian Shield is the edge of the wild. Land to the south grows wheat and cities, automobiles and people. Land to the north grows wolves.

It is said that a land that can grow a wolf is a whole land, a complete land. We wanted to test that premise; it matters in a world where whole land is vanishing. Is a whole land untouched land? There is little of that. Almost all "wild" land yields trees for newsprint and lumber, and minerals such as nickel and iron. It provides for fishing, hunting, and trapping, is sought after and fought over by resource exploiters, dam builders, multinational interests, local interests, government agencies.

Still, this contested land is nature-dominated, possessed of stark ecological truths and mysteries. Symbolically tying it together is the wolf, backbone of wild country in a nation whose art, literature, and culture is imbedded in wilderness. Ecologically tying it together is the wolf, too, as a summit predator, top of the food chain, sum of maples and balsam firs, moose and deer, bogs and rolling hills.

We picked a small chunk of central Ontario wilderness, Algonquin Provincial Park, on the southern edge of "up north" to study wolves. Our reasons were partly historical, partly biological. I had studied wolves there in my undergraduate years as an assistant to the internationally recognized biologist Dr. Douglas Pimlott. Mary – my research partner and wife – and I had continued together there in the mid-1960s and again in the early 1970s. Although discontinuous, this string of wolf data is the longest in Canada. That makes Algonquin Park valuable. It takes time to puzzle out the causes of changing large mammal numbers in dynamic, ever-shifting ecosystems.

We picked Algonquin, too, because it is a world-famous wolf sanctuary, a special place for wolves. Over the past thirty-five years, possibly more people have learned about wolves and heard them howl in Algonquin Park than anywhere else in the world. On August nights, park visitors jam a campground amphitheatre for a talk about wolves, then go out in a motorcade with park interpreters to listen to howls. Often more than fifteen hundred people take part in such a trip. Many leave with a new appreciation of wilderness.

Algonquin is a land rich in species, situated in a transition zone between southern hardwood forests to the south and the vast boreal forests to the north. As transition, it is called "northern hardwood-boreal forest," with maple and yellow birch covering its rolling uplands, spruce and balsam fir stringing along its waterways. The 7,725-square-kilometre park consists of a low dome of granite and gneiss rocks that were pressure-cooked in the bowels of the earth, smashed by continental collision, lifted up into towering mountains, then dismantled piece by piece by erosion until only the cores of those mountains remained.

Then the glaciers worked the land, repeated advances wiping out the handiwork of previous ones. As the last one retreated ten thousand years ago, it created a huge spillway on the east side of the dome that carried prodigious volumes of water. Today's Petawawa sand flats remain as the floor of that ancient waterway, and on those flats grow some of the finest white and red pines in eastern Canada – or did, as the whole landscape has been logged at least once, and more pines fall every year, despite park status. Logging has a place in our story, because it influences wolves along with everything else in the ecosystem.

Driving to our study area from the University of Waterloo is a trip across a threshold. Algonquin lies five hours north of Kitchener-Waterloo, four hours north of Toronto. It is upwind of southern Ontario's industrial air for the most part, unless storm fronts sneak up the Ohio Valley and cross the lower Great Lakes to brew up international smog. It is a trip from a cultural landscape – farmlands dotted only with remnants of forest – to a natural landscape – forests dotted with occasional farms. Thanks to the forces of continental geology, shallow, infertile soils make much of Canada economically unattractive to urbanization and agriculture. Despite overexploitive logging and creeping development, we always greet with relief the forest-clad rocks of the Canadian Shield where they first poke out of the overlying Paleozoic strata north of the city of Orillia.

Any place suitable to study a mysterious animal such as a wolf must have its own mystery, its own myths. The word "Algonquin" conjures up visions of voyageurs and the fur trade that represented Europeans' first assault on the Canadian wilderness. It was the famous explorer Samuel de Champlain who first met the indigenous people of the area and translated the name they called themselves as "Algonquin."

Maybe that is where the name came from. But there is a contending myth. The Hailstorm marshes on the north end of Opeongo Lake were well known by early loggers for their migrating waterfowl – good hunting. Sometime in the mid-1800s, two gentlemen were out in a boat poling through the marsh, hoping to bag a few ducks. It was a cold October day with grey cloud scuttling across the hilltops. Men in those early lumber camps came from a variety of ethnic backgrounds – Scandinavians, Irish, Scots, Frenchmen. One man in the boat was Irish, by the name of Quin; the other was a Scot – MacDonald.

To keep out the cold, MacDonald had brought along a flask of Scotch, which they passed back and forth between them. "Pass the bottle, MacDonald" and "Pass the bottle, Quin" were the repeated requests of one to the other as they poled or rowed along.

A bottle can only take so many requests, and soon MacDonald threw back his head and drained the last drops. Quin, his back turned to watch a flock of blue-winged teal get up off the water, did not notice. In a minute he requested, "Pass the bottle, MacDonald," to which MacDonald raised his hands, palms upward, and made a statement that has become enshrined forever: "All gone, Quin."

The principal humans in the story include Mary and me; together we have shared the highs and lows, the adulation and the hate that go with being wolf researchers. To conduct our research we lived in the bush, close to nature. That suits us. Our daughters, Jenny and Michelle, were part of the research team in the early years and periodically since then, working with us and then independently with other members of the crew, getting hooked on wildlife careers that they now both follow. Graham Forbes' five years of field work and an additional year of writing and analysis earned him both a master's and a Ph.D. He now follows an academic career at the University of New Brunswick. After the first three years, we were joined by Lee Swanson, who obtained a master's degree by answering some questions about deer ecology that related to wolves. A Swanson-Forbes marriage enhanced field efficiency. Joy Cook followed and earned a master's degree determining how wolves distribute themselves in winter. John Pisapio pursued the relationship between migratory and resident wolves living adjacent to the park. Hilary Sears studied wolf-coyote hybrids over a broader region.

Many undergraduate students have contributed to the study, adding various talents and idiosyncrasies and keeping the human side of the job lively. Some of them wrote senior honours theses. Most have gone on to careers in wildlife conservation.

Volunteers have played a big part, filling the gap between field needs and budgets. They have come from many places: Switzerland, Austria, Portugal, Germany, United States, and closer to home from Ontario too.

Most of our flying was done in a white-and-blue Cessna 172 owned by Pem Air of Pembroke, Ontario. Many pilots enjoyed the sky manoeuvring, doing the job safely and well.

Then there are the wolves, assigned pack names from lakes or other geographic features in their territories, given numbers in the order caught. They were allotted an additional pack name after the number if they later dispersed or showed themselves to be members of another pack. It was, at the very least, a fair trade – our intrusion into their lives resulted in fewer of them dying premature deaths. Gone now but not forgotten are alpha-female Basin 3 Foys and her mate, Foys 1, who headed up a pack of thirteen, and big, forty-four-kilogram (ninety-seven-pound) Basin 4 McDonald, who provided so much key information about the McDonald Creek pack. The howls of Nahma 1 will always ring in our ears. Alpha-female Jack Pine 3 wore three different collars over the course of five years and provided us with a thick file of data. We will never forget Billy 1 when we found her curled up under a tree, a light dusting of snow drifted over her, her neck one-third severed by a snare.

Our study has been and is supported primarily by World Wildlife Fund Canada (WWF), whose president, Monte Hummel, not only encourages us and helps forge both research and conservation strategies, but participates with us in many meetings with provincial government officials, township politicians, and sister conservation organizations where we present our data and make our case. Concerned individuals and corporations who care about the character of Canadian wilderness give money to WWF for our work or donate directly to us. In times when dollars for wildlife have been shrinking, they make our work possible.

Behind all our work lay the memory of one man who did much for the protection of both wolves and wilderness in Canada – Douglas Pimlott, who died in 1978. My years working for Doug formed much of my previous book, *Wolves and Wilderness* (Dent Canada, 1975). Doug shunned radio telemetry, which involves putting radio-collars on wolves, each one transmitting its own frequency, discernible by portable, battery-operated receiver. The electronics were new and undependable back then. But he did not shun the biopolitics of wolf and wilderness protection, and he made his mark. He founded the World Conservation Union's Wolf Specialists Group to address wolf conservation needs around the world. He helped found many conservation organizations that continue their important work today: the Canadian Arctic Resources Committee, the Canadian Nature Federation, the Canadian Parks and Wilderness Society.

When Doug had amassed too much ill will from a segment of government policy-makers, the status-quo clones, he gave his red Chestnut "Bob Special" cedar-strip canoe to me, and with it the Algonquin wolf study. He never promised that either the science or the biopolitics of wolf research would be easy. I know he would be interested in what we have learned.

AMBER FIRE

AUGUST 1987. The first of over 150 wolves to oblige us with data, albeit unwittingly, lay sprawled out full length under a spruce tree. A light, all-day rain had petered out; the wet bush hung suspended in early-evening hush. From a distance a hermit thrush played taps.

The wolf raised her head, struggled to rise, fell back. A few minutes passed. Phantom-like, a gray jay glided in, perplexed by the scene, and landed above the wolf. Cocking its head sideways, the bird uttered a confused-sounding squawk. Again the wolf lifted her head, this time trying to focus on the sound. Again her head fell back.

More time passed. We sat as motionless as we could on the mossy ground a few metres away and watched. Then, thirty-five minutes later, the wolf lifted her head for the third time, groggy from the drug, but more alert – she was remembering. She looked for us, found us, our eyes met and locked. She held her gaze for a full minute, two minutes, an eternity. Wolf – human – each searching for meaning in the eyes of the other. Eyes so alike – iris, pupil, cornea, lens, size, musculature, movement. But eyes so different, reflecting two different social orders that began diverging, like two continents drifting apart, hundreds of thousands of years ago. One species possesses great physical prowess – speed and endurance, night vision, a keen sense of smell. The other possesses an unprecedented mental capability.

Burning in those amber wolf eyes was the vital force of wilderness itself, a force that left our eyes some four thousand years ago as human civilization first began to separate man from nature. Locked in neural connections behind those eyes were ecological secrets we no longer remember, shared with the pines who whisper them from ridge to ridge, and the beavers who tell them in their lodges late at night. As a summit predator, the wolf ties species together, binds them into a marvellous functioning whole, provides the ecosystem glue.

Burning in those amber eyes, too, were deep and unsettling questions. They were about the capacity to hate another species, about persecution and population genocide. They asked what kind of future we were creating for wolves and wilderness, indeed for species, ecosystems, the very biosphere itself. They were embarrassing questions; they made us ashamed. They brought tears to our eyes, changed the buoyancy of success into a poignancy of self-recrimination. Did we have to do this, to capture and lay at our feet the very spirit of wildness? We tried to look elsewhere, at the trampled ferns, the open drug kit, the poke stick with syringe attached, but always our eyes came back to the wolf, because we could feel her eyes on us.

We had trapped the wolf in a foothold trap designed for scientific research. In Canada, commercial trappers trap a few thousand wolves every year. Those wolves not already dead from starvation and freezing must look up into the eyes of the trapper, as this wolf did. For them, the look is brief. The trapper puts rifle to wolf forehead and shoots. As a bucket of water douses a campfire, so the amber fire in a wolf's eyes goes out.

It has been said that wolf eyes are mirrors; what different people see in them is simply a reflection of themselves. Could they reflect even more, not just a person's attitude towards wolves, but towards the environment, wild lands, nature itself?

We named the wolf Nahma 1. She was the first wolf to be radio-collared in a pack whose territory centred on Nahma Lake. We did not call her Jane or Sue: it was enough to put a collar on her without further humanization. She was a yearling as shown by the limited wear on her incisor teeth, a medium-sized wolf with a slender build and long legs. She was tawny with black guard hairs along her back and flanks, reddish tinges behind the ears, and darker legs – a typical Algonquin wolf. She weighed twenty-seven kilograms (sixty pounds) by the bathroom scale, part of our handling gear.

Fifty-five minutes after injection she was on her feet, wobbly, and gone. We collected our equipment and left. Her radio signal showed that she had not gone far. Probably she was asleep again under a tree.

We hiked back along an abandoned railway bed once used to haul logs out of this hill country. Now healing, alders crowded the embankment's shoulders, moss and grasses buried the cinders, and wolf feet used the path for a trail. Our truck was parked at a washout two kilometres away. We felt encouraged, especially Jenny, whose trap set had caught the wolf. With our two student crews, we had been trying to radio-collar wolves for five weeks without success. Finally we had a wolf to follow.

When we returned the next day, we heard her signal weakly from the washout. Squadrons of deer flies accompanied us on our walk along the old railway, and cicadas hummed in the maples. Nahma 1 was up on a hill above what we suspected was the grassy rendezvous site where her packmates waited. From a strategic knoll beside a lily-covered beaver pond, we sat on a log and listened to her signal. Its irregularity told us she was moving. Five minutes passed, ten minutes. She was working her way downhill towards the rendezvous site on a trajectory that would have her pass within two hundred metres of us. We moved into the denseness of a hemlock stand and turned the volume of the signal down. Now she was close, now she was past, like a ship going by in the mist. Forest phantom.

In a few minutes she would be at the meadow's edge. We left the hemlock grove and followed, to be within hearing when she reached her pack. She was in the opening now, walking fast to its far end, maybe even loping. A whine and a soft bark of greeting floated through the trees.

We stayed, listening to the now steady beat of Nahma 1's signal as she slept among her packmates. At dusk we heard what we had waited for, first a single wolf voice lifting from the other end of the meadow, then another, and a third – the wolves were spread out. The howls of the third wolf came from exactly where she was.

On a map, Nahma Lake does not take up much space. From the ground it is almost obscured by big, rolling hardwood hills over which broad-winged hawks ride the summer thermals and in whose forests red-eyed vireos sing all day. The surrounding country is laced with bogs and streams. The loggers pulled out a few years previously, leaving old roads in the process of regenerating to one-moose-wide trails through raspberry vines and brush. Good wolf country.

Our interest in this northwest side of the park was to compare the ecology of wolves where white-tailed deer were scarce with the rest of the park where deer were more plentiful. This was to be the basis of Graham Forbes' Ph.D. thesis research. Partly because we could occasionally use a log cabin we had built nearby, Mary and I centred our work there; the student crews worked farther east.

A week before we caught Nahma 1, Mary, Jenny, and I had canoed Nahma Lake and part of Craig Lake in a heavy afternoon wind, returning in the calm after dark. We had heard wolves, faint and far away, so far that we decided to search elsewhere for a more accessible pack. So we drove thirty kilometres to a system of logging roads near the ranger station of Kiosk. No sooner had we arrived than the chief ranger there received a strange report. Back near Nahma Lake a wolf had approached some campers to within a few metres. It had stayed only briefly, then walked away.

So we returned to Nahma Lake, this time walking the overgrown railway by flashlight, pausing every kilometre to howl. Wolves respond to human howls commonly enough that howling is a useful research tool. We have used it more consistently over more years than other wolf researchers. The human howl does not have to be good, just loud. At each stop we howl three times with only short pauses between, then wait for about two minutes and do it again. On only our third stop, a pack with pups answered.

The next evening we returned to howl at them again, wanting confirmation that they were not simply on the move. The forest was calm, out of breath after a hot, hazy humid day. No leaves rustled. No birds sang. Too much effort. We walked for half an hour along the old railway, surrounded by mosquitoes. A woodcock flew off the trail ahead, the whir of its wings making us jump. Firefly flashes loosely defined the edges of the wet meadow where we expected the wolves to be. Pups answered our howl, but no adults; rarely do we hear pups only.

Because the howl had given us the information we wanted, we started back without disturbing them further. When we were almost to our truck by the washout, we howled one last time, wondering where the adults might be. A deep-throated wolf answered from a hundred metres down a stream, five or six long, beautiful, night-splitting howls, each like the other, dropping in pitch suddenly near the end. Following my notes made later that night:

"We sat on the old railroad and made no noise. In five minutes I howled again. Now it was closer and gave shorter, softer howls. A few minutes later we heard sticks breaking in the alders right beside us, and the wolf began to whine. Mary whined back and it whined some more. Then it gave some very short howls, one to two seconds long, deep in pitch, low in volume – obvious short-range communication. For an amazing one and a half hours the wolf stayed no more than four metres from us in the alders. We kept the flashlight off, wanting to see how events would turn out, periodically giving short little howls or whines that the wolf answered. It seemed like it wanted to join us but just couldn't get up the nerve to take those last few steps up onto the embankment."

Finally I stood up to ease my cramped legs. We heard the wolf move back a few metres (maybe to ease its cramped legs too). Then we made our way very slowly to the truck, thinking that the wolf might come out on the road, but instead its howls began to fade.

At the truck, we howled again, and now from a more distant ridge it gave us a final serenade of longer, louder breaking howls like the ones it began with.

Friendly, curious, perhaps it was the same wolf that had approached the campers a few days earlier. We had never experienced such a prolonged, close-range acceptance by, and back-and-forth communication with, a wild wolf.

A year later, the event was almost repeated. That summer the Nahma pack had not used the same rendezvous site, although wolf tracks along the old railway told that pack members occasionally swung through. One August evening, three wolves answered us, one beginning its howls with a bark, or trailing an initial series of barks into a howl, typical of a wolf disturbed at close range. We checked the receiver; the radio-collared wolf was not one of them. Three minutes later, while we were sitting on the embankment writing notes by flashlight, we heard the bark-howler again, this time even closer. Another wolf howled from the edge of a pond less than a hundred metres away. Moments later, one wolf, very close to us, began to whine. Mary whined back. We heard a wolf splash across the outlet creek and rattle stones as it climbed a bank a few strides directly behind us. We waited, breathless, not wanting to turn around for fear that movement would frighten it. Mist was rising from the moonlit surface of a pond. A few migrant passerine birds peeped overhead. Nothing happened; silence.

We waited for a full thirty minutes, then I howled, expecting to find that they were long gone. Two wolves answered from the outlet creek. What had they been doing all that time? Maybe they were exhibiting passive defence, staying between us and pups somewhere nearby. Or maybe they were just waiting for us to leave – so we did.

Through a long journey of over one million years, wolves have lived with humans or our immediate ancestors first in Africa, then Asia, Europe, and for the last forty thousand years or so in North America. As two species of large mammals, often hunting the same prey, it was inevitable that some ecological relationship would evolve between us.

If we had been equals in communication and reason, like early hominid species living at the same place and time, we might have become two warring species. But war requires a disagreement shared and communicated by members of each side, reciprocated hate, the ability to remember past wrongs, and the desire to retaliate. Wolves simply do not possess this emotional or intellectual equipment. So, while humans have waged war on wolves, wolves have exercised their only biological option, which is to behave as a hunted species. As such, wolves who react with fear have had an obvious selective advantage – they have been harder to exterminate.

How much fear is locked into the genetic make-up of a wolf? How much can be modified by experience? The Nahma pack provided us with other evidence that illustrated the various ways wolves regard us. One frosty October afternoon that first year, Nahma 1's signal was coming in loudly as we walked along the same old railway bed towards the now-abandoned rendezvous site. The signal from a radio transmitter is most audible when the wolf is in direct "line of sight." Trees have little effect, but just one or two high hills are enough to block it out.

She was close, so we turned towards some alders where the signal was loudest. Suddenly, there she was, standing face on, watching us. She trotted a few steps, seemingly not alarmed, then disappeared in the brush. Judging by her signal, she stayed within fifty metres or so for the next ten minutes. We sat on a mossy bank waiting to see what she would do. She may have been doing the same thing. Then she left. Curious, cautious, unafraid.

Other wolves from other packs exhibited similar curiosity. The Brûlé Lake wolf, for example, routinely urinated on vehicle tires and on occasion walked down an abandoned railway in full daylight and in full view of people. We received so many reports about that wolf that Graham thought he could radio-collar it by immobilizing it with our dart pistol. One afternoon he sat on the old railway waiting for the wolf to show up. It did, walking straight towards him. He didn't know whether to grab the camera or the pistol. As the wolf walked by, he took eye-level, full-frame pictures. Then as he reached for the pistol, the wolf galloped out of range.

And a wolf in the Lavieille pack was curious too. One night in a logging clearing, student assistant Carolyn Callaghan and Jenny howled and received no reply. Then while they were writing up their notes, a wolf walked through the sweet ferns into the headlights of their truck and just stood there. They howled softly to it, which seemed to increase its curiosity. After a while they carefully climbed out the truck window, not wanting to open the squeaky door, and sat on the ground near the wolf. Cautiously it circled them, staying about ten metres away. Finally, as in our encounter with the Nahma wolf, humans broke off the engagement, not the wolf.

At the park museum for a few consecutive winters before our study began, a wolf became habituated to humans and fed from the ground-level bird feeder attached to the window of the staff house. Nicknamed "Rosy" by park interpreters, it was the subject of several stories told by naturalists. Back when I was a student, another wolf raised ire at a children's camp in the park for its habit of tearing clothes off a clothesline.

It was not curiosity that Nahma 1 exhibited towards us early in the summer of 1988 when we found her at Mujekiwis Lake. It was dramatically different behaviour. On this occasion, she was the most aggressive wolf we have faced. That summer, the wolves were not around Nahma Lake. Graham's flights showed their movements centred on a big beaver pond-marsh complex near Mujekiwis Lake about nine kilometres away. We set out with two objectives: to radio-collar more wolves in that pack and to collect wolf droppings (scats) from a spring den and early-summer rendezvous site. The scats would provide evidence about the importance of moose calves in wolf diets when calves are small and vulnerable.

I flew with Graham to plot a route into Mujekiwis Lake. We took off in a float plane from Kawawaymog Lake, and in only a few minutes we were over the pond-marsh complex with Nahma 1's signal booming up to the antennas attached to the wing struts. Down below was a typical rendezvous site with a wet, post-beaver-dam meadow, an eye of water still in the centre, and tall grasses and alders around its edges. It was a good place for pups to explore and adults to watch for an unwary deer or moose coming to drink. Down below, too, stretched beautiful Mujekiwis Lake with rocky, pine-clad points, no canoes or people, and the Nipissing River to the south meandering out in wide sedge flats. The river was the obvious route in.

No people; no wonder! If you spot Mujekiwis Lake on the map of Algonquin Park, don't go there. Not unless it is early spring after a huge snow melt and it has rained for a week. Conditions were the opposite. The mighty Nipissing River, up there near its source, turned out to be a thin veneer of water on mud. We (Mary, Michelle, and I) put in, paddled, poled, hauled out around a beaver dam, put in again, got stuck, got off, stuck again . . . with supplies for a week, twenty-five heavy traps, drug kit, radio-collars, receiver, antenna. Early the second day, Mary, inconsiderate considering the circumstances, tripped and fractured her ankle while struggling along under her big voyageur pack. Michelle and I graciously relieved her of a jacket or two – we did not know her ankle was fractured then – and she hobbled on.

Finally at Mujekiwis Lake we made camp under the pines close enough to the pond-marsh to hear any wolves howl. Nahma 1's radio signal came in from a distance. That night the wolves did howl, seeming to make the water shimmer in the moonlight, stilling the bullfrogs along the shore.

The next day, hot and sunny, Michelle and I left Mary with her oversized ankle at camp and canoed down the lake. Striking through the bush, by good luck we found an old logging road going our way. We reached the pond-marsh and scanned it from a fringe of spruces. No wolves were visible, so we spent the afternoon and evening scouting the area back from the marsh, collecting scats and looking for the bones of kills.

Then suddenly, in the hush of early evening, we were challenged by a wolf – the most distraught wolf we have ever encountered. We were sitting on a log. On a rise above us, no more than fifteen metres away, a wolf shattered the stillness with a sudden burst of deep, throaty barks. Looking up, startled, we saw radio-collared Nahma 1 racing back and forth along the edge of the rise. She was so close and the evening so quiet we could hear her throat rattle as she sucked in air between each series of barks. No attempt at concealment, this wolf was aggressively challenging us.

Hurriedly we stood up. We faced her, talked to her, tried to quiet her down. Our voices often calm wolves when we are collaring them. But she continued racing back and forth and barking. Slowly we backed down the old road. When we were around a bend, we turned and walked away. Nahma 1 stayed where she was, barking less frequently. Finally she stopped.

Why so different from the previous October? We may have genuinely startled her. She may have been almost upon us before detecting us. Upon later inspection we found small pup scats on the rise. The situation was similar to an experience I had in my student days on Baffin Island when three adult wolves barked at me from close range while I was near their pups at a den. It was also reminiscent of a wolf who barked at student Paul Joslin while he stood with his back against a tree. Another wolf at Annie Bay in Algonquin Park once confronted Doug Pimlott, barking at him. Gradually it moved back to rejoin its pups and pack across a clearing. (That barking was recorded on the stereo record *The Language and Music of the Wolves*, narrated by Robert Redford, Columbia Records, 1971.)

These incidents were not attacks, as if we were prey. They were displays of angry, defensive behaviour, of a kind most likely directed towards natural dangers such as bears or threatening non-pack wolves. Wolves, like many other species, usually express ritualized aggression intended to cause the threat to withdraw. Such rituals are less risky than an actual attack and fight.

Michelle and I felt guilty for sneaking around the rendezvous site. Nahma 1 had a right to be angry. Den sites and the rendezvous sites where wolves move later in the summer deserve respect. We have a rule now for all our crews that nobody enters a rendezvous site to collect scats until the pack has moved on.

Three so-called "wolf attacks," as reported in newspapers, have occurred in Algonquin Park during our study. Like none of the foregoing, they all involved wolf-human physical contact. One of these wolves frequented the Pog Lake public campground week after week and often was seen trotting alongside the paved highway. One night it put its jaws around a girl's arm as she sat by a campfire. She received only a scratch from an animal that, if it wanted to, could have broken the arm into splinters with those same jaws in the same length of time.

Another night a little boy was bitten on the side by a wolf when he left the tent to visit the backhouse. Again, only a minor cut resulted. Nearby that summer, MNR and Algonquin Forest Authority (AFA) employees had unwisely habituated a wolf to approach them and eat doughnuts.

The third incident was different in that a little boy's nose and face were badly bitten. The child, sleeping outside a tent, was dragged a few metres in his sleeping bag. His calls, and the presence of other people, broke off the encounter, but the wolf was reluctant to leave and had to be chased away.

In these incidents, the wolves displayed neither angry challenge, defensive behaviour, nor vocalization such as we had experienced, so the same emotions probably were not involved. In none of these cases were the animals rabid. Nor were the humans regarded as prey, or the wolves would have been far more violent. Preceding all three contacts, the individual wolves had become nuisances to campers in the area. Perhaps the wolves were social outcasts. In all three cases, the wolves appear to have been more curious than aggressive. None exhibited the apprehension that normally prevents actual contact.

Wolves, like dogs, commonly mouth unusual articles out of curiosity, or each other in play. They grab foreign objects. Once, when Jenny was a child, a wolf took her jumper suit from where it was hanging beside our truck and carried it off to its rendezvous site. Maybe the sleeping bag was like this, the object of investigation, and the child in it a surprise.

Whatever the wolves' motives, these encounters represent rare, aberrant behaviour. To a wolf, we are neither prey nor competitor. They do not realize that in the latter case they are so wrong.

Where wolves rarely see humans, as in remote arctic places, or experience our lethal forms of aggression, they may exhibit more curiosity than fear. In 1997 on Banks Island in the western arctic, a white wolf approached our canoe to within a few metres, and was reluctant to leave. On Baffin Island in my student years, sometimes we found a wolf walking along behind us. At the other extreme, a wolf biologist working in Romania tells a story of a wolf that followed him when he left the forest and trotted behind him along a busy city street. Possibly at times European wolves exhibit fearlessness not through lack of exposure to humans, but excessive exposure, as long as they are not being persecuted.

Captive wolves are different, stripped of a wild environment, without any opportunity to disperse, hunt, or roam, all of which are needs encoded in genes. Sometimes with neuroses, always with artificial dependence forced upon them by humans, on occasion they can be unpredictable.

We followed Nahma 1 periodically for two years, learning a little more from each glimpse she gave us into her life. When I pull her records up on the computer, I find 185 entries, each with date, map coordinates, method of location, and a description of events. Most of the entries are from Graham's aerial fixes over two winters: eighty-nine entries for her first winter, twenty-one the next. Only once was she seen from the air, trotting along the edge of a frozen lake with two other wolves. Other times she was hidden in the trees. From tracking her on the ground, we knew her pack consisted of at least six wolves.

From another database, I can pull up on the screen a map of Algonquin Park with lakes and rivers shown in blue and coloured dots representing the locations of specific wolves. The first winter, Nahma 1's territory encompassed 110 square kilometres of prime moose and beaver habitat, with Nahma Lake towards its west side and the Nipissing River forming a southern boundary. Half the Nahma pack's territory fell in especially dense moose range, based upon Graham's analysis of winter data collected over a fifteen-year period by MNR biologist Mike Wilton and others. The second winter, her territory appeared to be smaller, but this is likely the result of fewer telemetry fixes.

The Nahma Lake rendezvous site where we first found her was used only temporarily. Maybe the pack had moved the pups there to be near a kill. In contrast, the site near Mujekiwis Lake, with a system of well-used trails, was used longer and probably included a den that we did not find. The two sites were only nine kilometres apart, a short hike for a trotting wolf.

We collected sixty scats in the Nahma pack's territory, all duly bagged and brought with others to the ecology lab at the University of Waterloo. Each scat was heated in an autoclave to 120°C for twenty minutes, then washed through a sieve. The remaining hair and bones were dried and put in an envelope for later analysis. Colleagues and students working in the west wing of the Environmental Studies Building knew without asking when scat preparation was taking place. When windows were open, they even knew two floors above.

Our analysis procedures involve randomly selecting three hairs from each scat, laying them on pieces of clear acetate, sandwiching the acetate between two microscope slides, and heating it in an oven for five minutes at 80°C. Heating produces a hair impression on the acetate through which light can pass, allowing microscopic examination. As a concession to help researchers identify hairs, evolution long ago decreed that each species of mammal possess a different pattern of tiny scales on the outside of its hair. By analysing the hair, we can figure out what the wolves have been eating.

For the Nahma pack, moose and beaver were represented about equally in the summer. Deer didn't show up much, as expected because of their scarcity. Beaver dropped in winter, when they spend most of their time in their lodges.

Wolf deaths figure prominently in our research; too many amber eyes into which we looked did not look back. On March 5, 1989, Graham phoned me at the university to say that when he dialled the wolf's frequency that morning from the airplane, the signal had come in at twice its normal pulse rate. Circuitry in the radio transmitter responds by altering the pulse rate when the collar has been motionless for eight hours. Nahma 1's signal was on mortality mode.

I rearranged my lecture schedule, and we drove north to the town of Sundridge stretched along the shore of Bernard Lake seventeen kilometres west of Algonquin Park. Graham flew over from the town of Whitney to the east. In a restaurant he pinpointed the location of the signal on a topographic map. The wolf was in a narrow valley about two kilometres east of a lake known to local fisherman as Carmichael. Nothing was unusual about the topography. She was, however, outside her territory, farther west by ten kilometres than she had ever been, even beyond the boundary of the park.

Jenny and I crammed in with Graham, the pilot, our snowshoes and some survival gear, and we taxied out beyond the ice fishermen's huts. Sun slanted in through the windshield as the engine revved for take-off. With the temperature a few degrees above freezing, wet snow lengthened our take-off run, and the pilot shouted in my ear that he hoped the snow wasn't too wet on tiny Carmichael Lake or we might be there until spring.

Nothing distinguishes the park from land next to it on the west side, at least from the air. Snowy lakes and bogs of all shapes and sizes, hardwood hills spreading like choppy swells on a grey sea, dark conifers stencilling the low places, rivers tracing out the valley bottoms. Only when you get to the ground do you notice the more heavily cut-over forests and a scattering of cottages around the lakes.

We circled over Carmichael Lake, sloped down, and landed. Jenny and I climbed out. Graham and the pilot taxied off to complete a circuit of other radio-collared packs to the east. The plane gained just sufficient altitude on its run down the lake to clear the spruces at the far end.

Before we landed, Nahma 1's rapid signal was coming in clearly through the earphones. Down on the lake, however, we could not hear it. We walked to shore, snow clinging to our snowshoes, pushed through the alders, and came upon an old snowmobile trail heading east, our way, which made walking easier.

After about seven hundred metres, a faint signal registered on the receiver. Encouraged, we followed the trail that ended at a derelict cabin on the edge of a clearing. Past that the valley narrowed, and we followed a small stream, gurgling with muted voice.

Crossbills were in the air, tossing melodious notes into the wind. A raven or two cruised the treetops, and an all-white snowshoe hare hopped out from beneath a snowy spruce branch and posed for pictures, white on white. Two sets of fresh wolf tracks ran our way. Clouds had obscured the sun, and the thought crossed my mind that if it started to rain, the pilot might not risk a landing back on Carmichael Lake at our designated time, two hours later.

The signal strength increased. Then, abruptly as we walked over a small rise, its direction changed, indicating that we had just passed the collar. The signal led us out of the conifers to the base of a hardwood hill. By turning around and pointing the antenna towards the snow, we located the spot to dig.

The snow was unbroken except for the wolf tracks a few metres away. The wolves had not paused, unaware or uninterested in what lay below. We began excavating an area about one and one half metres wide with our shovel, taking turns at the heavy work.

The collar lay about forty-five centimetres beneath the surface – but no wolf was in it. Its bolts were still fastened. The leather strap and acrylic casing around the radio parts had been heavily chewed. A small piece of frozen flesh stuck to it, and a spot of blood was frozen to the acrylic – nothing more. We dug farther, carefully excavating an encrusted layer shaped like a wolf's body. A few guard hairs were frozen in, but no carcass.

For the next hour we excavated a huge area right down to last year's fast-frozen ferns and bunchberry leaves without uncovering any more clues. The body could have been nearby without our knowing it.

Time was running out, so we packed up and snowshoed back along our tracks to Carmichael Lake, passing the snowshoe hare again, and the derelict cabin. The plane came in low to the west end and taxied to us. We climbed in and held our breath as the pilot took us back out. This time, by keeping the skis in their former tracks, he gained more speed, and we cleared the trees with ease.

We were left having to draw a most probable, instead of a definite, conclusion. Nahma 1 had been faithful to a defined territory until mid-December of that second winter. Then she went missing despite repeated flights over her whole territory. On January 3, Graham found her in an area where he had not been searching, south of the Nipissing River and well south of her territory. She disappeared again on three subsequent flights, neither on territory nor to the south. Sometime after early January, she had moved west to the place where she died.

She was a mature adult by then, three and one-half years old. While old for a wolf to disperse in search of a mate, she could have been doing that. Or, she could have been on an extra-territorial foray with other members of her pack. Alone or with others, however, she had been trespassing on land occupied by another pack. The evidence suggested that she had met a violent end. Humans could not have killed her or the collar would have been unbolted. Black bears, which at times kill wolves, were in hibernation. The verdict? Most likely she had been killed and dismembered by the resident pack. One wolf carried the collar off, lay down in the snow, chewed at it, then got up and left.

Nahma 1 and her pack illustrated something about wolf attitudes towards us, and especially their forbearance. They also showed us that harsh rules exist in wolf societies. In years to come, however, Nahma 1's death at the jaws of other wolves began to stand out as unusual. Based on the observations of other researchers, and the large amount of trespass we later recorded, we expected to find more wolf-wolf killing. That lack of killing eventually led our research in a different direction.

We left the Nahma area after that season, except for annual spring scat collections and moose-browse surveys. The old railway bed has had more years of reabsorption into forest, and so has the old logging road near Mujekiwis Lake. Maybe by now beaver have rebuilt their dam and flooded the Mujekiwis rendezvous site again. A new generation of wolves living there doesn't know us, and if any wolves are still alive from back then, they have forgotten. That is the way it should be.

CAMP AT THE RAPIDS

Limited Wolves

Wolves, like other large carnivores, live in low densities. Their numbers are limited by a set of environmental conditions that apply to all species, and are then limited further by their position as a summit predator.

The adage that "no population can expand indefinitely in a finite space," variously worded, shows up in most books on population ecology. If any population even came close, just once, it would quickly commandeer all the energy available on Earth, and global extinction would result.

Driven by all-powerful geometric progression, any population can grow at a staggeringly high rate. Illustrating its power is a question: Would you rather be given one cent on the first day of the month and allow it to double each day until the end of the month, or be given one million dollars? Answer: Take the one cent. On the thirty-first day of doubling, it will be worth $10,737,418.

Curbing the maximum potential growth of any population, however, is "environmental resistance." It operates as an unseen pressure pushing down on a population, a sleight of hand that increases the death rate, or decreases the birth rate, or both. It also operates by negative feedback, becoming progressively stronger on a population as it grows, eventually strangling any further increase. Then the population is at "carrying capacity," its environmentally set maximum size.

Measuring carrying capacity is difficult because it is influenced by so many environmental factors. Food quality, food quantity, weather, disease, predation – all can interact differently from one year to the next. All have a greater effect the larger the population. Disease is transmitted faster in a dense population; food runs out sooner when there are more hungry mouths to feed; predators increase when prey is more abundant. So, while each animal in a population lives and dies, and leaves more or fewer offspring because of the interplay of environmental factors on just it, simultaneously, every individual is subject to the influence of population size.

For the wolf, as for other predators, a maximum population is set by the total combined biomass (weight) of its prey, and it is surprisingly low. To start with, a wolf population cannot kill more than about one-quarter of a moose population in any single year without causing a decline in prey. This is because we know that moose populations can grow no faster than this to offset losses under ideal conditions. Ideal conditions, of course, rarely exist. So, already there must be a much greater biomass of prey than of predator.

About 20 per cent of prey is inedible bone and hide. And only about 10 to 15 per cent of what a wolf consumes actually becomes wolf biomass; the rest is lost through digestive inefficiency and the metabolic demands of life.

In addition, not all prey that die goes into wolf stomachs. Other predators such as bears take their share, and scavengers such as ravens can eat prodigious amounts. Furthermore, some carcasses are never found by wolves and end up feeding the myriad microbes waiting in the soil.

I calculate that wolf biomass ranges only between 0.15 and 0.52 per cent of prey biomass, based on studies in Alaska (interior and southcentral), Minnesota, Michigan, and northcentral Canada reviewed by Wisconsin biologist Lloyd Keith. Even the wide swings in moose and wolf numbers reported by Rolf Peterson for Isle Royale National Park in Lake Superior between 1965 and 1988 changed the ratio of wolf biomass to prey biomass only from 0.46 to 0.58 per cent. These figures mean that one 34-kilogram (75-pound) wolf needs between 5,900 and 22,700 kilograms (13,000 and 50,000 pounds) of prey on its range each year. In terms of actual animals, a single wolf must share the land with between 14 and 55 moose, or 86 and 333 deer, to assure it gets the fraction of that needed to stay alive.

This analysis implies that food abundance is of overriding importance to wolf numbers. It is, but only when all else fails. A wolf population may be limited by some other components of environmental resistance. Disease may intervene, or social factors may prevent its increase, even in the presence of abundant prey. Or humans may be lowering wolf numbers. In all the studies quoted except Isle Royale, wolf populations were exploited to some extent by humans.

Wolf-dominated systems are not unusual in showing low predator biomass relative to their prey. On the rich Serengeti Plains of East Africa, the biomass of predators is only 0.33 per cent of their prey. Paleontologist Robert Bakker concluded that the average biomass ratio of all modern predatory mammals to their prey is 1 per cent or less (three or four times less than the ratio in predatory dinosaurs).

Nature's economy is set lean. Behind all the greenery are populations of large carnivores such as wolves adjusted low, living near biological bankruptcy.

BIODIVERSITY is the multicoloured fibre in the tapestry of an ecosystem, each species a thread. Woven so intimately, each thread loses individual identity in the form and character of the fabric. Texture is physiography – rugged, wrinkled, warped, faulted, thrown up in rock ramparts, smoothed by glaciers down to the water's edge. Patterns emerge, if you stare at the tapestry long enough, from the order imposed on biodiversity by trophic webs and forest succession and species interrelationships.

The tapestry in northwest Algonquin Park differs dramatically from that in eastern Algonquin, because one dominant thread is missing – white-tailed deer. Deer threads were there thirty years ago, but they faded. Nature keeps tearing out and reweaving, experimenting with colours, altering patterns, inventing new designs.

We wanted to see how species relationships adjusted in the absence of deer. We were interested in the different patterns the wolf threads would form and, with them, the associated strands of moose, maples, aspen, beaver, and other species with a stake in the large mammal system. Would wolf packs be larger where their prey was predominantly moose? Would pack territories cover more land, adjusting to the lower biomass of ungulate (hoofed mammal) prey? Would wolf mortality be greater when tackling a larger prey? And if so, were any useful evolutionary messages hidden there in the northwest among the high hardwood hills?

Mary and I stuck with the northwest for much of two and a half summers, 1988 to 1990. Student crews took over at times, but we liked to swim in the rapids of the Amable du Fond River and dip water from a particular spring that welled up under a big yellow birch beside a logging road. It was exhilarating dodging the logging trucks there, avoiding the "crazy Frenchmen" driving like hell from the nearby town of Mattawa to the logging cuts in the early morning. Often we were coming the other way, bleary-eyed from lack of sleep after radio-tracking all night. Park officials later required us to equip ourselves with CB radios and issue warnings of our location every half-kilometre, just like the loggers do. Traffic control, even in the wilderness!

We also liked a particular beaver pond full of dead standing trees where we could watch moose any time, and where the biomass of moose exceeded that of any place we knew. Moose tracks made the sandy flat on the pond's east side look like a gridiron after a game, and the balsam firs around the pond's edge, pruned from moose browsing, met the standards of a formal garden. Usually, there were wolf tracks too.

Over these summers we managed to collar six wolves. Others tantalized us with their howls and tracks, first here, then there. It was a game, and often we were left thinking that they were study-ing us. In the end, which occurred surprisingly and suddenly, they donated some good data.

Kiosk is a near-abandoned ghost town along the then-active CNR railway, a few kilometres inside the park in its northwest corner. Mary and I first moved into the Kiosk area the summer after capturing the Nahma wolf, after that year's riot of birdsong dropped off to only red-eyed vireos singing among the maples on the ridges, after the peepers and treefrogs packed it in for the year. From Kiosk, a circulatory system of both logging roads and canoe routes fan out to the south. We set up camp at the far end of Kioshkokwi Lake, by the rapids, where the tannin-laden waters swirl across big, water-smoothed rocks on their fall into the lake.

Immediately on the very first night, the wolves fed us some false data that took us the rest of the summer to untangle. A worn-out, long-forgotten logging road that we called the Fassett Creek road ran west almost to the northwest corner of the park. Out at the end of it we began our first night's howling. Waiting for darkness where alders had finally reclaimed the road, watching a pair of olive-sided flycatchers swoop from spruce spire to spire, suddenly we became aware of wolf howls floating to us over the gurgle of a stream. We walked up a bank, waited fifty minutes, and howled back. They gave us a response loud enough for an accurate compass bearing.

The human ear is poor at measuring decibels, but accurate in determining direction. Mary and I both take compass bearings while wolves howl, and rarely do we differ by more than five degrees. Because wolves may howl at any time, day or night, our advice to our crews is that they always wear a compass.

This pack was north of us, but we could not plot a bearing on the map because we were not exactly sure where we were. We entered in our notebook: "22 degrees from somewhere."

After dark we began the drive back to camp, stopping every kilometre to howl. Wolf answers are classical examples of stimulus-response behaviour, well studied in the field of animal ethology and human psychology. An undefined drive to respond, called "action specific energy," is drained away by the animal's response, called the "consummatory act." Action specific energy might be compared to the water in a flush toilet. The act of flushing is the consummatory act that can't be repeated until the energy builds up again − or the tank refills. We normally wait at least half an hour before trying for a cross-bearing from another location.

A response of this type is a reflex action. Wolves benefit enough from howling for it to be favoured by natural selection. From my master's research, we learned both that individual wolves have characteristic harmonically related overtones in their howls that can serve to identify them, and that wolves can distinguish among these overtones more accurately than humans. Therefore, individuals probably recognize one another's howls, an advantage for pack animals often separated from one another. Wolves can pinpoint the source of the sound from a distance of well over two kilometres, as shown by the frequency with which they come to the exact place we howled. We also know that excited wolves howl at a higher pitch than normal. Group howls seem to be a spontaneous combustion of excitement, with wolves running around or grouping and jumping together, tails flicking. Undoubtedly there is a lot more encoded in howls known only to wolves.

What wolves think when they hear humans howl is unclear. Often they may respond as a reflex and not think, but other times they clearly do. They come to investigate, sometimes howling back first but often arriving silently. We know this from the increasing signal strength of those wearing radio-collars. That happens between one-third and one-half of the times. Then we are a temporary disturbance, probably of little consequence. Wolves discover us, then leave to continue whatever they were doing.

When humans howl near dens or rendezvous sites in the spring or early summer, however, they may cause a pack to move out, carrying the pups with them. We rarely howl in spring now, unless we know the alpha-female is not present, and we conduct fewer general howling surveys at that season. Instead, throughout the summer, we camp near known rendezvous sites and monitor spontaneous howling.

People travelling in Algonquin, or any wild environment, should consider the immensely more rewarding experience of hearing wolves howl spontaneously without the nagging fear that by howling themselves they have intruded into the wolves' world. The costs-benefits of howling as a research tool, used when necessary, differ from those of recreational users.

Exactly at midnight on that first night of searching along the Fassett Creek road, we heard wolves again, pups too, closer than before. In our notebook we jotted down 138 degrees from wherever we were, but this time we had just passed an old portage sign so we had a clue.

Never having located more than two packs in one night, so buoyed by success, we continued past our camp. It was wrapped in a light mist from the cool air. If we waited another night to finish covering the area, we could not be sure of the separate identities of packs we heard that may have moved. At 3:55 A.M., we scored the hat trick. By the time we had taken our three cross-bearings, the thin light of day was washing out our headlights.

The following afternoon we puzzled over the topographic map and our notes. Periodically the night before, we had tried to figure out our location from the stars. When we plotted our course, we found to our chagrin that the Fassett Creek road had taken a 180-degree turn in its first few kilometres. After identifying the creek where we had heard the first pack, and the portage where we had heard the second, and drawing our compass bearings on the map, we found they crossed!

Our hat trick was rescinded. The first two packs were the same.

Realizing we could approach the pack from Fassett Creek itself, that evening we drove back to the portage and unloaded our canoe. Fassett Creek meanders out in wide sedge flats with hills rising in the distance. Escorted by myriad mosquitoes, we paddled and poled our way downstream.

The calm air was burdened with light mist. A few hermit thrushes and a white-throated sparrow sang now and then, without vigour because the season was well advanced. We encountered a series of beaver dams that forced us to climb out on each side of the canoe and hoist it across. A moose heard us coming and beat a sloshing retreat to high ground.

In the gathering dusk we waited for the wolves to howl, but they were silent or not there, so after a while we gave a couple of howls ourselves. A lone wolf answered from back in the hills to the west with a series of remarkable treble-pitched howls, each starting with a half-bark. When the wolf stopped, all we could hear was mosquito-hum as before.

We manoeuvred the canoe into a backwater and sat quietly to see if the wolf would investigate. The thrushes fell silent, and the first stars appeared. Fifteen minutes later the wolf howled again with its unusual treble howl, this time much closer, halfway between us and the shore. The tall sedges and grasses completely hid us, and the gentle air currents were not flowing the wolf's way.

Three minutes of silence, then almost on top of us, the wolf howled again. We could not see it. By then it was too dark, and to shine the flashlight over the grasses would have meant standing up and becoming visible. So we sat there, breathless. In a minute we heard the wolf in the water, then all was silent.

Five minutes went by before the wolf howled again. It had swum the creek and was on the far side, halfway to shore. Having finished its reconnaissance and discovered the fraud, it launched into a long series of bark-howls. On and on it howled. Finally, its protest over, it disappeared into the night.

We were to hear that wolf with its distinctive voice again. Meanwhile, we found another pack the very next night, ten kilometres to the east, almost between the two-for-one pack that we had named the Fassett Creek pack, and the pack we had heard later that first night that we called the Ratrap Lake pack.

This new pack howled for us near the head of a deeply incised creek valley. The wolves had left plenty of tracks in an abandoned gravel pit nearby. Because we were uncertain of the pack's identity, and because it was wedged in an unusually small area between the other two packs, we gave these wolves only the temporary name Gravel Pit pack.

For weeks, we tried to catch wolves from all three packs – Fassett Creek, Ratrap Lake, and Gravel Pit – but they were elusive. More than once they investigated a trap set, walked all around it, and left. By late summer, when cicadas droned in the hills and the long-horned grasshoppers fiddled nightly from the meadows, we suddenly realized from our field notes that while we had occasionally heard the Ratrap and Gravel Pit wolves on the same night, never had that happened with the Fassett and Gravel Pit wolves. We had no confirmation that these were separate packs.

The wolves kept their identity a mystery until the last night of the summer. Then, just after midnight, from the edge of a bog three kilometres east of the gravel pit, we heard the same treble voice and bark-howl. It was the Fassett Creek howler well inside the Gravel Pit territory. Its presence there indicated that the Fassett Creek and Gravel Pit packs were the same.

We reinterpreted our data in light of this discovery and were surprised to learn that a whole pack, pups and all, would have moved ten kilometres between Fassett Creek and the gravel pit in mid-July when the pups were so young. Even more surprising was that they had repeated the trip. Maybe they were travelling back and forth to a moose carcass. We found a well-used game trail with wolf scats along it that led from the gravel pit south to a series of marshes and bogs that in turn ran west towards Fassett Creek, but our searches turned up no dead moose.

The Fassett Creek and Ratrap Lake packs had yet another surprise, and one disappointment, in store for us. In late August, Mary and I caught and radio-collared a wolf near the gravel pit that we took to be a member of the Gravel Pit pack. We were elated, hoping we could work out winter movements and territory boundaries. But it died in early October. Graham heard the collar on mortality mode and tracked it beyond the boundary of the park. He found it beside a lake, its body only a pile of fur, too decayed to determine the cause of death.

In early September, however, a student crew that had taken over our trapline caught a Ratrap wolf not far from Ratrap Lake. That wolf did give us winter data. Once, Graham and Jenny saw the pack from the air, feeding on a moose at the edge of Manitou Lake. Surprisingly, the lake was well within what should have been the Fassett Creek pack's territory. In later flights, Graham often located the wolf that far west. Repeated flights looking for the tracks of a different Fassett Creek pack turned out negative.

Our final interpretation was that Fassett Creek and Ratrap Lake packs were the same, but there had been two breeding females and two sets of pups. That happens in wolf packs sometimes, as other studies have shown, but we recorded it rarely. It is unclear why at times the social hierarchy in wolves permits it. In our population, experiencing high annual mortality as we discovered later, perhaps it was uncommon because vacant land was often available.

So, our three packs in one night shrank to two and finally to one. Still, its territory was only average size, 125 square kilometres (plus about 50 per cent for interstices between packs – land they undoubtedly used but where we lacked data points for sampling reasons). With few deer to supplement their moose-meat winter diet, hunting often must have been hard.

East of the Kiosk region along the CNR railway through the park lies the ghost town of Daventry. A logging road drops south to it and beyond. Park rangers had reported that loggers working there commonly saw tracks and heard wolves. We drove to a huge log-filled clearing to investigate. A big yellow log-loader was parked there, its long arm poised for action, looking greedy like the lumber mills it served. Ironically, given our feelings about logging in a park, the network of logging roads makes our research easier.

It was a Sunday when we first came to Daventry, so the big trucks were not rolling. Wolf prints plastered the sandy road on top of the tire treads. We spent the afternoon among the ghosts in the tangled clearing where the village once stood. In times past, the trains had stopped there on their way up from Ottawa to North Bay to take on water and disgorge an occasional party of adventurers into the back country. Raspberry vines and grasses now claimed the opening. Aspens and balsam firs grew from barely discernable ruins of buildings. Recovery, healing, memories of people fading into forest.

Back at the log landing we took our place and watched the lights dim and the curtain of night spread open to reveal a starry sky. We waited, but not for long. A whole pack tuned up in the darkness out across a beaver meadow behind the log landing.

The next day we set traps to the clang and clamour of heavy machinery. The loggers, of course, saw our truck and wanted to know what we were doing on their closed road. Our explanation was not greeted with enthusiasm. The crew was from Killaloe, a small town southeast of the park and a long way, about one hundred kilometres, for them to commute. Later, in the Killaloe area we would become the focus of public controversy.

Gathered around an eighteen-wheeler, feeling outnumbered, I tried to generate some interest by pulling out a radio-collar from the back of our truck and explaining how it worked. "I got a better rig for a wolf," responded a burly fellow who outweighed me by a ton. "It's called a bullet." Then I was regaled with the usual: "What good are they? No deer left. No moose." Their comments were laced with invectives about "friggin' wolves." I tried to explain that despite wolves we were standing in a forest with one of the highest moose densities in Ontario, but that didn't give anyone pause. What is knowledge in the face of prejudice?

The situation became tense. Every little while the conversation would get back to why we were wasting government money on such foolishness. Finally another big eighteen-wheeler rolled up, ready to take more of Algonquin Park to the mill. The circle of men gradually disbanded.

The next day we caught a large, adult male wolf. We had checked the traps in the early morning, again to the roar of logging trucks. At 4 P.M. we were driving back along the road, not expecting any action, when around a curve, only a hundred metres from the log landing, a trap was gone. We jumped out and immediately heard the chain clanking down in a thick tangle of alders. This was one of only two wolves caught in the daytime during our study, a mystery because we now know that wolves travel extensively both by night and day.

Daventry 1 was a feisty but fearful wolf, only wanting to get away. In a thundershower that suddenly blew up, we drugged, collared, measured, and weighed him, took ten cubic centimetres of blood from his right front leg, and lay him on the ground to recover. The cool rain must have helped revive him, for no sooner had we taken our hands off him than he jumped to his feet and ran.

Not far – his hindquarters could not keep up with his front end. We left him to sleep off the drug.

We wanted to know if the Daventry pack's territory abutted the Ratrap Lake pack to the west. Between Ratrap and Daventry runs a string of mostly long, narrow lakes roughly parallel to the CNR tracks. Believing Daventry 1 had to be there somewhere, Mary, Michelle, and I planned a night canoe trip. We set off from Kiosk, after arranging for volunteers Craig and Elaine Hurst to pick us up at the Daventry end at about 4 A.M. That gave us lots of time, we thought.

We waited for dark at the end of the first lake. After a hot, humid day, the temperature was dropping noticeably; that should have warned us of troubles ahead. No wolf answered our first howl, so, flashlights in hand, we set off across the portage. The canoe balances on my shoulders, so I can hold one arm down at my side and let the flashlight beam illuminate the trail ahead. Stars bright, no moon, traces of ground fog. As usual on such August nights, migrating birds cheeped faintly as they followed the broad sky highway.

Across Little Mink Lake, we picked out the next portage and walked it to Big Mink Lake only to find it bathed in fog. Casting off, immediately we were surrounded by invisible rocks. "Hard left . . . hard right . . . stop . . . back up!" We worked our way out from shore, now and then striking a rock and bouncing off or sticking and having to jerk our way off by shifting our weight in the canoe. Mary, flashlight shining on compass and map, calculated the bearing. No dark shoreline helped guide us, no stars.

At the far end of the lake we were unable to spotlight the portage and again ran into rocks. Finally at shore I climbed out and Mary took over the stern. A web of game trails disguised as portages ran into the forest, each one petering out.

We never did find the portage. From the map it looked like it ran uphill and down again to Cauchon Lake, with the railway bisecting the route, but fog hid everything. Finally I shouldered the canoe and we struck out through the bush, Michelle picking the "easiest" way. By then it was past 4 A.M. and we knew the Hursts would be wondering where we were. To pick our way down Cauchon in the fog, if we did manage to find it, would have taken a long time, so when we stumbled out onto the railway line, we stashed the canoe in the trees and walked out along the tracks. Daylight was working itself across the sky when we got to the Daventry road. The Hursts were asleep.

Daventry I was a data failure. We picked up his signal only once from the ground, and Graham heard him once from the air. The big hills where he came from just swallowed him up again. And the Daventry pack? It remains a mystery. We never managed to collar another member. The pack, however, had provided us with interesting information about tolerance. In their rendezvous site they must have listened each day, all day, to the clamour of heavy machinery and the shouts of men. The wolves even walked the roads in broad daylight, as Daventry I had done, barely out of sight of the unsuspecting loggers. Repeatedly in future years, we would find this curious correlation between active logging and the presence of wolves. Maybe more deer were there, feeding on the tops of downed trees. Wherever we are in the park, after the loggers leave for the day, or on weekends, we always check for wolf tracks around the skidders and trucks, and often find them.

Sometimes we have been asked to comment about regulating logging operations in wolf habitat – by other jurisdictions, not, unfortunately, by the managers of Algonquin Park, where we have proposed restrictions and have encountered indifference. Despite evidence such as that presented by the Daventry pack, we consider a no-tree-felling area around active and traditional rendezvous sites to be a common courtesy. The Daventry pack's rendezvous site itself, at the edge of a bog, had not been violated, so the wolves had stayed put. Cutting too close, or the presence of people – loggers, photographers, or anyone – in a rendezvous site is sure to trigger the pack's departure. Den sites are even more sensitive and should be protected from all forest activities to a minimum radius of one kilometre, as they are in several Canadian and United States national parks.

Nonetheless, wolves' acceptance of forest change and human presence – their tolerance of people – greatly exceeds our tolerance of wolves.

South of the Ratrap wolves lay the territory of a pack whose tracks we saw, howls we heard, and scats we collected. But for two summers we learned little about them. We called it the Namea Lake pack, but never liked the name because of its similarity to the Nahma Lake pack directly to the south.

Once, a Namea wolf put on a dazzling virtuoso performance of howling. It was a cool August night, and we were down in an ugly logging cut mercifully blurred by darkness. As usual, wolf tracks were all around the skidders parked for the night. The wolf was about three hundred metres away when it first howled, alone unless its companions were silent. In response to Mary's second howl, the wolf replied a record two hundred times! Normally, wolves howl maybe three or four, up to ten or twelve, times. This wolf went on and on like none we have ever heard. First came mouthed-over bark-howls, short in length and treble in pitch – twenty-five of them, followed by a brief pause and forty-six more. Another pause lasted for three minutes, then fifteen longer howls, a three-minute pause and twenty-one more, a two-minute pause and thirty-six more, now long, less treble, and breaking. The change in howls may have reflected the wolf's shifting emotional state, gradually becoming less perturbed by our auditory intrusions into its world.

We walked back to the truck, put it in neutral, and rolled down the hill to be closer to the wolf. One of Mary's howls set it off again, twenty-six times, a three-minute pause, then thirty-one more, its howl cutting up the night into small pieces and tossing them into the slash. The wolf did not approach. We waited for half an hour expecting to hear brush breaking nearby, but finally it gave up, or got fed up, or just went away.

Five days later we captured a Namea wolf a few kilometres away. Best of all, his capture was closer to Birchcliffe Lake than it was to tiny Namea Lake, so Birchcliffe became the official name of the pack. Graham was glad. After coming off telemetry flights and being spaced-out on motion-sickness pills, he could distinguish and pronounce the difference between Nahma and Birchcliffe somewhat better than he could Nahma and Namea.

Birchcliffe 1 was a light, tawny wolf who had threaded the game trails around there for six or seven years, judging by his well-worn incisors. He weighed in at twenty-eight kilograms (sixty-two pounds), a middle-weight. His eyes were wary, distrustful. He fought off the effects of the drug fast and was gone. A few days later we picked up his signal to the northwest along a boggy little creek, then, at other times, he was farther away, and we were able to start defining his territory. It fit nicely between Nahma and Ratrap, enclosing one large lake and a chain of small ones named after two of the famous Group of Seven artists: J. E. H. MacDonald and Lawren Harris. Some evenings we would slip our canoe into this chain of lakes and howl the route after dark; occasionally the Birchcliffe pack was there.

By spring 1990, three Ratrap wolves and one Birchcliffe wolf were on the air. From telemetry flights the previous winter, Graham had defined their territories. Mary and I were anxious to increase our sample size, so in July, we set up camp at the rapids again. We set traps in accustomed places, watched moose in the famous (to us) bog, canoed to distant corners of the region, listened nightly to wolf howls, fought mosquitoes at dusk, and collected water at the spring. Then, unexpectedly, our work in the northwest came to an abrupt end.

July 10, 1990, was a warm, sunny day. We slept late, having radio-tracked much of the night. After breakfast at the rapids, we drove over to the Fassett Creek gravel pit, climbed up on the back bumper of the truck, and searched for a signal. Distant from the south, Ratrap 3 came in. But wait! Fast pulse – mortality mode.

When you work for weeks to radio-collar each wolf, hearing mortality mode comes as a great disappointment. Somewhat dispirited, we took a bearing and started hiking through the bush. The signal took us down the Fassett-Ratrap wolf trail that two summers before had been heavily used by this pack when it was determined to confuse us. Where the trail ran down into a wet sedge-meadow, we left it and traversed a side slope of sugar maple-yellow birch forest. After walking another three hundred metres, the signal became loud.

Ratrap 3 was a medium-sized, adult male, captured and radio-collared by Carolyn Callaghan and Cam Douglas only thirty-six days previously. Nothing on the capture form had appeared irregular. He had been a healthy wolf, thin as is common but not emaciated. He had apparently taken the drug well and recovered quickly. Since collaring, he had moved extensively throughout the Ratrap territory. Now when we got to him, he lay stretched out full length at the base of a hemlock. From the lack of smell, he had been dead only a few hours, although long enough that his body was cold.

We examined the site for signs of a fight, wolf on wolf or wolf on moose, but the vegetation was not torn up. We felt his body for broken bones or bleeding, but he appeared in good shape. Puzzled, I hoisted him up across my shoulders and we hiked back to the truck. We would freeze him and later have him autopsied by our pathologist, Ian Barker, at the University of Guelph.

But we had noticed two peculiarities that bothered us. Unexplainable was a bit of exposed underbark at the base of the hemlock, as if the wolf had chewed there. Also strange was a stick lodged between the wolf's carnassial teeth, lying up against his hard pallet, and another at the back of his throat. Mary raised the possibility of rabies because an animal that is disoriented by this disease may chew at anything. We dismissed that idea because only one case in wolves had been recorded south of the tundra biome in North America, that one in Minnesota.

At the truck we bagged the carcass, tied it on top under the canoe, and headed out to Kiosk. We kept talking about the hemlock tree and the sticks, however, and finally convinced ourselves to have the wolf checked for rabies. On the radio-phone at Kiosk we called Agriculture Canada in North Bay and were given instructions on how to remove the wolf's head with a knife, of course wearing surgical gloves. We arranged to meet a veterinarian at a café along the highway.

The vet was sure rabies was not involved because of the two sticks in the mouth and throat. No wolf, he considered, could stand the sticks, and the one in the throat probably had punctured the esophagus, but he took the head anyway.

He was wrong. Two days later an MNR ranger drove up to our tent. "You should go get rabies vaccinations," he announced.

Although rabies is common in Ontario, mostly among foxes and domestic animals, we had trouble getting shots. For two days we phoned health clinics and hospitals in the area and were referred from one to another. We wanted to know, as well, if the wolf could have passed the virus thirty-six days earlier to the student crew, and found opinions divided. Rabies dies within a few minutes of exposure to air, but the danger to us was from contact with wolf saliva while routinely examining tooth wear. We followed the safe route and eventually all got vaccinated. From then on, pre-exposure rabies vaccination has been mandatory for all field crew members.

One dead wolf would have had little consequence to our study, but that was not all. After a flight a few days later, Graham left a message at the Kiosk ranger station that Ratrap 1, Ratrap 2, and Birchcliffe 1 were all on mortality mode, that is, all our other radio-collared wolves in the northwest.

It took a flight with an MNR floatplane to a remote lake to get to Birchcliffe 1 and one of the Ratrap wolves. They had died within a hundred metres of one another. The trespassing Ratrap wolf may not have been aware of its location. The remaining Ratrap wolf had died in its own territory. Two of the wolves were too decomposed for a rabies check, but the other Ratrap wolf tested positive.

Periodically throughout the rest of the summer, one crew or another would swing by and find some wolf tracks and scats. The next winter, Graham flew over a few times and once saw the tracks of some remaining Ratrap wolves threading across a lake, so the rabies epidemic had not annihilated them.

Rabies killed two more of our radio-collared wolves on the east side of Algonquin Park, for a total of six. If our sample of radio-collared wolves, then about twenty, represented 10 per cent of the park population, possibly sixty or so wolves died in the epidemic.

These results led us to investigate clinical records in Ontario more fully, some in files of the MNR, some held by Agriculture Canada. To our surprise we found fifteen confirmed or strongly suspected cases of rabies in wolves in Ontario since 1960, and fewer than fifteen cases of rabid coyotes annually. Most were in a zone of overlap between the two canid species, and identification was sometimes not confirmed.

Reviewing a decade of records south of the upper Great Lakes in Minnesota, Michigan, and Wisconsin, no cases of rabies were confirmed in wild wolves between 1981 and 1991. Why the difference? Two different strains of rabies were involved: a fox strain in all the Ontario cases, and a skunk strain south of the Great Lakes. We speculated in a paper published in the *Journal of Animal Diseases* that because foxes feed more commonly at wolf kills than skunks do, transmission of the fox strain to wolves might be easier. Nobody knows why rabies is so rare in forest-dwelling wolves, notwithstanding our results. We have not found rabies in the Algonquin population since then.

In his Ph.D. thesis, Graham concluded that the density of wolves in the northwest was roughly 27 per cent lower than in the eastern sector of the park. Pack sizes were only marginally smaller, so the lower density was primarily the result of larger territories.

These larger territories appear to be at least partially the result of less total prey. In winter, with almost no deer in the northwest, the biomass of prey there was roughly 12 per cent less than in the east. Besides less ungulate prey, snow depth may have reduced wolf efficiency, or lengthened hunting time. Moose come in packages roughly six times larger than deer, so there are fewer animals to find. Probably because wolves experience greater difficulty in obtaining prey in the northwest, wolf biomass there was 0.27 per cent of ungulate biomass compared with a slightly higher 0.37 per cent in the east. Both values, however, fall within the low, expected range from other studies.

In the northwest, wolves had a surprising 11 per cent snow-shoe hare in their winter diet, a high value for any wolf study, suggesting that wolves may have been experiencing some difficulty in obtaining enough moose or beaver. A small percentage of deer in their winter scats showed an ability to find them when few were around.

And were any useful evolutionary messages hidden among the high northwest hills? Only that, inexorably, the wolf population there reflected both the obvious – its prey abundance and the conditions of the forest – and the subtle – its diseases and the quiet flow of calories through the ecosystem. Wolves play the ecosystem game of life with the cards nature deals them, their social integrity and population fitness at stake, a new hand every season, a different deck on occasion, changing players, shifting odds. Large carnivores, at the top of the energy pyramids, need wide adaptabilities.

Each spring we still collect wolf scats in the northwest and walk a series of pellet transects to record changes in moose numbers. Volunteers Bill and Carrie Steer run some moose/deer track ratio counts along logging roads and locate packs. We watch for some major change in the system. Deer are recovering slowly, and if their numbers keep edging up, we may want to see if they migrate to winter range outside the park and influence wolves in that way.

Someday we may start up a full program there again. Until then, it is satisfying enough just to think of the Fassett marshes echoing from wolf howls, and tracks of a pack stitching the snow on Manitou Lake.

WOLVES ACROSS THE DOME

Coping with Chaos

Over time, the assembly line of nature slowly but inexorably rolls out genes, species, communities, entire ecosystems, making new combinations, tearing up the blueprints of the old and unsuccessful. It is the business of science to classify and find order in nature, to "search for systematic relationships and verifiable truths." Science has been wildly successful: we can place a spacecraft on the moon or Mars; we understand the behaviour of atoms and molecules; we have cracked the genetic code.

In the midst of such overwhelming success, however, a new science has emerged, born out of failure. We still cannot predict weather, nor changes in ocean currents, nor molecular movements of diffusion, nor the changing behaviour of ecosystems. The new science flies under the banner of "chaos," "complexity," "catastrophe and surprise."

When processes in nature are simple and straightforward, that is, keep going in a constant direction, we have a chance to understand them. When they are complex and chaotic, we are only now beginning to try. There are principles awaiting discovery.

"Catastrophe," when stripped of its everyday connotation as something undesirable, means only "sudden change." As such, it often comes in nature as a surprise. It may be a hurricane or ice storm or flood, a forest fire, or an

outbreak of spruce budworm. All share common features. There is an initial state before the event and a final one after and some silent pressure building up within the atmosphere or the forest that eventually erupts to move the system suddenly from the initial to the final state. The pressure may build fast, like the sudden formation of an atmospheric low pressure cell, or it may build slowly, like the initial population of spruce budworm. Finally, with the addition of just a little more atmospheric pressure or a few more budworm larvae, the catastrophic event occurs.

Ecosystems, while quietly going about their business and altering little with time, are full of hidden pressure gradients. Eventually pressure builds up to cause sudden change. Eruptions of moose or deer populations may be like eruptions of budworm. Time delays between a change in prey numbers and a resultant change in predator numbers may be like that too, while the predator adjusts its hunting behaviour. So predator-prey ratios may be stable at either high or low density but be unstable in between. A population of any animal may do well until it runs out of food, then suddenly collapse. A beaver dam may give way, draining the pond overnight. Dead wood accumulates to the point where the probability of a forest fire becomes a near certainty.

That ecosystems experience so many non-linear, minor to major catastrophic changes results in unpredictability and surprise. Some catastrophic change exhibits a periodicity making it partially predictable, such as fire that, on average, occurs about every hundred years in Canada's boreal forests. Others, such as a sudden shift in major species without any obvious change in the forest, are unpredictable.

After the catastrophic event, what then? Will nature run things back to the beginning so sometime later it can all happen again? The answer is yes and no. Sometimes forest succession after fire is reasonably predictable. If the soils remain unaffected, a predictable sequence of trees and other plants will grow again, reconstructing the forest of old.

In other circumstances, however, the system will flip out into something new. Conditions may have changed. Maybe after a forest fire, topsoil has eroded away, or without the insulation of trees, permafrost rebounds upward to preclude tree growth ever again. Or after a temporary cessation of moose browsing, a generation of saplings has grown permanently inaccessible.

Then, new ecosystem models run off the assembly line of time — new combinations of species, different adaptive responses, novel ways to survive.

IN A BROAD north-south band just east of the central crest of Algonquin Park, we came to know five wolf packs: Little Branch, East Gate, Annie Bay, Lavieille, and Charles Creek. These were the transition wolves, familiar with both the tolerant hardwoods of the west and the pine-poplar forests of the east.

Across their lands, going east, the subtle interplay of rain, snow, humidity, and soils shifts the forest from one type to another. The transition is discreetly achieved, with just a touch more poplar at first, or more pine, then less sugar maple and yellow birch. The hardwoods slip away as if a magician passed his hand across the forest. This change-over reflects a distant geological past, ancient, naked mountains there long before life left the seas. Now, the remnant dome of low, gently rolling land is still high enough to wring moisture out of air masses moving in from the northwest, leaving the eastside forests marginally drier. Coupled with shallow or sandy soils, the legacy of glacial outwash, the ecosystem responds with a cast of more drought-tolerant players.

To the large mammal system, the forest shift is of little consequence. Poplar and red maple are just as good moose and deer food as sugar maple and yellow birch. The small and finely adapted may feel the difference, but big animals tend towards greater generality, one key to their success. For wolves, as long as there are deer in the thickets and beaver in the ponds, they are all right.

The wolves across the dome gave us shreds and scraps of data. Although we studied them less intensively than wolves of the northwest or the east, without them, some pieces of the ecological puzzle would have been missing. Without them, too, wolves would be receiving less protection in Algonquin Park today. And they provided us with an ecosystem history, an all-important time-depth perspective. These packs or their forerunners lived in Doug Pimlott's "primary study area" during his years of wolf research from 1959 to 1963. I had known some of them as a student. Back then, the forest and its prey base were very different.

Some packs were primarily Graham's, especially Little Branch, although at times Mary and I filled in with summer howling to find them. The Little Branch pack occupied the southern portion of the park, living in the two townships that hang down on the map like an inert pendulum, one below the other. Its territory extended beyond the pendulum on the east side. The pack paid a price for that.

These two townships, Bruton and Clyde, were added to Algonquin Park only in 1961, sixty-eight years after the park was established. To try to please everyone, the government of the day allowed hunting and trapping to continue. Already, Algonquin native people held trapping rights throughout the eastern one-third of the park, but in Bruton and Clyde, trapping rights were extended to white trappers too.

Graham collared a Little Branch wolf very early in the study on August 30, 1987. The next autumn, two West Virginian hunters arrived at a hunting lodge near the town of Whitney. Non-resident hunters are drawn to our frontier for the spring and fall black bear hunts. Part of the package for the Virginians included the services of a resident guide who had prepared the site. He had baited it during much of the late summer and early fall with meat scraps or day-old doughnuts and constructed a platform up in a tree for the hunters to wait on.

Baiting bears, deer, and waterfowl like this is legal in Ontario but not in many states, although there are some regulations affecting how you do it to waterfowl. Calling moose, placing out scents, chasing with dogs – all are legitimate. Little Branch 1 took the bait. The hunting lodge reported the success. Why not? It was perfectly legal. The hunters took Little Branch 1's pelt back home to show the boys.

A second member of the Little Branch pack was collared in May 1988. Like Little Branch 1, this wolf was an adult male. He managed to live only seven months more, then one January day

Graham heard his signal from the air on mortality mode. The wolf was located well within the park, near the centre of his territory. Although the Cessna was on skis, there was no lake large enough to land on nearby. It was late May before Graham finally reached him and found a pile of fur and bones lying under a dangling wire neck snare. The local white trapper had not even bothered to check his sets.

In the official master plan for Algonquin Park, approved in 1975, is the statement that in Bruton and Clyde townships, "All species of Park furbearers, with the exception of timber wolves, may be trapped." Park officials were ignoring their own directive and allowing trappers to kill wolves there, as many wolves as they wanted – just like they can on land outside the park.

Graham met with park officials, armed with photos of the dangling snare and a copy of their park management plan. The statement in the plan could no longer be ignored. Soon after, the MNR applied a zero quota for wolves to all white trappers in the park.

Of course the action raised a protest. At the MNR's request, Graham attended a meeting of local trappers to explain our research. Tempers flared, and local newspapers carried complaints that wolves would eat all the beaver. That was only a minor skirmish compared to the battles that lay ahead, and it blew over – in part. The part that did not blow over was the now-aroused attentiveness of the Ontario Federation of Anglers and Hunters. This large federation seems to protest any erosion of hunting, fishing, or trapping rights on behalf of local rod and gun clubs scattered throughout the province. We would hear from them again.

Abutting the northwest corner of the Little Branch pack's territory, at the base of the pendulum, lies the territory of the Louisa pack. As a student I knew this area well; the Louisa pack provided my first wild wolf experiences, including the first howls I ever heard. This pack's responses lay the groundwork for the annual parkwide howling surveys I participated in for Doug Pimlott and my master's research on the meaning in wolf howls.

Back then, the Louisa pack lived in a landscape of mostly hardwood cut-over, a sad example of "high grading" where all the marketable trees were taken with little regard for the future stand. I remember a forest made up primarily of big, gnarled yellow birches, magnificent giants too bent or rotten for the mill. They were the last of a generation. Nobody in Ontario has the nerve to say that yellow birch has been managed under "sustained yield." Tiny, trident-shaped yellow birch seeds need to land on a mineral soil to germinate. Instead, in stands with sugar maple, the seeds encounter a blanket of fall leaves. The millions of seeds from these giant trees lie all over the previous autumn's leaf-litter and rot. Yellow birch needs ground fire to prepare a seed bed, or soil scarification such as happens accidentally in log skidways or landings.

In contrast, maple seeds are large and fleshy with stored carbohydrates that allow them to send a radicle rootlet to penetrate the fallen leaves and jump-start a new generation. Without fire, maples will claim these stands.

Other species gun for yellow birches too. Sapsuckers, attracted to the heavy run of spring sap, drill holes that provide easy access for the spores of bracket fungi that, in turn, clog the water transport system with hyphae. Seedlings have to live in fear of browsing deer. The 150-year-old yellow birch giants were products of a time when there was a much smaller, or non-existent, deer population in the early 1800s.

I also remember old stables, and manure piles not yet rotted away – remnants of horse-logging, the end of an era. It was harder work to skid logs that way than with the mechanical "bush pigs" of today, but horse hooves were gentler on the forest than lug-and-chain tires.

We would have enjoyed canoeing Harry and Rence lakes again, searching for wolves and trying to raise a howl from the Galipo marshes, but we were not destined to work long in the Louisa area. Like the Daventry wolf, Louisa 1 was a data failure. She managed to slip her collar and leave it lying on mortality mode among the trees. After that we left; our study area was just too big to handle the pendulum too.

WOLVES WE HAVE KNOWN

Above left: McDonald 7 Basin, an immigrant into the decimated Basin Depot pack, became alpha-female and raised litters from 1995 to 1997.

Top right: Basin 14 successfully raised the pups after his mate of three years, Macdonald 7 Basin, died in August 1997.

Above right: Basin 3 Foys, alpha-female in the Foys Lake pack, had a deformed hind leg that caused a permanent limp.

Below right: Basin 4 McDonald, alpha-male of the McDonald Creek pack, was the largest wolf of the study at 44 kilograms (97 pounds).

Below left: Redpole 3 was born in 1991 into the Redpole pack. He was still with the pack when recollared in 1996.

CATCHING AND
COLLARING WOLVES
Left: John weighs Mathews 11,
an adult male shot the
following March (1997).
Below: Mary with Jocko 4,
whose collar failed.

Above: Graham Forbes with Annie Bay 3, a long-lived wolf, grandmother of Jocko 11, 12, and 13.

Below: Our field crew, summer 1988, included (left to right) Carolyn Callaghan, Graham Forbes, Harry Vogel, Jenny, Mary, and Michelle.

TRACKING WOLVES
Top: Mary prepares for a telemetry flight with volunteer pilot Hank Halliday.
Above: A typical Algonquin landscape, viewed from the air. Sec Lake is in the foreground.
Left: Mary radio-tracking.

Above: Another Algonquin scene.
A beaver dam caused the
Bonnechere River to widen
where we often camped.
Right: Jenny howls to locate the
Nahma pack, summer 1988.

WOLF COUNTRY
Above: A typical summer rendezvous site.
Below: Basin Depot pack's den in 1996 was used only once, then flooded out by a beaver dam the following spring.

Above: Poplar and red maple take the place of pine after the area has been logged in the Bonnechere Valley.
Right: The growth of red maple is slowed by moose and deer browsing.
Below: A young bull and cow moose make an appearance.

WOLVES WE HAVE KNOWN
Top left: A young wolf in the Foys Lake pack, born in 1990, daughter of Basin 3 Foys.
Middle left: Jocko 11, a yearling male, son of Jocko 10, born in 1996.
Bottom left: McDonald 8 wandered widely for a year before returning to his natal McDonald Creek pack to become the alpha-male.
Top right: Jocko 13, a yearling female, daughter of Jocko 10.
Above right: Jocko 10, alpha-male of the Jocko Lake pack, usurped his father's dominant position.

Northeast of the Little Branch territory lay the land of the East Gate pack, so named because the extreme eastern corner of its territory extended just beyond the East Gate of the park – a mistake in judgement on the pack's part. The East Gate wolves lived mainly in pine-poplar forests, not quite reaching the sugar maples to the west.

This pack was not remote. The park's major highway bisected the northern quarter of its territory, and one major public campground lay within it. Thousands of people have heard the pack howl on wolf-howling nights run by park interpreters. These wolves have been tolerant of repeated human demands that they perform.

In 1987, the pack contained eight wolves, two of whom we radio-collared. Graham saw the pack occasionally from the air and, once, while ground tracking at Rock Lake found them on a deer. They spotted him watching from the barren lake-edge alders; agitated, they barked at him and ran back and forth trying to get a better look.

Occasionally they left their tracks in the snow up on Bluebird Lake to the northeast, and it took us a while to figure out that another pack hadn't made them. Back in Pimlott's days, a separate pack had lived there, but territories had shifted since then. Wolves don't leave fences or land deeds, only tradition, which is sufficient unless too many elders die. Here, the original wolves had died, non-consenting subjects of a research decision in 1963 to kill them to assess the age structure of the population. Attitudes have changed; such a decision would be impossible today.

Or would it? It is still acceptable for wolves to be trapped if they step outside the park. In the fall of 1988, a young radio-collared East Gate male dispersed to the northeast, perhaps looking for a mate. He was snared four months later in Alice Township, eighty kilometres away. Then in March 1989 the whole East Gate pack ventured just beyond the park to the edge of the town of Whitney – a fatal move. Four of them strangled in neck snares. When the ice broke up on Bluebird Lake that spring, only three East Gate wolves remained.

Late in April, these survivors found a highway-killed moose that road workers had dragged into the trees. We set traps, hoping to collar a remaining wolf and follow its fate. One evening we sat in our truck on the shoulder of the highway near the carcass listening for howls. Wood frogs were calling from the lake margins and a saw-whet owl repeated its single note from a distance. Warm air was sending lingering ice tinkling on its way. Suddenly we were aware of a tap-tap-tap – wolf toenails on pavement. The wolf walked right past the truck, intent on the moose meat it knew was in the trees. We watched its shadowy form climb the bank and disappear.

A minute later, after a car zipped past, the wolf reappeared, walked back down the slope and stopped, finally aware of us. It ran back a few steps, then stood looking up the road as if expecting another wolf to appear, then loped into the trees. Downslope, it splashed across a beaver pond and was gone.

The next morning, a blood stain and wolf hair on the highway told that another East Gate wolf was dead. We could not find its carcass, not even a blood trail, and concluded that whoever had hit it had picked it up.

Now the pack was down to two. We caught one of them the next day, an immature male. It was easy to feel sorry for him; he had suffered the anguish of seeing his pack destroyed. Unless the remaining wolf was an adult female, the pack was doomed. Unfortunately, we lost track of him; he slipped his collar. Not that summer nor the next did we hear an East Gate pack. Singles on occasion, but no pack. After that we quit working in this area.

The range of the next pack to the north, the Annie Bay pack, was and still is centred on a clearing where once there had been a lumber mill. Where the mill itself stood is still open grassland after more than half a century. In my student days I lived in an old trailer in the mill clearing and watched the pack from a hill one kilometre away that gave a good view across a burn. That pack was the subject of my first scientific paper: "Observations of Wolves at a Rendezvous Site in Algonquin Park." Here I witnessed many hours of pup play, the rudiments of hunting behaviour to be used when pups grow older. Over the years, the burn had grown back to young forest, and the wolves had shifted their rendezvous site to the clearings right at the old mill.

Anyone seeing the burn for the first time today could not imagine how different it was thirty-five years before. Back then, a wolf trotting across it was in full view between low blueberry bushes and patches of bracken fern that grew sparsely around blackened stumps and logs. In the burned-over landscape, bluebirds dipped from standing dead spire to spire, and nighthawks dove down on flying insects in the opening. Gone are savannah and field sparrows, replaced by white-throated sparrows. Among the aspen saplings, redstarts and chestnut-sided warblers nest – birds of young forest. Soon there will be ovenbirds and hermit thrushes – species of more shadowy places.

Fire has always been part of Algonquin forests. In an environmental battle zone between major biomes – boreal forest to the north and southern hardwood forest to the south – fire ushers in even more dramatic and longer lasting change than it does in more central places. The first explorers, such as Alexander Sherriff, looking for a safe water route to the west, recorded large areas on their maps as "burned land." At that time and even earlier, moose and caribou inhabited this highland dome, but no deer. Deer bones are absent in archaeological sites.

With the first loggers in the early 1800s, clear-cutting and burning opened up vast tracts of land. Deer living in hardwood forests to the south extended their range into this food-abundant, early successional landscape. Moose, it seems, may have declined, and caribou vanished. It was a dramatic ecosystem shift, an artificial one, human-caused, with its own built-in, hidden tensions to return to what it was. But rarely can ecosystems duplicate the past.

In the early 1960s, deer greatly outnumbered moose and ranged throughout the park at an estimated density of 5.8 per square kilometre. Cedar seedlings, a preferred food, had no chance to survive except on cliff faces. In many places, forest succession was being retarded by repeated browsing of poplar and maple leaders. Along the highway, traffic jammed up around deer habituated to human handouts, and individual animals were seen so often they were given names.

In contrast, you could travel the park all summer and be lucky if you saw one or two moose, then estimated at only one per six square kilometres. The wolves largely ignored them, eating 80 per cent deer in summer, 90 per cent in winter. It was a deer-dominated system.

You could argue that the ecosystem was artificial then, with so much early-stage forest and with the dominant herbivore being a recent immigrant. Nonetheless, the ecosystem was poised for change – it always is. The climate was warmer than it was when many of the forest giants grew, and beaver had just recovered from a province-wide outbreak of tularemia. Sure enough, in the early 1970s the deer population crashed, victim of winters of deep snow, less logging opening up the hardwoods, too many logged-over conifer stands so crucial to winter survival, rigid fire control, or some combination of these conditions much too complex to sort out. Wolves may have exacerbated the deer decline, once it started, until wolf numbers adjusted downwards too.

Then, for subtle ecosystem reasons or good luck, moose took over, more than quadrupling. Maybe they did so because with less deer there was less brainworm in the forest, or maybe because moose can reach forage higher than deer and can handle deeper snow. Spruce budworm may have helped; it hit parts of the park in the mid-1970s. Graham's moose-forest analysis showed that some of the highest moose densities were in areas of heaviest budworm infestation fifteen years earlier. Whatever the reasons for the moose eruption, wolves were incapable of preventing it.

Through the 1980s, deer increased in most of eastern North America, the result, many biologists think, of more than a decade of increasingly milder winters and less snowfall. Climate warming? El Niño? In Algonquin, however, the increase was only moderate and occurred only in the eastern and southern sectors of the park.

Finally, in the past few years deer have fluctuated and declined. We examined a range of possible reasons including wolf predation, and then we found the answer. It was not what we expected – that is a later story.

The Annie Bay pack's rendezvous site at the old lumber mill was used more consistently than any other pack used any site – tradition successfully passed on. Once, shining our flashlight out the truck window, three pairs of wolf pup eyes reflected back from the grasses at the edge of the road. The pups, tiny balls of fur, walked this way and that to get a better look. It was midsummer and we had come upon them by surprise. In a few minutes, their curiosity satisfied, they scampered back out of sight.

We radio-collared three Annie Bay wolves over the years. The first gave us good territorial boundaries for a year and a half before going missing. The second, a young female, dispersed from the park and died a year later from an unknown cause. We found her collar near the town of Wilno.

The third Annie Bay wolf was on the air for three and a half years. She was a yearling when we radio-collared her in 1990. After two years we were forced to stop following her because of budget restrictions; to fly to Annie Bay added half an hour to our telemetry flights. Until then, she had never gone south as far as the park boundary, staying at least five kilometres inside the park. Then in February 1994 a trapper notified the MNR that he had snared a radio-collared wolf adjacent to the park. When Mary and I retrieved it, we were surprised to find it was her. Like so many wolves, her collar, still transmitting, had outlived her.

The next spring we returned to Annie Bay, this time with Wayne Rostad, the host of the popular CBC television program "On the Road Again." The producer, cameraman, and soundman brought all the paraphernalia with them for night filming: floodlights, big white reflectors, special film. The peepers were going full blast, and a couple of woodcocks were sky-dancing in the dark. Now and then a snipe winnowed by.

There wasn't the same aura of other times, not with the producer saying "stand here" and the cameraman saying "can we try that again." To provide a whimsical interlude in the film, we were to "teach" Wayne how to howl.

I howled to show Wayne how to do it. No wolves responded. Then Wayne tried it. Mary tried it. Just the peepers, never missing a beat, and the woodcocks undisturbed.

Halfway up Dickson-Lavieille lakes, the Annie Bay pack's range abutted the Lavieille pack. With big Lake Lavieille on its west side, this pack ranged to the east among stately red and white pines, some of the most persistent escapees still at large from the logging mills. Fortunately, a new wilderness zone designated there in 1995 has granted them a life-time pardon.

Various student crews worked with this pack and put on five radio-collars over the course of three summers. Mary and I took part in only one capture, made by Jenny and Carolyn. We came to visit them with our veterinarian colleague, Ian Barker, who wanted to inspect our handling and drugging techniques. Ian witnessed the collaring of Lavieille 2, who was lying prostrate and drugged in a grove of balsam firs.

The first summer of tracking showed us a clear demarcation between the boundaries of the Lavieille pack and a pack named Charles Creek to the north. Between them ran two roughly parallel east-west roads only five to eight kilometres apart. The roads were used by logging trucks, wolves, and us. The Lavieille pack claimed the southern-most road and the Charles Creek pack owned the northern road. Two collars on Charles Creek wolves gave us data on their movements. Never did we record an actual meeting of the two packs, but often they were close.

The next summer, the Charles Creek pack stayed a few kilometres to the north, not using their road at all. They were inaccessible most of the time.

The third summer, Charles Creek wolves again stayed to the north, but this summer, Lavieille wolves took over both roads. Had they won a boundary war, or was this an example of "use it or lose it?" If it was the latter, why had the Charles Creek wolves stopped using the southern edge of their territory? They could have travelled across the full diameter of their territory, about twenty kilometres, in only a few hours. The boundary road was not in a prey vacuum; we routinely found moose tracks there, and beaver ponds were plentiful. For whatever reason, ownership had changed.

Lavieille 1 and Lavieille 3 both went off the air only a few months after having been collared. In neither case do we know their fate. Lavieille 2 was hit by a car twenty kilometres south of the park. Lavieille 4, a lactating female when caught, slipped her collar. Lavieille 5 gave us a year, then died at the northeast corner of Lake Lavieille among the big pines. It took a canoe trip by a student crew to recover her collar. Her carcass was too decomposed for us to determine cause of death.

In this transition zone across the Algonquin dome, changes in snow depths and temperatures, logging practices, and fire will shift forest composition as they have in the past, subtly or suddenly. Hidden tensions, coiled for release, lurk in ecosystem gradients found there. With luck, the adaptable wolf will ride them through. Human killing of wolves is a bigger problem.

Recovered now, the East Gate wolves howl again for tourists and take their chances with the wolf killers in the town of Whitney. The Louisa and Little Branch wolves do not have to fear walking into snares so long as they centre their territories inside the park. The Annie Bay wolves will continue to prowl the clearing at the old mill and with luck keep away from the park's southern boundary. We no longer work with these packs, not because they have no more to tell us, but because of a shortage of research dollars and shifting priorities. People will undoubtedly continue to kill them; we won't be collecting their carcasses.

LASTING KINGDOM:
THE JACK PINE PACK

Dispersers

A desire to leave home is typical of young animals, usually as they become mature. They may need a push, subtle or otherwise, by parents or other group members, but when the time comes, most of them move on.

In leaving, young animals are responding to the dictates of their genes – ancestors who left home contributed more genes to future populations than those who stayed. Against staying is the threat of inbreeding depression. Close relatives may produce sterile or unhealthy young often enough to handicap their genetic future. Also against staying may be a population build-up and overexploitation of resources. By leaving, younger animals and social subordinates normally increase their chances of meeting their needs; inadvertently, they help the entire population meet its needs too.

There is, however, a counter-pressure. Leaving home means going into an uncertain world where chances of getting killed increase. Therefore, competing in an animal's make-up are the genes of ancestors who stayed, survived longer, and eventually bred.

Highly evolved social vertebrates have an enhanced ability to behave beyond the narrow dictates of their genes and make decisions based upon an assessment of their situation. Young animals may make a pre-dispersal reconnaissance to see if land or mates are available, or if members of other social units accept or repel them. Their sex bears on the decision too; in mammals, usually only males disperse, but that is because the males of most species mate with more than one female. If subordinate males stay home, dominant, multimate males may prevent them from ever breeding. Among monogamous mammals, however, normally both sexes disperse.

Variations in the way animals disperse characterize different species. Dispersal influences social organization, spatial distribution, genetic structure, population size, and even whether a population will persist. Wolf dispersal has been scrutinized intensively, especially in Dave Mech's twenty-year study in northeastern Minnesota. He and Eric Gese published detailed results along with a review of the observations of François Messier in Quebec, Warren Ballard in central Alaska, Rolf Peterson in southeast Alaska and on Isle Royale in Lake Superior, and others.

Typically, about half to three-quarters of the wolves in a population eventually disperse from their natal pack. Among those who leave, about one-quarter do so as pups (animals less than one year old), half as yearlings, and the other quarter as young adults. Occasionally wolves wait to disperse until they are three or four years old. Young females tend to leave about one year earlier, on average, than do young males. Gese and Mech found that although heavyweight pups were just as likely to stay as to disperse, all lightweight pups dispersed, likely the result of their social inferiority and perhaps resultant food stress.

Most dispersers either establish new packs or, less commonly, join existing packs. Most settle down next to their natal pack or close by, although some young animals travel hundreds of kilometres. Yearlings tend to travel farther than adults. Adults may be more successful in staking out land and obtaining a mate close to home because of their maturity and experience. In dense wolf populations, dispersers have to travel farther to find what they are looking for than in exploited populations with vacant lands nearby. The older a dispersing wolf, the greater its chances of successfully mating.

Dispersal most commonly occurs during the breeding and early denning season from February until spring; some studies describe a second peak of dispersal in October and November.

Dispersal rates are high in both increasing and decreasing wolf populations, presumably influenced by the availability of food. When wolves and prey are increasing, existing packs may be more willing to tolerate new pack formation. When wolves and prey are decreasing, greater food stress within packs may lead to greater intolerance and so greater dispersal.

Dispersal rates are also high in sparse populations and unstable ones. Steve Fritts, who studied both an exploited and then protected population in central Minnesota, found that exploitation increases dispersal by increasing the chances of dispersers finding vacant territories. As follows from his observations, in exploited populations packs tend to be smaller; in unexploited ones, with less dispersal, pack sizes build up.

Non-dispersing wolves are betting on eventually taking over positions of dominance in their natal pack and breeding. More wolves take this option in a non-exploited, dense population where, because of less dispersal, fewer females breed. In contrast, in a heavily exploited Alaskan population, Robert Rausch found that 90 per cent of females bred.

From these studies we know many facts about wolf dispersal. But how do we interpret them? What do they tell us about wolf societies? The single most interesting feature of wolf dispersal is that rarely do territory holders kill dispersing wolves even though the dispersers are trespassing. Is dispersion an exemption to the fundamentally competitive, territorial system in wolves? Or is dispersion a manifestation of a more flexible social system, sometimes characterized by indifference, sometimes even cooperation? The answer may be based as much on expectation and outlook as on fact.

SPRAWLING across the driest parts of the Petawawa sand flats, once a broad, ancient river bottom that drained glaciers to the north, is a forest dominated by jack pines. Dry and hot in summer, even red pines struggle here. White pines have to search for the scattered, higher rocky places where there might be more soil moisture. It is the kind of place for jack pine budworm, a natural monoculture. Because of an outbreak about thirty years ago, a "salvage cut" took place, so the forest still has the scraggly, awkward appearance of youth. That is just fine for spruce grouse, who nest here more abundantly than in other places, and for the flashy budworm warblers such as Cape May and blackburnian.

The Petawawa sand flats form the heart of the Jack Pine wolves' land. In summer they leave their footprints on the sandy logging roads and in winter trace the creeks and bogs. They range north-west to the Petawawa River, whose waters foam over rocks before disintegrating in extensive Lake Travers. They travel south beyond the hills cradling Dawn and Dusk lakes, two forest teardrops. Several times they denned under a big spruce growing on an old stream-bank where a creek wound through tangled alders out front.

We became acquainted with these wolves during the first summer of our study. Over the years we radio-collared eight Jack Pine wolves, getting to know some of them well. Then, nine years later the pack vanished, all but one. In that interval, despite suffer-ing their share of losses, the Jack Pine wolves maintained more constant boundaries than any other pack. Now, claiming the same lands, there is even a new Jack Pine pack, different wolves, slightly altered boundaries, same kingdom.

Midsummer heat. Oppressive humidity. Storm-feeling in the forest. I climbed a ridge to a rocky crest overlooking a sweep of pine forest to the hills beyond. The signals of the three Jack Pine wolves came in clearly. Quietly, I searched for a level place to set up my tent.

The rocky crest provided an excellent vantage point to monitor movements in and out of their rendezvous site without disturbing them. We had collars on the alpha-male, alpha-female, and a year-ling female. In addition, the previous afternoon an unprecedented event had occurred. Basin 6 Jocko, a male from a pack to the south-east, joined the Jack Pine pack. Later, genetic analysis confirmed our impression that he was the alpha-male of the Jocko Lake pack.

He arrived near the Jack Pine pack's rendezvous site in the late morning. Graduate student Joy Cook flew over and reported his signal about two kilometres from us. When Mary and I located him, he was only half a kilometre away and ten minutes later was on the same compass bearing as immature female Jack Pine 7. We quickly drove a few hundred metres for a cross-bearing and confirmed that they were together. Their signals moved in tandem as they entered the rendezvous site, where one of them began a long sequence of bark-howls. The other collared wolves were absent, but the pups must have been there; they always were.

We could not imagine a strange wolf being allowed right into the rendezvous site. Never in three years of tracking had there been any association between the wolves in these two adjacent packs. We expected to hear sounds of a fight.

A few seconds later, a different wolf began barking just off the bearing we had on the two wolves. That must have been an uncollared baby-sitter. Barks changed to howls, then silence.

We sat beside some alders and waited to hear more, unable to approach closer for fear of disturbing them. This was wolf-only business. Nothing else transpired. Soon Jack Pine 7 drifted out of range, leaving the interloper with the pups and whatever uncollared adults were home.

Two hours later when we returned from checking another pack, alpha-male Jack Pine 8 had come in and was on the same bearing as Basin 6 Jocko. Variation in the trespassing wolf's signal showed that he had not been killed.

Because we were anxious to monitor developments, I had climbed the hill for my night's vigil. Mary was back in our other tent near the truck in the semi-shade of a budworm-sickened jack pine tree, the best we could find nearby. We had returned only recently from a month in Costa Rica visiting Michelle, who had a summer job studying bats, and Mary had contracted what was diagnosed later as histoplasmosis, a fungal disease spread in bat guano. The hilltop was too close to the wolves for her to cough without disturbing them in the calm of night.

From 9 P.M. until after midnight, I sat on the rocky crest in a patch of sweet fern surrounded by scraggly maples and oaks. During that time, the day shift went out – hermit thrushes and white-throated sparrows stopped singing – and the night shift came in – nighthawks overhead and whip-poor-wills lashing the forest with their repetitive songs. As darkness came, I watched big cumulonimbus clouds build up above a salmon streak on the western horizon. Now and then the clouds were illuminated by flashes of lightning that caused static on the receiver.

Summarizing my field notes, initially, JP8 and B6J were together at the rendezvous site, and alpha-female JP3 and her immature daughter JP7 were about six hundred metres upstream near their den abandoned a few weeks previously. A half-hour later, JP8's signal was coming in from close range. Apparently he was investigating me, or I was inadvertently on his travel route. He made a semicircle around me in the dark staying about a hundred metres back and kept going. Without hearing his signal, I would never have known he was there.

Not much happened until 11:35 P.M. when I was startled by two treble howls from an adult at the rendezvous site. I had fallen asleep despite the mosquito attack. A few seconds later, one pup gave a few high, nasal howls. I got up to check the receiver. JP8 had returned.

By midnight it was obvious a storm was approaching. The aspens began talking and the lightning was more persistent. A loud clap of thunder rolled over the forest. B6J was still at the rendezvous site, JP7 was distant to the north, JP3 was gone, and JP8 was close to me once again.

Suddenly the sky split apart with a long, dazzling flash that lit up the entire ridge for about four seconds. The thunder came almost immediately. There I stood on top of the hill, antenna raised above my head. So to hell with JP8. I put the antenna flat under a tree a few metres away and headed for the tent. One minute later I heard the first hiss of oncoming rain. Quickly the rain rheostat turned up.

By 2 A.M. the storm was over, and I was left lying in a pool of water on the tent floor. In veiled moonlight I walked up to the top of the hill through the wet sweet fern to find that JP8 had gone and only B6J was on the air. Was he the designated baby-sitter? Back in the tent, I killed all the mosquitoes and set the alarm for 5 A.M.

At 3:52 A.M. pup howls awakened me. An adult must have returned. I climbed out to check and found that, sure enough, JP7 had come back. The signals of B6J and JP3 were weak to the north; possibly she had returned to take him to some distant kill. For a while I sat on the hill. Forest dripping. Soft, wet, warm. Diffuse moonlight. Then I returned to the tent, killed all the mosquitoes again, and set the alarm for 6 A.M., but I couldn't sleep. Instead, I lay in the wet, hot tent and listened to a nighthawk practising percussion dive-bombing. At 5 A.M. a slight hint of daylight touched the tent wall.

My notes seem to reflect the typical coming-and-going home life of a wolf pack in summer. One or more adults nearly always stay with the pups. Howling occurs when wolves change guard. Wolves leave singly or in groups and return when they want.

Most remarkable was the casual acceptance of Basin 6 Jocko, as if he had always been a member of the pack. We understood why three years later from genetic analysis done on blood collected when he was collared. Jack Pine 3 was his mother! After three years and founding his own pack, he had returned to mother and his natal land. We were amazed that this would happen. Later we learned why.

We kept as close to a twenty-four-hour vigil as possible, obtaining additional locations from Joy's twice-daily overflights via air-to-ground radio. Most often the wolves went southwest when they left the rendezvous site, and often we found their tracks on a road there. Never were they in one place long enough for us to suspect a kill, but they may have stayed at one only briefly before returning to the rendezvous site with food for the pups.

One evening we inadvertently disturbed the pack. All three collared Jack Pine wolves were about four kilometres south of the rendezvous site, and Basin 6 Jocko was out of range. Wanting to confirm the number of adults in the pack, we returned directly to the rendezvous site and Mary howled. There was no response. The signals of Jack Pine 7 and Jack Pine 8 were barely audible in the distance, but thirty minutes later both wolves had returned, travelling at eight kilometres an hour – a trot – to get there. Because alpha-female Jack Pine 3, the most sensitive pack member to howling near the pups, was not present, we believed that our howling would not be intrusive. So we howled again. This time the wolves responded. Although Jack Pine 3 was not close enough for us to hear her signal, she must have heard us, because only three minutes later, she was there too. She must have been running flat out. Realizing we had disrupted their routine, we backed the truck out, turned around, and, with only the parking lights on, slowly drove away.

The next two days in succession we found the tracks of two wolves along eight kilometres of a sandy road right to the southern boundary of the pack's territory. The wolves urinated and scratch-marked all the way. Probably our howls, sounding like an unknown wolf in their territory, had stimulated this territorial behaviour.

The Jack Pine pack gave us some surprises and provided some insights into wolf social dynamics. Even one that did not live long, Jack Pine 1, surprised us. He dispersed from the Grand Lake pack to the Jack Pine pack as a four-year-old, his age confirmed by cross-section tooth analysis performed at G. Matson's wildlife ageing laboratory in Montana. In other studies, most dispersing wolves are young animals just becoming sexually mature. As our study progressed, we found more instances of adult dispersal and adoption into other packs. Possibly because so many wolves in our study were killed by humans, more adult wolves were left wandering and packless. Prior to Jack Pine 1 joining the Jack Pine pack, that pack's alpha-male might have been killed, leaving the position up for grabs.

Another surprise was the tendency of the Jack Pine pack to split up in winter. They did this more commonly, or for more prolonged periods, than other packs. In 1990–91, three wolves spent the entire winter together outside the park while the other five stayed on territory. The next winter, four wolves spent the whole time as roving trespassers in the neighbouring Mathews Lake, Pretty Lake, and Grand Lake packs' lands while the remaining six wolves stayed home. Once, the trespassing group was within two kilometres of the Pretty Lake pack, but that is the closest we found them to any residents.

Jack Pine 6

She has survived a long time for an Algonquin wolf and is still out there threading the hills around Zigzag Lake. We classified her as large for a female, based on our index of weights and lengths, but she barely made that category. The second time we caught her she was 2.3 kilograms heavier, likely the effect of a good meal.

She was born in 1989 or 1990, daughter of Jack Pine 3. During her first winter on the air, when she was either two or three years old, she stayed with the Jack Pine pack only until late December. Then we found her trespassing with her mother in the Jocko Lake pack's territory to the southeast. Her older brother, by then the alpha-male of the Jocko Lake pack, was only one kilometre away. She had known him in 1990 before he dispersed. Accepted relatives?

Then she disappeared for six months, showing up again back in her home territory, sometimes alone, twice with her mother, Jack Pine 3, and the rest of the pack. Obviously she was remembered and still welcome. Later that summer she vanished again, and over the next fourteen months we found her only once even though we kept her frequency programmed into our receivers. By then a four- or five-year-old, she was ranging widely, apparently still shopping around for a mate.

In September 1994, MNR biologist Mike Wilton found her while flying south of the park. He was radio-tracking black bears at the time and had our wolf's frequency programmed into his receiver. That winter she was part of a pack of seven, and extended her range to define a territory in the extreme southeast corner of the park.

Mary and I caught her on a hot July day in 1995 and replaced her well-worn collar. She was lactating, the alpha-female of what we named the Zigzag Lake pack.

The following winter, with the help of local forest technician Colin Fabian, we snowmobiled and snowshoed to a moose she and her pack were attempting to eat. The moose had gone through the ice in the middle of a small lake and had been unable to climb out. Only its head, neck, and shoulders were exposed, and they were frozen solid. Although the wolves returned periodically to this food source, they could never get at the rest.

She denned that summer under a big pine by the water's edge of a scenic, unnamed lake, and by winter her pack had grown to nine. They spent most of the winter outside the park living close to houses. By winter's end, her pack was down to five, for unknown reasons.

In the summer of 1997, a set of early-June flights showed scattered locations back in her home territory but not centred at a possible den site like they did the previous year. Maybe she had lost her dominant position in the pack. Two collared offspring from the previous year rarely travelled with her.

She received her third radio collar in January 1998, when we contracted with Helicopter Wildlife Management from Utah to net wolves. Mary, in the spotter plane, found the pack on the ice of a small lake, then radioed the location to the helicopter and circled as it came in below the Cessna to net the wolf. The wolf was measured, weighed, and recollared without being drugged, and was off again in only a few minutes.

Now either seven or eight years old, she is one of the older wolves in the study. She has been a survivor, both as a lone wolf and an alpha.

Jack Pine 3

She was the matriarch, maintaining her alpha position while wolves in her own and surrounding packs came and went with alarming frequency. Captured first in 1990 and recaptured twice after that, she gave us six and a half years of data before she died. Nothing about her physically suggested superiority. We classified her as a medium-sized wolf.

Where she denned in the old streambank, the creek provided a curvilinear alder-grass tangle through jack pine flats. Beaver operations had strung the creek with small ponds, drowning standing trees that olive-sided flycatchers perched on. The surrounding jack pine stands offered little browse for moose and deer, causing them to concentrate in this riparian strip. Even the rendezvous sites where Jack Pine 3 moved the pups each summer were only short distances away from the den along the same creek.

Mary and I saw her only once, tracking her signal one day in early December with our daughters. She and her mate, Jack Pine

8, had ambushed a deer near the foot of a lake, twenty-five kilometres off territory. Jenny and I followed their signals, but they had left the carcass. Mary and Michelle were guided to the kill by the raucous calls of ravens. The wolves went up a creek and out onto the lake ice. We watched them, just the pair, reluctantly walking away, glancing back at us every few seconds.

The partly eaten carcass lay half-submerged along the edge of the creek where the deer had broken through thin ice. The wolves had been tugging at it, unable to get at the deep-water side.

Jack Pine 3 first became the alpha female of the pack either in 1989 or 1990 and maintained that position for six or seven breeding seasons, an unprecedented length of time. Genetics analysis done by Sonya Grewal and Paul Wilson in Brad White's laboratory at McMaster University later revealed that we had collared three of her offspring, four of her grandchildren, four of her great-grandchildren, one brother, and two nieces. Before pairing with Jack Pine 8, she had mated with another male who must have died or had his position usurped (wolves are normally monogamous). Her genes end up today in six different packs and will spread even farther in the next generation. All but one of these packs hold adjacent territories to hers or are one-pack-distant; one granddaughter lives three packs away.

All this dispersal based on knowing the fate of just three of Jack Pine 3's pups over a period of seven years suggests much more. It shows that the population was unstable, as we also know from our mortality data. Territorial vacancies and part-packs, characteristic of an exploited population, apparently provided many opportunities for wolves to disperse and breed successfully.

This dispersal meant, as well, that if Jack Pine wolves trespassed anywhere nearby, they would likely be on a relative's land. They might not know each other if they had never lived together, such as if the territory holder was a grandparent, niece or nephew, or sibling born more than two years apart, but they would if it was a son or daughter or a sibling from a successive year. Such close relationships may lessen aggression and be one way an exploited population heals itself.

Whatever ways dispersal aids the population, Jack Pine 3's genes — so adaptive, so successful — live on though she is dead.

The railway was a boon to the Jack Pine pack. In the ditches beside the track were plenty of moose bones with wolf scats nearby. One winter's day we radio-tracked Jack Pine 3 and Jack Pine 8 through deep snow and dense bush to the railway, where a crowd of ravens flew up. Instead of finding a carcass strewn along the embankment, this moose, to our surprise, came pre-packaged. Its legs had been cut off and were in a torn cardboard box; its head was in another. A short distance down the tracks was the railway siding of Travers Station with a couple of cabooses where linemen lived. Wolves were not the only large mammals to scavenge on train-killed moose.

Another moose fell victim to a train on the east side of the Jack Pine pack's territory in late August 1994. On a windy afternoon we heard the signals of all three collared wolves from a high hill. A cross-bearing established their position along the railway. When we drove closer, we noticed ravens sail over in the direction of the wolves. We left the truck carrying our camera and binoculars and headed uptrack and upwind. More ravens skimmed the trees ahead.

Near the second bend, we left the tracks, edged slowly along the trees, and crawled to a rock outcrop. Slightly below us, only twenty-five metres away, an uncollared wolf was tugging at the mangled remains of a moose. Although we were almost completely exposed, the wolf had not detected us. Slowly I raised the camera and got off a few shots. The wolf gripped the skin of a leg with its incisor teeth and pulled back, the whole leg moving without the counter-pull of another wolf. Then it crouched down and chewed with its carnassial teeth. The collared wolves, satiated, were out of sight in the trees nearby.

After a few minutes, the wolf raised its head, turned, and started moving directly towards us. At ten metres it bounded up over a rock, saw us for the first time and froze. Nerve impulse travelled from eye, to brain, to its cognition centre, to legs, and a second later it jumped back and bounded up the embankment onto the tracks.

There it looked back as if in disbelief that we were really humans and it had been so careless. Then it was gone.

After dark we came back and put up a tent at the edge of the trees. The next morning at daybreak, again the collared wolves were just out of sight. Ravens were working over the carcass, so full of meat they could barely hop. We spent a long morning in the tent without seeing any wolves.

Sometimes after a period of inactivity, events occur so suddenly and unexpectedly that only later can you piece together what happened. We climbed out of the tent, and I started to unhook the fly. Mary walked about ten paces to pick up a piece of notepaper we had dropped the previous evening. I heard a stick snap just behind the tent, and looked up at an uncollared wolf in full bound towards her. By the time I exclaimed "Mary," the wolf was almost there. Glancing up and seeing the wolf so close, only a second or two from contact, Mary involuntarily straightened up. The wolf arched its back in mid-air, hit the ground, turned, and bounded off.

We have considered various possible interpretations of the event. If Mary had not stood up, we might have known what the wolf intended – an experimental error on her part. Likely the wolf had been sleeping very close to the tent and, hearing movement, either thought it was a member of its pack or a deer. Its high, bounding leaps were typical of a wolf's approach to both. Perhaps it did not know what had made the noise and would have responded appropriately at the last instant. Or, maybe being the same wolf that almost walked into us the day before, it was not at the head of its class.

The incident was the stuff that reported wolf attacks are made of, but, of course, it was not.

The trains were not the sole source of human-killed moose. With a change in provincial governments in 1992 came a political decision to give the Golden Lake native people hunting rights to moose and deer on the eastern third of the park. They are allowed to use trucks, all-terrain vehicles, and snowmobiles anywhere they wish. The decision was made without any consideration of its environmental and biological impacts. Conservation organizations objected, and so did I in the Toronto *Globe and Mail*. To the extent that land is used and wildlife exploited inside the park the same way it is outside, there is no reason to have a park at all. However, despite our objections, a new predator entered Algonquin's large mammal system.

One January day during the first winter of native people hunting the unsuspecting and relatively tame park moose, we followed the signal of Jack Pine 3 down a snowy logging road grooved with fresh truck tracks. Three kilometres along, the tracks stopped, and a crimson trail of blood led from there to a moose carcass. Its legs had been axed off at the knees and piled together, and its head and a gut pile lay nearby.

More than one hundred butchered remains of moose, and possibly even more of deer, are laid out in the park each fall and early winter by native hunters. Undoubtedly the wolves welcome this unexpected food source, but it is unclear how it changes their pattern of movements in this season when they are adjusting to the onset of the annual deer migration. It further erodes the functioning of the park as a natural place.

In mid-December 1995, graduate student John Pisapio flew the circuit of collared packs accompanied by Jenny, home from her grizzly research in Alberta. They reported Jack Pine 8 on mortality mode. On the next flight, John found Jack Pine 3 on mortality as well, about six kilometres from her mate. We had lost both alpha animals; as it turned out, the whole pack except Jack Pine 7 was gone.

Snows had come early and heavy that year, so retrieving the dead wolves was not easy. On a grey, late-December day, Mary, Jenny, Michelle, and I tried to reach Jack Pine 8 with two snowmobiles borrowed from the MNR. The snow was deep, trackless, and powder all the way to the ground. We lost speed on the slightest rise, gunning to a snow-grinding halt where the snowmobiles commenced to dig themselves down. We lifted, shovelled, pushed, lifted, shovelled. Mary and Jenny even tried snowshoeing ahead to make a trail, and while that helped, even a slight mound of snow would edge the snowmobile off its centre of balance. When the driver tried to correct for that, it tipped farther until it capsized.

We made only eight kilometres in six hours. By then it was dark and the temperature was dropping, chilling us in our sweat-soaked clothes. The wolf was still three kilometres away, so we turned around, with difficulty, and headed home – all the way home for Christmas.

On December 28, cold and sunny, we returned to try again accompanied by forest technicians Tom Stephenson and Colin Fabian. With no snow over the Christmas period, this time the trail was broken most of the way. Where we left the truck, we could hear Jack Pine 7's distant signal, and all the way along our old snow-mobile trail we could see a fresh set of wolf prints, likely hers.

We zipped down to Dusk Lake, crossed a bay, and parked, not trusting the ice any farther. Then we snowshoed across the lake and into the woods where I made an energy-draining miscalculation. A steep hill rose from the shore, difficult to climb in the deep snow. I was concerned that we might be following a deflection in the signal, but could not be sure until we got to the top. For almost an hour we struggled uphill, confirmed that we were going the wrong way, then made our way back down. Jack Pine 8 was in thick lowland conifers close to the lake.

What we found was a shock. The wolf was on top of the snow-pack, so he must have died after mid-December when the last snows fell. He was frozen solid, legs extended, but his body cavity had been opened, and, more significantly, when we turned him over we found that one shoulder and foreleg had been eaten off. Wolf tracks were there, one set leading out on the lake, the same set we had followed in from the main road. Ravens had been at the carcass too, and maybe a fox. No fisher tracks were evident, an animal that might be able to turn over a wolf carcass. We concluded that this was a case of wolf cannibalism.

It is tempting to apply human values to nature, but ethics pro-hibiting human cannibalism are our own constructs. In a non-human context, especially when killing is not involved, cannibalism may be adaptive. Regardless of the cause of death, Jack Pine 7 had been left alone, packless as it turned out, and likely in a difficult situation. The deer had all left the Jack Pine territory, and the severe cold had driven the beaver into their lodges. Under such conditions, natural selection would favour cannibalism over starvation.

We tied a rope to Jack Pine 8, dragged him back to the snow-mobiles, lashed him on a sled, and trucked him home. In early January, John and Colin retrieved Jack Pine 3. They had to shovel for her; she had died in mid-November, just before the heavy snows.

Veterinarian Doug Campbell performed the autopsies a few weeks later. Lying on the stainless-steel table next to Jack Pine 3 was the body of her mate. These two wolves were the only ones in the entire study for whom Doug, Ian Barker, or the other veterinarians could not determine any certain cause of death. Both wolves were in excellent condition with plenty of body fat. Neither wolf hosted any unusual parasites. Lab results for canine hepatitis, the only viral disease that would not have shown obvious symptoms, came back negative. Rabies checked out negative. Strychnine was negative. Antifreeze, sometimes used as a poison, leaves crystals of glycol in the kidneys that were not present. The only clues were a bruised leg with internal bleeding and some blood in Jack Pine 3's urine. Rodenticide poisons cause both disorientation, which may have accounted for the leg injury, and internal bleeding, which may have affected the urine. By process of elimination, poison became a suspected but unconfirmed cause of death.

After the deaths of Jack Pine 3 and Jack Pine 8, John made a special effort to aerial-track Jack Pine 7, the remaining collared wolf, and repeatedly confirmed that she was alone. In the summer of 1996, Mary and I drove through the old Jack Pine territory past Dawn and Dusk lakes. The forest looked the same, but the heart of the wild was gone, or maybe its soul. No wolf tracks embossed the sandy road. No use getting out to howl. No use turning on the receiver in hopes of hearing a signal. We missed the Jack Pine pack like you miss a friend.

But there is more to tell, and it centres on the one remaining wolf.

Jack Pine 7

She was the daughter of Jack Pine 3. For a while, dispersal clearly was on her mind; she made forays into the territories of adjacent packs, but never stayed long.

One cold March day in 1994 while the Jack Pine pack was still alive, we heard her signal well beyond her territory on land that once belonged to the Grand Lake East pack but was vacant. Carrying our snowshoes, we hiked the railway towards her. She was still ahead, down Stratton Lake, so we continued until we judged we were opposite her, then dropped down into the shoreline trees. There she was, by herself, trotting down the centre of the lake towards a dark object on the ice. When she got there, she nosed around it for a few minutes, then hoisted it up to reveal that it was the vertebral column and remaining ribs of a deer, picked clean. Carrying it in her mouth, she trotted to the far shore, disappeared, then a few minutes later re-emerged minus her booty and continued down the lake. Had she made the kill alone and was revisiting it, or had she made it with her pack, or was she examining a kill that other wolves had made? Anyhow, she was making no efforts to stay concealed.

Whatever her plans to disperse, they changed late in 1995 when, at two and a half years of age, she became orphaned. Within a month the Pretty Lake pack, next door, realized the Jack Pine pack was gone and enlarged its boundaries to take in about one-third of the Jack Pine range. At first, Jack Pine 7 seemed to keep her distance from the invading Pretty Lake wolves, but then, one March day, she was with them. The Pretty Lake wolves seemed to have taken over not only Jack Pine's land but the remaining wolf as well.

Pretty 6, particularly, showed an interest in her, so much that by the denning season, in April and May, they were constantly together. They stayed mostly on the west side of the Jack Pine territory while the rest of the Pretty Lake pack stayed to the east. It seemed like his pack was giving him room to help re-establish a Jack Pine pack. At that time, he was at least a four-year-old wolf.

That entire summer, Jack Pine 7 and Pretty 6 were inseparable.

The field crew suspected they knew the location of the den, and in midsummer after the wolf pair had moved elsewhere, Mary and I took a bearing and hiked in. The sand that John had seen from the air and suspected was a mound in front of the den turned out to be only a patch in the middle of an old log landing still unclaimed by sweet ferns and grass.

By late summer, it was clear that they had no pups. If they had mated and denned, it had been a failure. Still they were always together, by then claiming almost all the old Jack Pine territory, although they tolerated a few intrusions by the Pretty Lake pack and vice versa.

Then, in December 1996, Jack Pine 7 lost her new companion under strange circumstances. John pinpointed Pretty 6's signal on mortality mode coming from a dense stand of conifers just south of the recently abandoned railway. He made a trip to recover the wolf but could not find her even though the signal showed he was in the right place.

On a cold, blustery day, Mary and I gave it a try. We hiked down the track and into the conifers until we got to a place where a few steps one way would put the signal behind us and a few steps the other way would do the same. We shovelled for two hours, eventually clearing a huge area right down to the frozen mosses. We both tried the receiver and repeatedly returned to the centre of our excavation. We pounded out frozen roots with the shovel and tore up rotten logs and still could not find the collar.

Finally I climbed a spruce tree in the centre of our excavation, because the collar could be nowhere else. After breaking ice-coated limbs I saw it almost at the top, cradled against the trunk in a tangle of branches. When I reached it, my bare hands were numb. Mary gathered twigs and started a fire, and it took a painful ten minutes to thaw them out.

The collar was still bolted up. No blood or tissue clung to it, nor was it badly chewed. Certainly a wolf had not deposited it in the tree. No human had climbed up because that was impossible without breaking branches. Our best guess is that a fisher was responsible, or a raven.

Now Jack Pine 7 was alone again, for the second winter in a row. For a while she wandered outside the park, then back on territory. The day after we retrieved Pretty 6's collar she was at Dusk Lake, and, close by, we were surprised to find four trespassing wolves from the Northeast pack. As it turned out, these wolves were doing more than trespassing; they were taking over the territory. Could they have been responsible for Pretty 6's death?

Jack Pine 7 left the park again the next day, alone. In the farmlands, she formed an alliance with four other wolves of unknown origin, but she must have been thinking about home because in late February she returned to the southeastern fringe of her territory. John saw her there, lying on the ice of Loonskin Lake with a new potential mate, Travers 8, only two metres away.

Travers 8 was a thirty-two-kilogram (seventy-pound) male, between three and five years old based on our incisor-wear index. He seemed like a suitable suitor. On the capture form, however, students Doerte Poszig and Jennifer Neate noted some scars, clotted blood, and new hair growing in various places on his body, as if he had been in fights at different times with other wolves. Since collaring, he had been wandering to the west beyond our study area. This was the first time he had showed up all winter.

But tragedy struck again. The night after John saw Jack Pine 7 on Loonskin Lake, she travelled more than fifty kilometres out of the park. Travers 8 did not accompany her. We pieced together the events after a long snowmobile trip to retrieve his body.

Travers 8 must still have been on or near Loonskin Lake with Jack Pine 7 when three wolves appeared and attacked – that must be why Jack Pine 7 left again so soon and travelled so far so fast. The three wolves chased Travers 8 in a straight line for three kilometres – that, in any event, is how we interpreted the tracks leading from the kill site. They ran across frozen beaver ponds, down through thick conifers littered with broken branches, up one near-vertical ridge until finally, in a log landing dotted with young red pine, the chasing wolves flanked him. They killed him with little struggle. A later autopsy showed that one wolf had grabbed his throat, another his chest. His lung collapsed and he was dead.

Every mate of Jack Pine 7's seemed to die mysteriously. Who did it? We cannot be sure but again suspected the Northeast pack. The following day, John found them from the air at Greenleaf Lake only four kilometres from the kill site. For some time they had been focusing much of their activity in this southeast corner of the land they had usurped from Jack Pine 7.

Why hadn't the Northeast pack accepted Jack Pine 7 as the Pretty Lake pack had done the year before? The answer may lie in some subtle difference in social context. Or perhaps the Northeast wolves are just aggressive by nature. In Yellowstone National Park, biologist Doug Smith tells of the Druid pack that seems to have an inclination for killing wolves from other packs rather than passively defending its land.

During the remainder of the winter, the crew occasionally found Jack Pine 7 with one or two other wolves outside the park, twice at deer kills. When melting spring snows brought the deer back into the park, she returned too, possibly alone. She stayed clear of the Northeast pack in her former territory, crossing the Petawawa River that had formed her western boundary and set-tling next to her usurped land in a very small wedge of Travers pack land, as if hoping not to be discovered. Then, in July, she went off the air. If she had died, we would have heard her signal on mor-tality mode. Either her collar went dead prematurely or, landless, she dispersed. We still have her frequency programmed on our receivers, hoping to find her.

In summer 1997, students Lou Chora and Willie Hollett recollared the former Northeast pack wolf still in the Jack Pine territory, his new land. They collared the other three wolves as well, one a daughter confirmed by genetics, one an unrelated adult female, and one the lactating alpha-female, and they found her den. Back in the Northeast territory itself, north of the Petawawa River, there was another pack, and it also produced pups. So, apparently the North-east pack had split, one part staying, the other taking over the Jack Pine territory. Here was a new social twist in the wolf's wide array of adaptive strategies. Although we had recorded permanent pack-splitting at Grand Lake, that case only involved re-allocation of land within the pack's territory. This time, part of a pack went in search of a new territory and appears to have used force to get it.

Now, a new, unrelated Jack Pine pack holds the land. But that is not all; across a broad sweep of central Algonquin Park, in other surrounding packs, original Jack Pine genes live on.

TRANSIENT KINGDOMS

Turf Wars

The territorial imperative is deeply ingrained in the animal psyche, especially in birds and mammals, including us. Because of it, we nail up no-trespassing signs, build fences, arm nations, and fight wars. Often, in both individuals and groups, it is an expression of selfishness and aggression – not a value judgement but a biological truth. Always, it has survival value.

In its simplest terms, territorial behaviour confines the movements of an animal, or a social group such as a pack of wolves, to a particular locality where it enjoys exclusive use. But that definition hides complexity.

Considerable research and debate centre upon two competing ideas about the function of territorial behaviour. According to one theory, it acts to space animals out so that resources are shared equitably by all members of a population. According to the other, it acts to limit the size of a population to the "haves" – the bigger, stronger, or the first there – who exclude the "have-nots." Those excluded from prime habitat either die or produce fewer young. Both outcomes are prejudicial to the future of their genes.

The population-limiting function makes more sense, because in times of severe resource shortage, a system of merely parcelling out available resources may spell doom for all. But it is difficult to obtain field evidence to establish territorial exclusion, a good example of simple experimental difficulties that sometimes restrict what science can explain. You have to first find individu-als that are clearly excluded from the population; secondly, determine that the aggressive behaviour of territory holders caused the exclusion; and thirdly – the acid test – determine that if those territory holders were not there, the excluded animals would become territory holders and breeders instead.

In only a handful of studies have these requirements been met: song sparrows in British Columbia, white-crowned sparrows in California, magpies in Australia, red grouse in Scotland, and a few others. So, which of the two possible functions of territories predominates is still not clear.

A defining feature of territorial behaviour is defence, which implies aggression. Not all aggression is overt: ritualized, passive aggression may serve the same evolutionary function, although from the observer's point of view, it is harder to detect. It is safer for an animal to defend land with posture, bluff, and ferocious appearance than to get in a fight and risk being killed. On the one hand, passive aggression explains the evolution of much that seems excessive and flamboyant in nature: gaudy colours, crests, plumes, horns, antlers, and dramatic display behaviour. On the other hand, some expressions of aggression are exceedingly subtle, such as a direct stare or tail or body position.

Different from territorial behaviour, with its obvious or inconspicuous expressions of defence, is simple "home-range behaviour." By definition, the landowner stays in one general area but makes no effort to exclude other individuals or groups of its species. An animal that knows a place well benefits because it can find food and avoid both predators and accidents with relative ease. Home-range behaviour is a more benign, sometimes even cooperative, spacing mechanism.

Home-range behaviour may be characterized by simple avoidance between the landowner and intruder. Then, it is enough just to detect one another's presence, enough for a wolf at times simply to smell where a member of another pack has been to send it packing. Home-range behav-iour with avoidance is so difficult to distinguish from passive territorial behaviour that, in practice, often the two terms are used interchangeably. The wolf literature is full of both.

Nonetheless, wolf populations normally are thought to exhibit a text-book example of group territorial behaviour, capable both of passive defence through scent marking and howling, and active aggression, even killing.

Because territory size adjusts to prey densities, this behaviour may be shaped by the availability of food – "resource partitioning" in the jargon of ecology. Or the motive may be defence of a mate.

What about dispersing animals with the free pass they seem to hold to trespass anywhere they like? What about kin affiliations in a wolf population that make aggression and competition illogical from a genetic standpoint? What about successful trespass and even carcass sharing? What we found was not so simple.

T RAVERS PACK, Mathews Lake pack, Grand Lake pack, Pretty Lake pack. For a while, before things changed, these wolves provided winter experiences that intermingled over the years to convey an impression at once harsh and harmonious. The oneness of life and land is easiest to sense in winter when the superfluous is stripped away, and the soft and sensitive are sleeping it off or have migrated. When a snow-laden gale lashes the limbs of the maples and whips through the pines, and the wolves hunch into the wind as they travel up the lake, then the system reveals some of its inner workings.

We lived during those winter field sessions well within the park in a ramshackle, brown, three-storey MNR staffhouse at the abandoned railway stop called Achray. A few other buildings disturbed the pine forests there: a once-elegant, small stone house with wide porch, perched on a scenic bank above expansive Grand Lake, and a small log cabin used by one of Canada's famous artists, Tom Thomson, when he worked there in 1916 as a park ranger. A couple of white shacks for workers lined the railway track, along with a long bunkhouse and garage. They all spoke of a different age when Achray was a logging centre. Better roads and pickup trucks ended Achray's prominence; now loggers can drive all the way home each night. Today even the railway is gone – rails, ties – all trucked away in 1997. With only its few remaining buildings, Achray is left closer to being nothing, more appropriate in a park.

During the early years of our research, the MNR leased out its oversized staff house to Algonquin College, whose teachers brought classes of forestry and wildlife students out from the campus at Pembroke for two weeks at a time to train them in bush skills. We made an arrangement with Tom Stephenson, who worked for Algonquin College, to give evening talks about our research in exchange for accommodation. It was a satisfactory arrangement, except for the all-night student partying. Through the thin walls of the staff house we often heard informal evaluations of our talks. Although laced with expletives, the commentary, when discernable, showed a lively interest in our work. Young wolf haters were outnumbered by students who were developing a wider appreciation of nature.

Along one wall of the kitchen ran a vast cast-iron stove meant to cook meals for work gangs of fifty or so men. Across the long dining room was a row of windows looking out over scenic Grand Lake. No wonder Tom Thomson was inspired when he lived at Achray. The original sketch of his famous *Jack Pine*, today a Canadian icon of "the true North, strong and free," was painted from a similar view of Carcajou Bay across Grand Lake. Out back, a large bird feeder kept stocked with food configured blue jays into a colourful node. Evening and pine grosbeaks or red and white-winged crossbills coloured the platform when the blue jays were off on other business. Often a richly coloured red fox sat in the snow nearby, hoping a chunk of suet would fall off or someone would toss out some table scraps. Both happened frequently enough to make the wait worthwhile.

We sort of backed into an arrangement with Tom Stephenson to stay at Achray. At the beginning of our first winter's field work, we thought we would have to camp. Winter camping is fine when you devote a significant portion of your time to being comfortable at best, or staying alive at worst. We have done well in central Labrador on two metres of snow, but then we had an eight-by-ten wall tent, a bed of spruce boughs, and a small, airtight wood stove. The camp took hours of maintenance each day: cutting wood, melting snow for water and other survival chores, a necessary but weighty time-loss from collecting field data.

By poor luck, our first night out, in mid-December 1988, was blistering cold, bottoming somewhere between -35°C and -40°C. Before dark, Graham, Mary, and I scraped away the snow from under the pines beside tiny Pretty Lake and set up our tents. Then we went out searching for wolves, returning before midnight. The night was cold yet bearable, but in the morning I froze a finger against the metal plunger while trying to light our one-burner stove. Graham's plastic ground sheet disintegrated in his hands. Our feet became numb in our frozen boots, forcing us to run around until we could get a fire going. We had nowhere, and no inclination, to write up the previous night's field notes or fill out data forms.

We put in a good day tracking wolves, but with clothing wet from perspiration, the prospect of a cold camp again was not pleasant. That is when Graham remembered Achray. Graham and Jenny had stayed there once the previous summer when the staff had invited them in, and Graham remembered that the window of his room had a broken latch.

Nobody was there when we rolled in. The latch was still broken. The unheated bunk room turned out to be even less comfortable than the tent, but in the morning we heated it up a bit with our little stove and ate breakfast in relative comfort.

After that, Graham made the informal arrangement with Tom Stephenson. Happily for us, Achray turned out to be strategically located near the interface of a number of wolf packs. Often we could stand in the parking lot and dial up three or four wolves from more than one pack.

Not only that, but big, redheaded Tom, the image of a nineteenth-century woodsman, strung many entertaining wolf stories. Sometimes it was difficult to distinguish fact from fiction. We were particularly intrigued by his description of how the wolves would come down long, narrow Grand Lake from the west, then fan out, one or two staying on the lake, others in the bush, and hunt their way back, all travelling parallel to the shore. We were interested by the use of topography in the hunt that Tom's story implied. Over the course of a few winters, other people told us similar tales, such as how the wolves on the west side of Lake Travers would drive deer down the point and catch them on the ice.

It is easy to overinterpret observations like these, and coupled with Tom's propensity to round out his stories, we were not too sure what to conclude. However, a number of times we did observe the Grand Lake pack moving fanned-out as he described. Once, our departure from Achray was delayed because our truck would not start. We have memories of many such truck malfunctions, usually resolved by draping sleeping bags and coats over the hood and putting a Coleman stove under the engine until it warmed up. Achray, buried in the hills, seemed to be a cold sink. While we were waiting for the truck to revive, a single wolf came trotting down the lake. To test Tom's idea, we hiked up the road to see if we could find parallel tracks of companion wolves, and we did – one wolf back about one hundred metres from the shore, another back two hundred metres farther.

The pack obviously benefited from this pattern of movement. A deer flushed in the trees by a wolf might run to the lake, where better footing improved its chances of escape. But there it would meet one or more lake-travelling wolves in a good position to bring it down. In the 1960s when wintering deer were more common, Doug Pimlott found that many deer were killed on lakes, presumably because they made some effort to escape there.

An intelligent species such as the wolf, adapted for group hunting, should be able to use topography to its advantage. Such application of intelligence would require only memory, and knowledge of one's territory, which wolves certainly possess. It would be a highly selected trait. Nevertheless, thinking over the bulk of wolf kills we have examined over the years, in only a few places have wolves repeatedly ambushed deer. Most kills seem to be at happenstance places.

In the core of winter, the sun throws little warmth, the nights are brittle. Trees crack, and ice on the lakes booms until muffled by snow. Snow curtains the streams, silencing them. Grouse remain buried in their night-beds and snowshoe hares stay in the deep recesses under the spruce trees. Living things hunker down, husband their precious calories. Northern lights flicker at night, backlighting the uplifted arms of the pines and etching the lattices of maple limbs against a translucent sky.

Among those many illuminated nights, the night of March 12, 1989, stands out, described in newspapers at the time as the "northern lights display of the century." It was seen as far south as Texas. That evening we had given a talk to the Achray crowd in the dining hall. Later, with our daughters and Graham, we went out to see if we could tune in a radio signal from one wolf or another along the Sand Lake road. After a warm day hovering around freezing, the temperature had plummeted to -25°C. No breeze, moon less than half full, no human-caused light pollution in the night sky, conditions were excellent for the show. I follow my notes, made later that night in the Achray bunkhouse while the student party raged in the rooms around: "At the jack pine stand near Lake Travers we became aware that the northern lights had changed from a subdued horizon-glow to bright bands shooting across the sky. We stopped the truck, got out, and watched as the sky grew brighter, then suddenly, in a broad swath, turned pink. The pink deepened to crimson and mounted all the way to directly overhead where it became a pulsing, full corona. Across the red sky played white, pink and greenish searchlights, expanding, contracting, flaring up, expiring, reviving, pulsing, 'dancing heal and toe.' Gigantic magnetic shapes, soon expanding to within 20 degrees of the southern horizon, glowed and pulsed rhythmically, west to east, each cloud lighting up in sequence. One moment they were shaped like cumulus clouds, another like wispy cirrus strands. Wave after wave of colourful light crossed these magnetic clouds, wrapped in an intense blood-red sky. It was unreal, unworldly. We felt transformed to somewhere else in the universe. In the face of all that galactic power, human endeavour seemed scarcely to count."

We drove with our headlights off to Pretty Lake, then to the bridge over the Petawawa River to listen for signals or howls but heard nothing. Back to Achray at 1 A.M.

Across a broad range of species, territorial behaviour is found under circumstances of a favourable cost:benefit ratio. Where the cost of staking out, marking, and defending a territory is greater than the benefit of exclusive use of the prey in that territory, then territory is replaced with some other social system running from active co-operation to nomadism. So we looked for examples of these systems, as well as evidence of boundary marking and defence.

Once, the Mathews Lake wolves made a three-day circuit around their territory. They started close to their southeast boundary at a moose they had run off a little lake and killed in a thick stand of balsam firs. The struggle had left tree limbs broken and trunks splattered with blood. After the wolves had consumed about three-quarters of the carcass, they left, heading west. Suspecting they were travelling their southern boundary, we snowshoed along a hydro right-of-way to intercept them. Five sets of wolf tracks crossed our path.

Back at our truck again, some campers driving by reported seeing wolves at Pretty Lake ten kilometres farther on. There we found wolf tracks and heard the Mathews wolf's distant signal. The pack had swung north, by then almost six kilometres beyond its normal boundary, and was trespassing on the Pretty Lake pack's land. The next day, Graham found the Mathews wolves from the air back on their own northwest corner, and from there they travelled downstream along the Petawawa River, their northern boundary. The following day they were back at their moose kill. The Pretty Lake pack had not detected them, as far as we know. Although the Mathews Lake pack had pushed beyond its normal range on this foray, the evidence that it had made a boundary patrol seemed to fit expected territorial behaviour.

Their patrol cost them a modest price. While away from their moose carcass, Grand Lake 2, an adult female, not only trespassed, but treated herself to a meal. The day before the Mathews pack left, she had been stationary right on the edge of her territory less than one kilometre from the moose kill. That night she moved in. We followed her signal across a bog, the soft light of the moon casting our shadows ahead of us and sparkling off a thousand snow crystals. Her single set of tracks showed that she was trotting as she left the bog and plunged into thick lowland conifers. She was travelling straight, as if she knew exactly where she was going. Eventually we turned back for fear of pushing her and drove a short distance down the road for a cross-bearing. The bearings crossed exactly at the Mathews pack's moose kill.

That was the only night we caught her poaching. This was not a case of willing prey sharing because she had picked her time to avoid being discovered. All that really was involved was avoidance behaviour. Even before the Mathews Lake pack returned, she was back on territory again.

Although poaching was not common on these winter territories, there were some other interesting cases. On December 18, 1991, four wolves from the Jack Pine pack killed a deer on a pond within the southcentral sector of the Grand Lake East pack's territory. Meanwhile, the Grand Lake East pack of six was eleven kilometres to the northeast and, as far as we could tell, stayed there for the three days their "guests" were dining, so they may not have known about the kill. Perhaps they had their own carcass, not visible from the air, but if they detected the trespassing pack, they did not take offence.

Two days later, surprisingly, a new pack was at the remains of the same deer, although by then not much was left. The new Grand Lake West pack of four, who had never before travelled in Grand Lake East territory, was on the carcass when Graham flew over. Meanwhile, the Jack Pine wolves had left the carcass and were about three kilometres away. Unfortunately, we do not know what transpired earlier between them at the kill. Still the landowners, the Grand Lake East wolves seemed to keep their distance.

Another two days later, unbelievably, yet a third pack was at what was now only a blood patch on the snow. The Basin Depot pack of seven had moved up from the south. By then, the Grand Lake West pack had gone back home and the Jack Pine pack was even farther south, killing a fawn in the territory of the Grand Lake East pack, who again did not seem to care.

Years later, in February 1998, a pack of four Jocko pack wolves gave way to seven Jack Pine pack wolves at a half-consumed moose. Both packs were trespassing. Michelle found the pack of four from the air on her morning telemetry flight – she was working for us again that winter. The wolves were hidden by the trees on the southside of Grand Lake. By the time we got there by snowmobile and snowshoe in the afternoon, the Jocko pack was gone, but the Jack Pine pack was there, feeding on the moose. Again we do not know if the carcass was conceded or won.

Trespass sometimes occurred just beyond territorial boundaries, making zones of overlap between packs. No known prey poaching was involved on the occasions when Mathews Lake wolves would swing across Johnson, Berm, and upper Stratton lakes at the eastern end of the Grand Lake pack's territory. Occasionally collared members of both packs were less than one kilometre apart; we could hear their signals from the Achray parking lot.

We made it a practice first thing every morning to go out and swing the antenna. Often enough we heard signals from one or both packs. One cold morning just after daylight we got the signals of the Foys Lake wolves from the parking lot, loud enough that we realized they must be within sight, so we ran out to the lake. The Foys Lake pack lived to the south, normally separated from Grand Lake by a long, high ridge that neither pack used. This morning, they had crossed the ridge to trespass along the shore of Grand Lake itself. We saw them strung out in single file where two days previously we had watched the Grand Lake wolves. Meantime, the entire Grand Lake pack was thirteen kilometres away at Clemow Lake at their own moose carcass.

More than just boundary overlap was a ten-kilometre intrusion a pair of Pretty Lake wolves made one night along a road into the Grand Lake territory. Tracking was easy; the road had been freshly ploughed, then lightly dusted with snow. Similarly, a Jack Pine wolf once spent two days well within the Pretty Lake pack's territory while that pack was three kilometres away, stationary and possibly on a carcass. Another time, Grand Lake wolves travelled deeply into Jack Pine territory. No charges laid, no penalties exacted.

Boundary overlap like this, even the occasional deep invasions, were minor events compared with the redefinition of whole territories. In 1991 the Grand Lake pack shuffled the deck. Our data

were good on the Grand Lake wolves partly due to viewing opportunities out on the lake itself and partly because the railway along
the shore provided easy access. Our longest string of data, almost
five years, came from Grand Lake 2, collared in July 1988 by
Graham and Jenny. Her den was dug into the top of an esker that
lined a fast-flowing creek not far from the west end of Grand Lake.
She was part of a pack of six. Late one grey afternoon, we watched
her and her packmates trotting in typical easy fashion down the
centre of the lake. We crouched behind some spruces beside the
railway and howled. The wolves swerved our way to investigate. A
March thaw had left slush on top of the ice, and soon we heard
wolf feet sloshing close by. Feeling guilty for deceiving them, we
abandoned any effort at peering out and crouched even lower. The
sloshing stopped in front of us; undoubtedly they were scenting
the breeze. We were revealed as surely as if we had been in full
sight. They loped away.

Another time we watched Grand 2 with the big wolf Grand 4,
her mate, and four other wolves as they picked their way along the
far shore of the lake. We managed to stay parallel to them, walking
through shallow snow. A strong wind bent the trees and covered
our movement. Eventually they lay down in the sun on the snow-
covered ice, and there they spent the afternoon, getting up, walking
around a bit, lying down again, as "stationary" wolves always seem
to do. It was a harmonious winter scene – snow, sun, forest, wolves.

Then in January 1991 something disturbed the pack. Maybe
the death of the big male, trampled by a moose, destabilized them,
but that had happened a year earlier. Maybe the recent dispersal of
a young, radio-collared female was involved, but dispersal of young
is common and not disruptive to wolf packs. The month before,
the territory of the six wolves in the pack extended beyond both
ends of Grand Lake. Then, Graham found Grand 2 with two other
wolves outside the park in the Petawawa Military Reserve, ten
kilometres northeast of her territory. They stayed there for two days,
then moved another ten kilometres southeast. By mid-February,
when Graham flew in search of them again, they were back in the
eastern part of their territory and we thought the trio had only been

off on an extra-territorial foray. After that, however, they never travelled beyond the midway point of Grand Lake, and Grand 2 never associated with her old den along the creek. And never that winter was she with more than the two other wolves. Meanwhile, the other three wolves of the original pack stayed put on the vacated west end of her old territory.

The pack had split in two, not because it had become too large, as happens occasionally – there had been only six – but because of some internal social dynamics known only to its members. Each pack maintained somewhat smaller territories than the original Grand Lake pack, although the following summer the eastern trio expanded its territory another few kilometres to the east into the range of an uncollared pack. In a new den, Grand 2 produced pups to become a pack of five. The western trio added one disperser from somewhere, then either lost adults or produced only one pup, because by winter they also were a pack of five. Despite probable genetic affiliations, and knowledge of each other, the two packs never associated again.

For a long time the Pretty Lake pack was an enigma. We knew it was there; several times each summer we heard its howls from our campsite among the pines. When we plotted the fixes of the Jack Pine and Mathews Lake packs to the west and east respectively, there was obviously a gap between them. But the missing pack eluded us until August 1991, when a yearling female was collared and began to fill this vacant place on the map with dots.

Pretty Lake, accessible from the Sand Lake road, turned out to be near the southern boundary of the pack's territory, which extended north to, and sometimes beyond, the fast-flowing Petawawa River. The river posed a psychological more than real barrier in summer because it could be swum, and no barrier at all in winter. The collared yearling was in a pack of four. That December, as the deer migrated away, the pack made two extra-territorial forays south into lands occupied by packs in the Bonnechere Valley. On one of these trips the trespassers killed a deer.

In mid-March, Graham plotted aerial fixes after three consecutive flights that all fell close to the same little creek buried in a deeply incised, conifer-filled valley. A stationary pack such as that normally signals a moose carcass, so Mary, Michelle, and I loaded our snowmobile and drove to the "Pretty Lake trapping road." The snow was hip-deep, and a strong wind left the sun cold. We cut down the two-metre-high snowbank at the edge of the road to get the snowmobile up onto the snowpack, then headed off with Michelle behind me on the seat and Mary in her accustomed place on the sled runners.

Six kilometres later, Pretty 1's signal came in weakly. Our rule is to keep the snowmobile one or two kilometres back from any wolves, so we cut the noisy engine and donned our snowshoes to continue on foot. A trio of gray jays sailed in silently to look us over, concluded we were not good for a handout, and vanished. The paired tracks of a pine marten showed where, sometime ago, it had decided that red squirrel hunting was better in the pines on the opposite side of the road. In the spruce-fir low places, the tracks of snowshoe hares revealed where they had been dancing in the moonlight. The snow had enough body to hold them up; even the wolves sank only a few centimetres. Moose, though, were going in half a metre, deep enough to make them lift their hind legs high and run with knees splayed in an awkward gait. Wolves, under these conditions, can run circles around a moose without fear of its deadly hooves.

As we continued, the signal strengthened from the far side of the same gully Graham had seen from the air. Too steep and too densely covered with small, snow-bent pines, we took off our snowshoes and slithered to the bottom. Over another ridge we followed the wolf's tracks to a knoll where she had been lying with a good view all around, as is typical. There, she had first heard us coming and bolted away with long strides, clearing a snow-laden log with a metre-high jump.

After searching unsuccessfully for the moose carcass, we floundered back to the snowmobile. In our absence, two wolves had come up the ravine, encountered our snowshoe tracks, and turned to walk beside them. They continued half a kilometre before crossing them and heading back into the ravine. Wolves have hesitated to cross our tracks on other occasions, but we have also seen instances of wolves walking right in them or crossing without hesitation.

We drove the snowmobile south for a couple of kilometres, set off again by snowshoe, and soon found the tracks of what looked like the same two wolves. They had crossed a beaver pond and scratched all the snow off the top of a lodge, undoubtedly smelling beaver through the top vent. We have yet to find a successful excavation; the frozen mud and sticks form an impenetrable roof. Some freshly cut birches on shore indicated recent beaver activity. To get a meal, wolves must come upon beaver away from their lodges, which they do often enough, judging by beaver hairs in winter wolf scats, to make checking out beaver ponds worthwhile.

The collared wolf's signal was still to the north, so we waited in some fir trees where we had a view across the pond. By then, late afternoon, the cold sun had disappeared, and an icy wind whipped the pines causing them to convulse in disarray. Tracks showed where a moose had browsed balsam firs, then bedded down making an ice-lined depression with its body. We watched a black-backed woodpecker flick bark scales off a red pine in endless pursuit of bark beetles. But the day was in shut-down mode.

Soon a full moon veiled by thin cirrus strands sailed into view among the tossing pines. The collared wolf was closer, but by then all we could hope to see was its shadow out on the pond. We were not going to find its moose. I howled; the wind grabbed the sound and transported it elsewhere. The wolves heard it, though they didn't respond immediately but waited until we had started back along our snowshoe trail. Then they broke out into a wild chorus from the beaver pond where we had been, accompanied by the stereophonics of wind gusting in the pines, rising on one side of us, falling, building up again somewhere else.

We wound our way back in the moonlight, flashlights off. Twice we stopped to listen to the voice of a single wolf. No breaks in pitch, just smooth up, then down, in long, beautiful solos.

Pretty Lake wolves trespassed on occasion in Grand Lake West's territory and in turn got trespassed on by the Mathews Lake pack. Once, a Pretty Lake wolf joined a Jack Pine wolf next door. But other than occasional winter excursions in response to migrating deer, they remained reasonably faithful to their own lands.

Our winter experiences with the Travers wolves were limited. Because they lived on the west side of Lake Travers, and only the southern tip of their territory was accessible by road, we rarely could reach them. They provided a few moose carcasses for us, and made their share of extra-territorial forays. Once, in mid-December they split into two groups, one of them feeding on poached moose in the Foys Lake pack's territory while the other group was also off territory, twelve kilometres away. They appear not to have shared the moose, a puzzling lack of pack coordination.

Then, tragedy befell the pack, repeated tragedy that made the Travers lands vacant through much of our study.

When we look at a handful of computer-drawn maps showing the locations of these wolves, most fixes fall within the loose boundaries of what we came to expect for each pack. Strings of dots occur where Graham backtracked a pack from the air, most frequently along lakes; linear Grand Lake looks like a highway. In places, concentrations of dots occur along roads, reflecting where we searched most intensively rather than wolf behaviour.

Except for the Grand Lake highway, we can discern no tendency by these packs to use distinct travel routes repeatedly, although we did for the Foys Lake pack to the south. Pack movements within territories seem to be largely random. Minimum pattern represents maximum flexibility. That undoubtedly is adaptive for wolves under the circumstances of the largely patternless and unpredictable movements of moose and deer. If wolves were creatures of habit, prey would be able to predict their movements and avoid them better.

Boundaries differed somewhat from one year to another. This tendency was partly due to the outer locations we managed to detect, but also to differences in the way various wolves used their territories over the years. The packs were definitely not nomadic. But they did not seem preoccupied with defending boundaries, either – we recorded only a few instances of boundary patrolling. If boundary patrolling was common, many more fixes would have helped define the outer limits of their territories. Instead, the points seem to peter out away from an ill-defined core. Boundaries must have been marked, or remembered and recognized, however, otherwise pack overlap would have been much more common.

Against this matrix of territoriality were frequent instances of trespass and even some cases of prey poaching or sharing between packs. Part of what we saw could be attributed to dispersing individuals with their apparent free pass to travel on any pack's land. We tracked young dispersers, such as a young, female Grand Lake wolf who travelled widely before joining a pack to the south, and a few adults, such as Grand Lake 1 who wandered much of one winter before settling down in the Jack Pine pack. Until we realized that these dispersing wolves held free passes, their trespassing escapades perplexed us.

Then we developed an entirely new perspective on our population from the genetics work of Paul Wilson and Sonya Grewal. The genealogy of the population showed that we were studying one big extended family! Not only the Jack Pine pack had scattered its genes in most of the surrounding packs, but so had many others. The Basin Depot pack in the Bonnechere Valley, for example, sent three dispersers north to the Travers pack, one in 1994 and two in 1995. As in rhesus monkeys and chimpanzees, one sibling dispersing to a new pack may open the door for later ones who would have known each other back in their natal pack.

We found that we had collared eight great-grandchildren of the oldest wolf in the study, Redpole 4, who died when fifteen years old (confirmed by tooth cementum analysis), and these great-grandchildren lived in four different packs. We identified other relationships forged by dispersal between the Mathews and Pretty packs, Grand and Mathews, Redpole and Travers. . . . Our conclusions about the difficulty of Jack Pine wolves going any-where without meeting kin was true for most other packs too.

The dispersal we found differs only by degree from that described by other researchers. The greater amount of dispersal in the Algonquin population served to increase interrelatedness among packs and may help explain the tolerance and lack of aggression that characterizes our population. But Dave Mech and colleagues in northern Minnesota have found more killing and inter-pack rivalries than we have, despite a great deal of dispersion in the pop-ulation they study.

Perhaps the difference in our results reflects differences in prey density or ease of capture, that is, some sort of cost:benefit analy-sis of defending a territory depending upon resource availability. Widely accepted theory explains that when prey is sparse and scattered and takes a long time to find, the energetic cost of main-taining a territory over a large area may be greater than the benefit of keeping all the prey to oneself. Under such circumstances in other species, nomadism may occur. But, scaling upward in prey availability, a situation may arise at moderate prey density where territories can be smaller and so defended at lower cost. In that situation, the predator benefits by not having to share prey and risk prey depletion by others. Then defended territories make sense. With even more prey, however, in the face of plenty of food, there may be little to gain by defending a territory.

The Algonquin wolf system, with some evidence of boundary patrolling but little active defence, may lie somewhere between the latter two situations. Subtle differences between years or even between seasons in prey availability or snow conditions may influence the level of aggression and territorial behaviour. The pop-ulation may be balanced on the edge of an indifferent or avoidance-based home-range system and a competitive territorial system, depending on immediate resource availability.

A good analogy found in ecology books for what we were seeing is a "compressible rubber ball." The more you squeeze it, the harder it is to squeeze until you cannot compress it any more. The behaviour of a landowner can be like that. The pack may be willing to make room for others for a while, but the more land it gives up, the less it is willing to concede.

As well, wolves with different temperaments, tolerances, thresholds of cooperation and competition may come and go in a population. Individual wolves have both behavioural plasticity and personality programmed in their genes.

The early Algonquin Indians faced many of the same survival problems as wolves. Both needed to strike a favourable ratio of energy expended to energy obtained where prey was sparse, discontinuous, scattered, its location unpredictable, and its chances of escape good. Both were co-predators on moose.

One winter, Mary pieced together a picture of the lives of these native people from archaeological and historical writings. She relied especially on the seventy-three-volume *Jesuit Relations* written by the first priests to make contact with them. Each winter the native people left their summer fishing camps along the Ottawa River and broke up into small family hunting units that spaced themselves out across the Algonquin dome, each with its own territory. Many family groups were related through a grown son, or a brother or sister. In times of need, one family could hunt on another's land. It was much like the system used by the northern Cree even today.

With this flexible system of land allocation, the early Algonquin people did not operate in the stereotypic ways described for wolves. Their spacing mechanism was largely a kin-based, cooperative land division with undefended home ranges.

Direct comparisons are complicated by differences in mobility, efficiency in both detecting and dispatching prey, and ability to hunt at night; wolves have the edge in most of these traits. But, despite the evidence we found for competition and territoriality among wolf packs, we have just as much evidence for a home-range system similar to that used by the early Algonquin people. Admittedly, in our study we could not identify the importance of passive forms of defence such as howling or scent-marking to keep trespassing wolves away. And accommodating the needs of one another out of compassion is more highly developed in humans than in other species.

Nonetheless, the Pretty Lake pack appears to have behaved cooperatively by leaving room for a re-establishing Jack Pine pack. Similarly, there were many instances of trespass permitted by various packs on each other's lands. As a survival strategy, some blend of competition, indifference, and even cooperation, some ability to show one or another depending upon circumstance, may be a fundamental part of the wolf's success. At least in the Algonquin wolf, that is the way it is.

Harmonious relationships between the MNR, the landlord at Achray, and Algonquin College, the lessee, did not last. One winter we had the place much to ourselves, then it was declared surplus. The water pump was turned off, pipes drained, generator disassembled. One winter's day a year later, we drove into the familiar parking lot and found the big building gone. As if it had never been there, a smooth blanket of snow extended from the pines out back where the bird feeder used to be across to the parking lot in front. We sat for a long time in the sun-warmed truck cab reliving memories. By then the focus of our winter work, and most of the wolves, had shifted to the southeast, outside the park in a much more dramatic example of wolf territorial flexibility. Everything changed, for the wolves and for us. The system of land tenure we had been observing, it turned out, was only part of the social order, and the territories more transient than expected.

THE RED QUEEN AND
WOLF-MOOSE RELATIONSHIPS

Predator and Prey

Predators can kill members of a prey population, yet not depress it — an apparent contradiction. A sharp-shinned hawk pinioning a flicker, a mink eating a shiner, a wolf killing a deer all result in one less prey animal. Predators get a bad rap, however, because the dramatic act of killing does not always lower the prey population in the expected way.

Several adjustments operate in predator-prey systems to accommodate such losses. Most significant are the compensations, first explained by Wisconsin ecologist Paul Errington. For example, prey populations drawn down by predation may increase their birth rate in response to better nutrition for the remaining animals.

Some species exhibit a greater capacity to respond in this way than others, most notably furbearers. Humans acting as predators can trap a densely populated muskrat marsh and induce the muskrats to breed two or three times a year instead of only once. Similarly, though less dramatically, moose can increase their rate of twinning and calve at a younger age in response to better nutrition. Species that physiologically cannot produce twins or rarely do, such as caribou, are more restricted in their ability to offset the effects of predation in this way.

Another mechanism, compensatory recruitment, leads to better survival of young to breeding age. It also is a response to improved nutrition. Normally in wildlife populations, especially in dense ones, losses of young are high and often related to poor nutrition.

But most importantly, Errington focused on compensatory mortality, the idea that if one environmental factor does not kill members of a prey population, another will. Compensatory mortality works most commonly in a prey population near its carrying capacity for food. In this situation, if predation does not lower prey numbers, more animals will simply starve – so predation is of little consequence. This potential for interplay between mortality factors introduces considerable complexity into deciphering the importance of any single factor.

Besides these compensations is the idea that if breeding opportunities limit the size of a prey population, any non-breeders beyond that limit represent a doomed surplus. Predation on them will not reduce the number of breeders. Hole-nesting birds may be limited by the number of trees with suitable holes, making members of the population expendable beyond those using all the holes.

Finally, there is the deflating idea for males that in a polygamous species, a few males can do all the breeding. As long as enough males are present to breed with all the females, the rest are superfluous. Numbers may drop accordingly but not the continuing productivity of the prey.

When these principles are applied to wolves, it appears that as long as they are living off capital that will either be replaced annually or die anyway, the effect of wolf predation is small. Or, if wolf numbers stay low, their effect may be only to slow the growth of a prey population. Doug Pimlott estimated from his Algonquin work in the early 1960s that when a deer population exceeds seven or eight per square kilometre, a wolf population cannot hold its numbers down. At this point the prey has escaped from the "predator pit," envisioned as a low place on a graph of its numbers. Bill Gasaway and colleagues in Alaska concluded that moose escape the effects of wolves at approximately thirty per wolf, whereas below twenty per wolf, predation may be limiting. In multiple-prey systems, a predator:prey ratio means little because the effect of predation may be spread out and thus minimize its consequences on each species.

Ultimately, available energy, lost in the metabolic costs of life and siphoned off between trophic levels, sets the maximum density a predator population can reach. But below that upper threshold, there is still plenty of room for wolves to have either a big or little influence on the numbers of their prey. Doug Pimlott concluded that over evolutionary time, wolves, perhaps in consort with other predators, have limited their prey commonly enough to be the norm. David Gauthier and I concluded in a 1985 review that in slightly more than half the reported studies, wolves acted as an important limiting influence on their prey populations.

But bedevilling complexity still surrounds the interpretation of inter-acting environmental factors and compensatory mechanisms. Nobody has discovered any universal set of conditions that, in anything but the short run, determines the role of wolf predation. Until that is uncovered, if such a generalization exists, there will be more to learn.

A WOLF PACK is a superb hunting device, coordinated, tactical, efficient. It fans out through the forest, swarms over hillocks, braids across lakes. With senses fine-tuned, it is ready instantly to turn on speed, dispatch flankers, cut off, corner, and outmanoeuvre its prey. Wolves instinctively know the rudiments of the hunt, and through additional training they learn how to kill. Time-tested, they have survived where more than ten thousand years ago the larger, stronger dire wolf and the smaller, weaker edwardian wolf died out.

A moose is a formidable prey. Its strong legs and hooves are lethal weapons. One of few surviving large herbivores from the Pleistocene Epoch, it managed to live through environmental change and technical advances in human hunting to which other species succumbed. Past successful strategies, such as calving on ridges or on islands where visibility is good, programmed survival into its genes. Long legged, snow adapted, moose have been shaped by eons of tough winters. They have also been shaped by wolves.

Wolf and moose: they first met in Eurasia or ice-locked Beringia (now Alaska and central Yukon). Dispersing south in an interglacial period, they have lived together in various places in North America for the past eighty thousand years. Across the broad, shifting boreal forest on both continents, moose sustain wolves. Despite the vicissitudes of deep or shallow snow, sickness or health, good or poor nutrition that at times favour one over the other, they have co-existed in tandem over the millennia in a remarkable, tenuous balance, like every other predator-prey combination that persists.

In Algonquin Park, moose are one of three major species of prey. Wolves think about deer and beaver too as they search their land. A particular focus of Graham's Ph.D. work was to understand wolf-moose relationships in this multiprey system.

In the deep snow and penetrating cold of an Algonquin winter, almost everything just seems to be hanging on. Not wolves, however; they do well. We have recorded no winter deaths by starvation. Life looks good when you see them from the air curled up in the sun on a south-facing lakeshore where snow is shallow or the ground is bare.

One March day the Cessna landed to pick up Mary, Graham, and me on the ice of Grand Lake. Graham handled the telemetry in the front seat. I, as usual, was barely keeping my stomach down in the back. Soon we were circling over the Grand Lake pack, the signals from the two collared wolves loud on the right side of the banked plane. What I thought at first were red pine stumps on the sunny edge of a pond suddenly stood up, stretched, and gazed at the plane. When we circled again they were all lying down. Likely they had fed on a moose carcass nearby.

Life may be relatively good for moose too, whose ratio of surface to body core alone favours heat retention. Living a negative-energy balance in winter, nonetheless, they know how to conserve what they need to stay alive. They know to seek out the dense conifers on cold nights to take advantage of any vestiges of trapped daytime warmth away from the heat sink of open sky. They know to head for heavy cover when the deepening snows make travel difficult.

Rumour had it, when we began our study, that the small Algonquin wolf was unable to kill moose. That incapacity was thought to be an important reason moose numbers had increased to roughly one per two square kilometres, high by eastern North American standards (although in Newfoundland they may reach three per square kilometre). Yet our analysis of hair in wolf scats showed that roughly one-third of both winter and summer diet was moose. We wanted to find out why.

Our routine for getting to moose carcasses in winter was for Graham to fly early-morning telemetry flights and Mary and I to be waiting at the Pem Air hanger when he landed. We would cross-examine him in his motion-sickness-fatigued state to find out what wolves were accessible. On bad days, Graham returned to Achray to sleep off the effects of the flight; on good days, when he was more coherent, he would join us. We drove the ploughed logging roads, or used a combination of snowmobile and snowshoes to reach whatever radio-collared wolves we could. Sometimes the wolves were on the move so when we got there we found only their tracks. Other times we located their bedding sites, suddenly abandoned. Often enough they were at a carcass.

A kill is a place of biological success and failure. Here is the most immediate moment of an ancient evolutionary drama – natural selection at work. This is the moment when genes succeed or fail. There is something solemn about such a place. We talk quietly and keep our visits short, staying just long enough to collect mandibles and femurs, take some measurements, and make a few notes.

The first moose provided by the Grand Lake pack died only a few kilometres from Achray under dense spruces at the side of a bog. A chickadee watched our approach from its perch on a chewed rib. A pair of gray jays flew up from inside the abdomen. The collared wolves had vanished into the trees.

The moose lay on its brisket as if it had just collapsed. The wolves had not dismembered it, rather they had tunnelled into its carcass from the abdomen, then up into the thoracic cavity where they had consumed heart, liver, lungs, and other delicacies housed there. The rumen lay to one side, its outer lining eaten off but otherwise intact, a football-sized frozen ball of half-digested browse. All the evidence added up to one thing. The wolves had not killed this moose but had found it already dead and waiting for them at the frozen-food counter.

It was the same for the first moose we found belonging to the

Travers pack. Late one afternoon we snowshoed towards them, pushing through conifers that too often released their burden of snow down our necks. When we thought we were close, I gave one short howl to find their exact location. The whole pack answered from the trees just ahead. We stood still, expecting wolves to come pouring out into the open, but nothing happened – only silence as if we had imagined their howls. When we advanced again, the radio signal changed direction as the wolves suddenly left. We found the same scene: moose on its brisket, legs still attached. Again, the wolves had tunnelled in from its abdomen.

The calls of squabbling ravens help guide us to many winter carcasses. Ravens keep an eye on travelling wolves, flying loose aerial patrols over them. Food is scarce, and wolves undoubtedly are a principal means of support. If the wolves detect us and leave before we have pinpointed their carcass, we are faced with the choice of following the signal coming from one direction or the ravens raising hell from another. We have learned to choose the ravens; they typically stay put on a carcass even after the wolves have left. Only when we are in sight do they lift off in a rush of wings, a black avian shroud unveiling the carcass below. They fly up into the trees or circle overhead waiting for us to perform our post-mortem ritual and leave.

Native people have speculated in legend about the special relationship between wolves and ravens. Bernt Heinrich's research in New England has shown that ravens can consume a prodigious amount of meat. Yet, apparently not resenting what goes down each other's throats, wolves and ravens feed side by side, sharing the banquet. Never have we found as much as a single raven feather at a carcass to suggest hostilities. Some speculate that ravens "deliberately" call wolves in to a carcass because they need wolf teeth to tear it open. Heinrich concluded, however, that ravens call at carcasses for a complex variety of reasons that includes, for example, recruiting a mob of juvenile ravens to swamp out a defending pair of adults.

Our data gave us even more to speculate about. Do ravens rather than wolves find these frozen moose carcasses first? Frozen meat is considerably less odorous than fresh meat, making its discovery difficult for the wolves. Although these moose were typically dying under heavy conifers, maybe ravens flying just above the treetops, as they normally do, could still spot them. If the ravens find carcasses first, are their calls a dinner gong for the wolves?

Evidence of what was killing these moose lay abundantly around each carcass. Ticks – thousands of them, each engorged with moose blood to the size of a nickel. If blood loss approximates one cubic centimetre for each ten ticks, then ten thousand ticks remove a thousand cubic centimetres, or one litre, of blood. Twenty thousand remove two litres. That is about one-fifth of a moose's blood volume, enough to make it anemic. However, the cause of death normally is attributed to hair loss rather than anemia. Each of these tick-infected moose displayed significant patches of skin – entire shoulders, rump, and flanks – where it had tried to rub the ticks off. Hair provides vital insulation; if a moose is only partially clothed when temperatures plummet to -30°C, hypothermia results.

Hypothermia is just the final blow. Depleted fat in the bone marrow of these moose showed that they had suffered for weeks before they collapsed. As they became increasingly temperature-stressed, they utilized the fat stored in their bone marrow, turning it from pasty, off-white to a crimson jelly. Bone marrow is a fat reserve of last resort. Hair and blood loss slowly drained them of energy until an especially cold night finished them off.

Winter tick is a classic parasite whose population rises with its prey population as transmission becomes easier. In that way, the probability that the tick may curb the size of the moose population increases with the density of moose. Characteristic density dependence such as this is the basic condition for population regulation of most species.

But nothing in ecosystems is ever simple. If winter snows stay late, engorged ticks fall off moose onto snow and perish instead of laying eggs to complete their life cycle. So, variability in weather superimposes its lack of pattern onto what otherwise would be a more cyclical moose-tick relationship. In the end, moose die of tick infections brought on by both their own density and snow conditions the previous spring.

Winter ticks took their share of moose in our study and may have helped prevent the moose population from becoming larger, but they were never prevalent enough to cause a moose decline. They can do that and did on Isle Royale in the winter of 1995 and 1996, according to Rolf Peterson. In 1992, Graham and I published "Importance of Scavenging on Moose in Algonquin Park, Ontario" in the journal *Alces*. At fully 83 per cent of the carcasses we examined, wolves were scavengers not predators – the moose had already died. In subsequent years we found slightly less tick effect, and that figure fell to 71 per cent. Despite this drop, MNR biologist Mike Wilton continued to document some heavy tick years, but for some reason, tick killing occurred in late March and throughout April rather than in February and early March. The reasons are shrouded in the tick's still poorly understood ecology.

Wolves and ravens are not the only species to benefit from the table set down in the conifers by winter ticks. So do foxes, martens, fishers, gray jays, blue jays, and chickadees, placing these tiny invertebrates in a pivotal position in the ecological circuitry. Without winter ticks, little "invertebrate agitators" of big ecological systems, fewer birds and mammals could live in the winter forest.

Not all the moose we examined had died of ticks. Algonquin wolves are not too small to make their own kills. Moose put up a good enough fight to leave obvious signs. There were plenty of signs where a moose was killed by the Grand Lake pack at Clemow Lake. It took us three attempts to reach it. Our battered and ageing blue pickup by then had developed terminal electrical complications; not always did the engine deliver sparks to the cylinders. Worse were the snowmobiles. We tried to get to Clemow first using graduate student Lee Swanson's ancient Alouette borrowed from her father, but the very first hill stopped us. Every time we throttled, the snowmobile ground its way down instead of forward. We pushed and pulled until exhausted, then reloaded it on the trailer and returned to Achray.

We made the second attempt directly up Grand Lake from Achray, setting off from the garage. The snowmobile died just past the dock. We pulled on the rope for a while, then manhandled the machine back. Tom Stephenson looked it over, pulled on the rope once, and it started. Anyone familiar with snowmobiles knows that the first place to check when it stalls is at the kill switch on the handlebars – which we had inadvertently knocked down.

Our third try began back at the road with the hill, but this time Tom had broken a trail part of the way with his smaller, lighter machine. Our truck died two kilometres short of the snowmobile road, so we unloaded there. The day was bright and sunny with wind sweeping up wisps of ground snow, but not enough to cover the tracks of three wolves on Tom's trail made the night before. Down beside a creek, three more wolves joined up, confirming Graham's aerial observation of six.

The snowmobile seemed to be running well. After a while I glanced back expecting to see Mary standing on the sled runners, but she was gone. This was no trivial matter, because it forced me to get off and jerk the heavy machine around. I found her a couple of kilometres back, floundering along in the deep snow. On the second turnaround, the snowmobile stalled, but Tom had shown us the trick of pouring some ether-based engine starter into the carburetor, and that worked.

Five kilometres farther on, the machine died again and this time refused to be whipped alive, so we put on our snowshoes. Soon we heard Grand Lake 2's signal from the east end of Clemow Lake. As we walked along, the number of tracks increased until the road was plastered, especially where it swung into the trees near the lake. The wolves had not heard us coming and one ambled across the road into the alders ahead. About twenty metres farther on, we came upon their moose, splayed out on the open snowy road.

Unlike tick-killed moose, this one was on its side and partly dismembered. Wolf teeth had punctured its rumen before it had frozen, and its semifluid contents had poured out onto the snow. We reconstructed what had happened. The moose had been browsing red maples and balsam fir, judging by the clipped twigs nearby and the needles stuck between his teeth, when the pack jumped him. He may have stood his ground for a while. Plenty of moose tracks pummelled the snow, but none showed him running. However, his days were over, wolves or not. He was an ancient moose who had experienced nineteen winters, making him the oldest we have found. His premolars and molars were worn flat to the gum line. When I split his femur with my hatchet, his red bone marrow flowed out. This time the wolves were merely overeager scavengers.

We scouted around looking for more evidence and flushed collared Grand 2 from the trees in a flurry of snow. While we were at the kill, the wolves had stayed within fifty metres, undoubtedly anxious to resume their feast. So we packed up our carcass kit and left.

The snowmobile leaped to life again after about the fiftieth pull, and carried us to within five kilometres of the truck where it died a final time. No amount of pulling or ether in the carburetor made it go, so finally we were forced to walk. Our truck started okay, and as long as we kept the speed over fifty kilometres an hour, much too fast for a winding, ice-covered road, it didn't stall. We careened our way back to Achray.

One moose donated by the Mathews Lake pack put up an even greater fight. In the Mathews pack was a gigantic wolf whose tracks we had observed periodically for more than two years. We collared other Mathews wolves but never the giant. On March 13, 1991, Mary and I took our new research snowmobile up the snow-filled connector road north from Achray into the Mathews territory. A few kilometres along, we heard the signal of Mathews 4, an adult female, off to the north. Simultaneously, Graham and Lee were circling in the Cessna over the wolf, and we judged the centre of their circle to be about one kilometre from us. We encountered a trail of wolf tracks following a little creek, and among the tracks were those of the Mathews giant.

Every wolf study has its mythical wolf, one that is bigger and stronger than all the rest. We wanted to see him (we assumed a male), and here was an opportunity, so we put on our snowshoes and struck out. Mathews 4's signal led us farther to the east than we expected, but we kept on it in dense conifers for a while. Late winter sunshine dappled through the trees, softening the snow in the forest openings and making it cling to our snowshoes. Eventually we came to a small marsh-lake where the signal was loud. Approaching very slowly, we parted balsam branches and looked out. Four wolves lay there, one of them dwarfing the rest with its enormous neck and shoulders and deep chest. Two smaller wolves lay flat out on their sides, absorbing maximum warmth from the sun; the other two were up on their haunches, occasionally lifting their heads to look around.

A raven flew by from the south carrying a chunk of red meat in its beak, so we knew the pack had a carcass nearby. Soon two of the wolves stood up and walked slowly to the trees on the south side of the lake. We wanted to photograph the giant wolf, and moved a few steps, but he sensed us immediately. When he stood up, he looked as big as a pony. Together he and his companion loped for the trees, the big wolf occasionally stumbling as he broke through the soft crust.

We snowshoed to where they had been, examined the familiar large tracks, then followed them to their moose. Mathews 4's signal evaporated as we approached. A few ravens lifted off the carcass, this one a young bull, its body parts scattered under the spruces. Branches were broken all around, many splattered with blood. Where the moose made his last stand the snow was pounded flat. His bone marrow was still rich in fat. Here was a clear case of predation, a moose that otherwise would have lived.

So, too, was the moose at Narrowbag Lake, where evidence at the scene allowed us to reconstruct the attack. The moose had been browsing red maples on a ridge 150 metres from the lake, then lay down under a balsam fir. Some wolves came upon her there, at least one of them making contact, judging from the blood on the snow at the bed-site. She jumped up and plunged down the ridge towards the lake, taking big bounds, mowing down saplings and crashing through brush. But she did not get far. More wolves had been hunting along the lakeshore, and they turned up to meet her. She was dispatched quickly in a clump of firs. A four- or five-year-old, her bone marrow showed only slight pink.

Among other memorable moose kills was one made by the Pretty Lake pack in 1996. Snow-covered Emma Lake glistened in late-afternoon sun as Mary, Tom Stephenson, and I trekked up it. At its north end we heard the signal of Pretty 6 and saw ravens circling overhead. We slipped behind some scraggly jack pines along the shore and I howled. Within seconds, five wolves materialized from some small, lake-edge pines. They looked our way but could not see us. Obviously excited, they milled about, flicking their tails vigorously. First one, then all lifted their heads in a group howl. Then, one by one, they ran across the narrow north end of the lake and into the trees. The moving radio signal showed that they came down through the shoreline trees towards us, but, when they were opposite us, stopped. They either picked up our scent or saw us. We waited to see what would happen next, but nothing did, so we snowshoed the rest of the way to the carcass.

The snow that winter was heavy enough to break records, and the big bull had been sinking in hip-deep. Making things worse for him, he had been wading through small pines that were bent over under their load of snow, with a tangle of brush beneath. When the wolves attacked, he ran but was up to his belly. Extracting his hooves for defence was impossible. The wolves killed him with apparent ease.

Moose survive in wolf country because they are a dangerous prey. They do not typically outrun wolves, although they may be able to do that with ideal footing and little to impede them. We once clocked a bull moose with half-grown antlers running down a logging road ahead of us at thirty kilometres an hour over one and a half kilometres. At a gallop for two hundred metres, he made thirty-five kilometres an hour. Wolves reportedly can run as fast or even faster. A cow and calf in January could only make twenty kilometres an hour on a ploughed road. Successful moose, however, stand their ground, as observations from several studies have shown.

In our heavily forested study area, we were not privileged to watch attacks, only assess their outcome. Sometimes the moose wins. Grand Lake 4 was a large adult male weighing in at thirty-six kilograms (eighty pounds). In December 1989, Graham heard his signal from the air on mortality mode. To recover him we snow-mobiled from Achray, across Johnson and Berm lakes, then down Stratton Lake to its east end.

We cut into a high-canopy stand of white and red pines at a point where the snow was shallow enough that we could walk without snowshoes. Grand 4 lay about fifty metres inland, his hindquarters exposed but his midsection and head under a few centimetres of snow. One set of fresh wolf tracks led up to the carcass and then away, and some older tracks were scattered near the shore. We carefully brushed off the snow and examined him.

He had some obvious wounds: scalp cut through to his cranium, and cuts on the right side of his face, top of his hip, and left flank just behind his foreleg. None of these wounds, however, seemed serious enough to be fatal. No human tracks were around, or snowmobile, or moose, or any signs of a fight. He was on his own territory so was not paying the price of trespass.

We carried him to the sled, lashed him on, and drove back. Eventually he ended up in a snowbank by our house, awaiting the reopening of the lab at the University of Guelph after the New Year. Upon autopsy, the cause of death was more apparent: fractured skull, broken ribs.

About the only conceivable way he could have been injured so seriously, considering his prime condition, was by a moose. His wounds were consistent with what would happen if a wolf lost its footing in front of a trampling moose that was standing its ground. He must have travelled some distance before he collapsed.

Grand 4 was not the only loser. In my student years I discovered a dead wolf with massive hemorrhaging on one flank and a ruptured kidney, the victim of a swift kick. Moose, even deer hooves, can be lethal. At both Isle Royale and Denali national parks, research showed that up to 90 per cent of wolf attacks on moose are unsuccessful. Wolves test a moose, then make a tactical decision and often leave.

How predators shape their prey, and prey shape their predators, is an example of co-evolution. Two species are bound together, influencing one another over time, like two clowns with feet and hands tied together doing somersaults at a county fair. One is the driving force for the other. As the prey gets better at escaping, it puts pressure on the predator to get better at catching it. And that, in turn, puts pressure on the prey to improve even more.

Under the constant pressure of co-evolution, everything that is not prey in wolf-dominated ecosystems but large enough to provide wolves with a decent meal has had to come up with some adaptation to avoid predation. It either goes into the ground, climbs trees, is large and fierce, runs fast, kicks, has quills, or tastes bad. By forcing these adaptations, wolves have structured the characteristics of species that share their ecosystems. Wolves, in effect, have lost out to these non-prey species, failed to make counter-adaptations to catch them.

Other species, however, have less perfect predator defences than do bears, porcupines, and the mustelids (mink, marten, otters, skunks), just imperfect enough to support wolves but still allow their own populations to persist. Beaver stay near water, their means of escape, and the dams they build can be interpreted as adding to their safe foraging range. Moose and deer spend most of their time, like almost all forest ungulates, singly or in small groups; they find safety in dispersion. Savannah and tundra ungulates, in contrast, gather in herds; they find safety in numbers where they can see and not be taken by surprise. Deer deviate from this rule in winter, as discussed in a later chapter. Despite these adaptations, enough moose, deer, and beaver succumb to support a wolf population.

Why the prey manages to outstrip the adaptations of the predator and develop immunity, sometimes but not others, is a central question in ecology. If wolves shape their prey by culling the vulnerable, making even faster and fiercer moose and deer, why haven't wolves always responded by getting better at killing?

They have responded in times past. The characteristics of the prey have forged the characteristics of the predator. This phenomenon is called the Red Queen Effect. In *Alice's Adventures in*

Wonderland, the Red Queen said, "Now here, you see, it takes all kinds of running you can do to keep in the same place." The predator has been forced to keep improving to match each improvement in the prey just to maintain the same level of killing efficiency. The Red Queen Effect has been important in the co-evolution of predator-prey systems.

.But the wolf has remained relatively unchanged since it first showed up in the fossil record about one million years ago. Making that more remarkable is the dramatic variety of its prey. Environments have changed too, going through glacial and non-glacial periods. Under the influence of changing environmental conditions such as these, you would expect to find the Red Queen Effect, an ever-adapting predator, or else it would fall back and become extinct.

Why the Red Queen Effect has not driven changes in wolves can only be answered speculatively. The wolf owes its success to being a generalist predator. Like the king or queen on a chessboard, it is capable of many moves. Wolves are able through their behaviour to adapt easily from one prey to another. They could shift with the diverse species that paraded through the Pleistocene: various deer, camels, pigs, horses, elk. In contrast, the sabre-toothed tiger could not; like a bishop or a rook, it was limited in its options. It evolved as a specialist on the mammoth, capable with its long, sharp canines of penetrating its tough skin. When the mammoth became extinct, so did it.

Also limiting the never-ending Red Queen Effect is the fact that predation is only one selection pressure working on prey species. Other pressures include unfavourable microclimates, accidents, and the ability to win mates and raise young. Life is a compromise. Getting better at avoiding predation may work a disadvantage in other ways. For a moose, environmental fitness involves surviving cold winters, which it achieves in part through efficient heat retention and a slow metabolism, both a function of being so large. But by being large, moose are less manoeuvrable when attacked by wolves. With such bulk, they also have little chance to stay on top of boreal snows. Large antlers have an advantage in attracting a mate but reduce speed in dense forest. A moose is an environmental compromise, shaped by wolves in some ways, shaped by other factors too. It is left with an average stable vulnerability instead of an ever-improving ability to avoid predation.

The wolf, too, is a compromise, driven in part by the Red Queen to match improvements in its prey's ability to escape, compromised by other environmental demands. Its long denning period restricts mobility, especially inhibiting for wolves that inhabit tundra where caribou migrate away. Energetic and time investments in pack rivalries limit the wolf's efficiency as a predator. Its large body size, driven upwards in part by selection for dominance within a pack, demands more energy.

Such a compromised situation for both predator and prey is like a chessboard with only certain squares open. Either the game goes on – the Red Queen – or the players reach a stalemate, and nothing changes for a long time until some drastic environmental event creates new moves.

Moose and wolf have not been locked in co-evolution for long, not much more than a hundred thousand years. Moose are latecomers in evolutionary history. Wolves evolved over longer periods with the ancestors of moose, such as the Gallic elk and the broad-fronted elk, although the latter was much bigger than modern moose and perhaps immune to wolf predation. Roe deer and Irish elk lived in Eurasia; stag-moose, white-tailed deer, and mule deer lived in North America; and caribou, camels, horses, muskoxen, beaver, pigs, red deer (wapiti), and bison lived in both. All have ancient histories. Wolf adaptations to kill moose are mainly a spillover from adaptations to kill these other, older prey.

Today in Algonquin Park, wolf hunting strategies may be some compromise between what is best to find and kill moose, white-tailed deer, and beaver. Optimum pack sizes and group hunting strategies may not be the same for hunting them all. Of the three prey species, we concluded that wolves were responding primarily not to moose, but to deer (subject of a later chapter).

Graham concluded in his Ph.D. thesis that wolves were not a sufficient, single limiting factor on the moose population, largely because alternative prey provided close to two-thirds of wolf diets. As well, we found only 15 per cent moose calf in summer diets, low compared with other studies. A declining rate of twinning in moose, documented by MNR biologist Mike Wilton, suggested that the population was experiencing some nutritional stress so was near its range carrying capacity. In such cases, losses from wolf predation are largely irrelevant because they just reduce deaths from starvation. Low production because of the lack of twinning roughly balanced some combination of tick-caused deaths, energy-stress, accidental deaths, human killing, and predation.

Killed or scavenged, most moose meat not taken from Algonquin Park by native people is cycled through wolves, despite the immediate or predisposing natural causes of moose deaths. Relatively little is left uneaten, or it is eaten by other things. Moose give their atoms another fling with life, in wolves, before they are handed back to decay organisms and the soil. This gift of life after death, given only because moose can make no effective move to avoid it, is the big herbivore's lasting contribution to its evolutionary companion.

WOLF WEB

Top Down or Bottom Up

Nothing is more basic to understanding wolf ecology than the drive-it–ride-it conundrum. It generates heated debate and calls for better research design.

At issue is the question of what predominates to control change in an ecosystem. Does the wolf, as summit predator, drive change down through the trophic levels, or does the wolf merely ride change caused by other environmental factors?

Why this conundrum has been so difficult to solve is obvious if you flip to the chapter on predator-prey theory in ecology books. It is full of graphs, tables, examples: functional response to increasing prey numbers, numerical response, principle of inversity, principle of compensation, models of predator-prey relationships, models of multi-equilibrium predator-prey states, relationship of predation to extrinsic factors, to intrinsic factors. . . . There is no shortage of theory, all looking for field evidence, nor any shortage of field evidence looking for theory.

Rephrasing the conundrum, the choice is between ecosystem control from the top down (wolf driving change in the herbivore, then herbivore driving change in the vegetation) or bottom up (soil and vegetation driving change first). If top down, changes in wolf numbers would precede changes in prey numbers. That is, if wolf numbers go up, then as a consequence prey numbers go down. If bottom up, however, vegetation changes first, then prey, and wolf numbers follow. In the latter case, the wolf is more passively riding the system.

To detect which population changes first and identify consistency over several cycles requires long-term study. That requirement severely limits the evidence. As well, most studies examine only the controversial wolf-prey link and not the vegetation.

On Isle Royale in Lake Superior, Rolf Peterson has found evidence that the system may run both ways depending upon circumstances. He published a top-down evaluation because he and his students observed changes in wolf numbers influencing moose numbers that in turn influenced the amount of browsing and seedling success of balsam fir. But then a crash in the moose population in 1995 and 1996 was precipitated by a heavy tick infestation, not by wolves. So the answer to the conundrum is not simple.

Where the possibility of conducting a controlled experiment does not exist, such as in studies of top-down or bottom-up control, scientists look for pattern over time or space. It seems reasonable that in very changeable environments, ecosystem control might be bottom up simply because something is continually altering conditions. One place you can expect natural environmental change is in boundary areas between biomes, where one type of ecosystem, such as forest or tundra, grades into another on some knife edge of differing physical conditions such as soil or climate.

Algonquin Park lies between two great biomes: boreal and southern deciduous. The park is range-edge for moose who make it no farther south except at higher elevations in the eastern United States. They need a cold climate. Algonquin is also range-edge for deer who peter out in deeper snows farther north. It is range-edge for gray wolves as well, on the southern fringe of their range in eastern Canada. The park, then, is a tension zone for the large mammal system. On top of that, humans are altering the forest with logging.

So we set up a hypothesis that we would find the system operating from the bottom up and that wolves would be largely free riders. Unfortunately we had no control area for comparison. No large enough place free from human influence is left in either adjacent biome.

Nobody made this web. Incongruously, it made, maintains, and runs itself. More intricate than humans can ever devise, it does not claim to represent virtual reality. It is reality.

Different parts of the web provide life support for different species. The wolf draws almost totally on the large mammal strands, themselves deeply embedded in trophic connections. To understand the wolf, you need to understand its ecosystems links. You surf for them better with binoculars than with a computer. Binoculars and patience.

Hot leaf-filtered sunlight angles through the stunted ridge-line oaks while cicadas drone from somewhere below. A red-eyed vireo, the most persistent songbird in the forest, repeats its monophrasic song twenty or so times a minute until its occasional silence, not its voice, attracts attention. A languid forest wrung out by summer heat stretches to a distant blue haze.

Mary and I have climbed this rocky ridge many times. It provides a vantage point to pick up signals from the seven McDonald Creek wolves that have been on the air at various times. Often we have leaned back against the same lichen-encrusted rocks with a view over the McDonald marshes and into the folding hills beyond. At dusk, the hills look like ranks of waves from a small boat.

Up there we can imagine ourselves out of ecosystem. Not totally detached, as you are in an airplane. Most of what is going on, however, takes place down below, connected to us only by thin oak strands, a tracery of blueberry bushes among the rocks, the songs of cicadas, and the vireo. It is a good place to wonder about the web, to wonder about how soils and forests and herbivores and the Algonquin wolf all fit together, to ask questions and design ways of trying to answer them. Doing that relieved hours of down time between half-hour checks on the wolves, especially when they were somewhere beyond the hills. It turned out to be productive time.

First we needed a map of forest composition. Not all types of forest support wolves equally well. Hills marching into haze, more than seventy-five hundred square kilometres of them, would not be easy to map. Fortunately, there was a high-tech solution. Employing it required plenty of patience – Mary's. It took her four months in front of a computer. Really, it took eight months because one summer while we were in the field, a computer technician inadvertently wiped the disk.

Mary's computer-drawn map was made from a coded image as seen by a satellite orbiting above the Earth on May 12, 1986. She chose that image because of the cloudless conditions, and because in early May the flower colours of different hardwood species make them distinguishable by the sensors onboard the satellite.

The trick to classifying forests from such a satellite image is to know a few sites from field work with selected species of trees. This information is plugged into the computer, which then finds all similar species throughout the park and builds up a map of major forest associations. This method beats the pre-satellite approach, which involved staring down a stereoscope at black-and-white air photos and trying to detect different shades of grey.

When finished, the map showed that Algonquin's principal energy processor on its eastern side is mostly "pine-poplar" forests. Closely coupled within these forests are white, red, and jack pines in that order of abundance, trembling and largetooth aspen, and red maple. There are also areas of black or white spruce and balsam fir, and stands of pure hemlock, all coming in seemingly chaotic combinations. However, as you stare at the computer screen, various broad groupings begin to stand out, and you realize that the forest types are not randomly situated. They reflect the roll of the hills, the warm, south-facing or cold, north-facing slopes, the cool lowlands, the wet places, and the locations of past logging or fire.

Here is the solar panel of the ecosystem, this complex canopy, capturing the energy that eventually works its way along various pathways to drive a wolf along a forest trail. The map would allow us to relate forest type to wolf activity. What species provide wolf support, where are they, and how are they connected?

The immediate "what" was obvious: moose, deer, and beaver. Our scat analysis gave us seasonal details. One step removed are the plants that provide these herbivores with food and shelter: primarily the two species of poplars, red maple, beaked hazel, balsam fir, the pines, and hemlock.

Recognizing where these components are found and connected, however, is more difficult; that came into focus only gradually. First to appear were the broad outlines of the conifer component.

Balsam fir share the lowlands with spruce. Graham's task in his master's research was to search for a relationship between spruce-fir forests and wolves. His examination of aerial moose surveys flown in fifteen consecutive winters by Mike Wilton or his staff showed that moose densities were highest where the spruce-fir forests had been disturbed sometime in the previous ten to fifteen years.

Two agents of disturbance had been at work. The first, spruce budworm, is a seemingly innocuous, drab, one-centimetre-long larva. Its assault on the forest in countless, voracious millions, as occurred during an epidemic in the mid-1970s, results in the death of extensive spruce-fir stands. After a budworm epidemic, young balsam fir normally grows aggressively, outcompeting spruce for a time because fir grows better in full sunlight. That is just what moose want. Fir is a favourite moose food; spruce is ignored. By promoting the growth of fir, budworm changes the forest in favour of moose – and wolves. So important is spruce budworm to the wolf subsystem that, along with winter tick, we gave it the dignified label of "invertebrate agitator."

The other important agent of disturbance that favours moose does not eat its way to prominence. It uses chain saws, log skidders, bulldozers, eighteen-wheelers. Graham discovered that lowland areas logged within fifteen years held more moose and, for the same reason, more young balsam fir.

That should have been good news for forest managers. They can log in a park and create better moose browse. Ironically, Graham's thesis and its recommendations almost cost us our research permit. The trouble arose over hemlock.

Uncut, undefiled old-growth hemlock stands are north-country cathedrals. Graceful limbs, bowing branches, fluted trunks. Tiers of delicate dark-green archways filter the sunlight like a stained-glass window.

Hemlock logs lying on the forest floor, the skeletons of generations past, decompose slowly because of their tannin- and resin-embalmed trunks. Among the logs grow shade-loving goldthread, the pale flowers of wood sorrel, flushes of red moccasin flowers. Blackburnian warblers nest here, repeating their thin, upwelling notes from the hemlock spires. Sapsuckers embroider the trunks with neatly aligned holes. Few places are more enchanted.

Hemlock stands such as these are cut down, even in a park, to make wharf pilings, railway ties, and little wooden crates used to store and ship commercially grown mushrooms. In the past, hemlock bark provided tannin to cure leather. Once prominent in pre-crosscut saw, pre-chain saw Ontario, we have succeeded in breaking the back of this species. No longer does golden hemlock pollen float great distances on the spring breeze. Instead, only a little is wafted into the air, too often searching in vain for a reproductive partner.

Hemlock first appeared on Earth, according to the fossil pollen record, in the Eocene Epoch, fifty-five to thirty-eight million years ago. It arose most likely in Asia, on a side branch of the evolutionary tree that earlier gave rise to the pines. A few million years later, it had radiated as far as western North America and China. Time and isolation fashioned approximately ten species, some found in Japan, China, and the Himalayan Mountains. In Canada, we have three species. One of them, eastern hemlock, makes its last, thinned-out stand today across its historic range from Nova Scotia to Ontario south of the height of land.

A desecrated hemlock cathedral near McDonald Creek alerted us to this species' plight in Algonquin Park. One winter day, Graham, Mary, and I followed the signals of two wolves in the Foys Lake pack into a big cut-over. After struggling over branches and treetops concealed by snow, we stopped, looked around, and realized that the standing scattered remnants consisted of hemlock. Only a few trees were left.

We photographed the carnage, resolving to return in spring to see if any hemlock seedlings were hidden beneath the snow. That was unlikely because hemlock seedlings need shade.

By the following summer we had forgotten the incident until, again tracking the Foys wolves, Mary and I recognized the raspberry-choked cut-over we had photographed before. We broke off our tracking to look for hemlock seedlings and found what we feared – none. Plenty of red maple and white birch seedlings and some aspen were coming up, but not a single hemlock. The stand was destined to become part of the extensive hardwood forest that surrounded it.

We tried to forget the McDonald Creek hemlock massacre, except for the bothersome possibility, suggested by our spring pellet and browse surveys, that moose favour these hemlock stands. Each spring, we and our field crews walk about forty kilometres of three-hundred-metre straight-line transects in various wolf-pack territories, estimating winter use by deer and moose from their droppings. On a hunch we added a few columns to the data sheets to detail hemlock regeneration.

The next spring, sure enough, we found hardly any hemlock regrowth even in uncut stands. Some bands of seedlings grew in dense, thin lines at the edges of abandoned logging roads, and some on hemlock–hardwood forest edges, always where the forest shaded them for much of each day. In contrast, we discovered many other logged-over hemlock stands growing back to hardwoods.

We still might have let what was becoming in our minds the "hemlock issue" go. Then the first drafts of Graham's master's thesis showed that hemlock stands were the most heavily used forest type, per hectare, by wintering moose in Algonquin Park. Moose find shallow snow and shelter from cold winds there, and can wander out into the surrounding hardwood forests to browse, an ideal arrangement.

Even more ideal is the strategic location of many hemlock stands on the west side of the park. They crown the big, rolling hardwood hills, responding to moisture trapped in shallow soils above bedrock. Smart moose hole up for the winter in these hemlock galleries, leaving no scent trail through the lowland conifers that wolves habitually hunt, daring the wolves to wade up through the deep snow to reach them.

We discussed the ramifications of this discovery one day in my office at the university. It could be risky to criticize the management of the forest because our access to much of the park depended upon the possession of a permit to drive logging roads for research purposes. But research is research. Graham agreed he had no choice but to present the findings. In the recommendations at the end of his thesis abstract, he wrote: "Due to the importance of hemlock to moose, and the threat of a significant decrease in hemlock, it is recommended that the Ontario Ministry of Natural Resources prepare and make public a policy statement regarding the cutting of hemlock as it affects ungulates in Algonquin Provincial Park."

Feeling he should not take the heat alone, I wrote a short position paper calling for all hemlock logging to stop in Algonquin Park until it could be done in a way to allow more adequate regeneration. It was an action sure to bring a response. However, I was buttressed, even motivated, by two confidence-builders. One was an exchange of internal correspondence not meant for the public eye. I still cannot reveal how I obtained it. The exchange was between senior administrators of forestry in the MNR and the Algonquin Forest Authority (AFA), the Crown corporation responsible for logging in the park.

What the letters, the MNR to the AFA, said, paraphrasing broadly, was: You are overcutting hemlock and there is insufficient regeneration in cut-over stands. The AFA response: You know as well as we do that hemlock is difficult to bring back so instead of complaining, tell us how.

From a technical standpoint, the problem is that you cannot cut more than about 30 per cent of a hemlock stand without flooding the forest floor with too much light for these shade-loving seedlings to grow. However, to allow seeds to germinate you need to scarify the ground, scrape away the deep accumulation of needles so the tiny seeds can reach a mineral soil. Fire does this naturally, but fire is fought and extinguished almost everywhere. Alternatively, you can scarify the soil with a bulldozer, but it is difficult to drive one around if you have cut so few trees.

My other confidence-builder was the detailed technical instruction and even editorial help I received from one of the MNR's most highly qualified forest ecologists, who totally agreed that the problem needed to be addressed. I could not reveal his name, of course.

Two weeks later I received a telephone call asking for a meeting with senior MNR and AFA staff. The meeting took place at the Algonquin Museum staff house on a cold winter's day, appropriate to the frosty mood of the government. Right away, as people trooped in, we noticed a general lack of levity.

They questioned the quantity and quality of our seedling data and scored a point because we had begun it only the spring before. They countered our concern over the McDonald Creek stand with the explanation that they were forced to do a "salvage cut" after a windstorm. They asked why our research and the privileges it entailed gave us the right to question their management.

We let them corner us. When it became apparent the next topic might be the continuance of our research permit, I reached for my briefcase and tossed the two letters on the table. They recognized them. There was an embarrassed silence.

The meeting had two outcomes. The MNR hired a hemlock specialist to study the problem and recommend how to solve it. The other was heightening discomfort among some MNR people whose park-management practices had been criticized. That discomfort was to have future ramifications for us.

Maybe it had a third outcome. Some hemlock cathedrals may still be out there, where moose spend the winter. And there may be fewer mushroom boxes.

While the hemlock groves and fir forests are special places, the rank on rank, hill after hill of pine-poplar forests provide the main energy pathway through the ecosystem web, provisioning most abundantly the wolves' three prey species. Beaver selectively fell the poplars close to their ponds. Moose and deer strip new leaves off poplars and red maples and browse their winter twigs. The pines provide shelter.

"Pine-poplar" rings poetically as a name for these forests, but it short-changes red maple, an equally common species, and ignores white birch as well. "Pine-intolerant" is a better name that encompasses them all. Seedlings of poplar, white birch, and red maple are intolerant of shade. In contrast, the seedlings of "tolerant" species do well in shade: sugar maple, yellow birch, and beech.

Both the shade-intolerant and -tolerant hardwood species are locked in continuous war with the pines. In various places, one or the other mounts the heaviest attack or they are evenly matched. Most of the action takes place where forests have been disturbed, providing an opportunity to gain new ground. Our entire study area has been logged up to three times except for a few small nature or shoreline reserves. The huge pines fell more than a century ago, then spruce and fir, then the hardwoods.

From the AFA we obtained a map of areas logged since 1975 and transformed it into a computer-screen product for later comparison with wolf locations. The AFA's method of logging in the pine-intolerant forests is called "shelterwood," a misnomer from the perspective of a moose, considering that only 40 to 60 per cent of the forest crown is left. Foresters, however, think of shelter for seedlings. Twenty years later, the chain saws and skidders will be back again, and in twenty more years the original stand will be gone. That schedule does not leave much time for forest types to replace each other in natural succession. What comes up immediately after logging will be the future forest stand.

Sometimes little pines poke up through the ubiquitous bracken fern and hazel. That is what foresters like to see; there is a good market for pine. Other times no pines show up at all. Each May along our transects we collect data on these differences.

To run these transects, Mary and I, or pairs of other crew members, walk parallel to each other fifty metres apart, pacing out our distances and counting moose and deer pellets. Then we retrace our steps counting browsed and unbrowsed stems of poplar, red maple, balsam fir, oak, and hazel. Sometimes we wade through lingering soft snow in the low places. At other times, we find ourselves on sunny warm slopes where the tiny, red brushcut flowers of beaked hazel are in bloom. The forest is full of the songs of newly arrived winter wrens, hermit thrushes, and white-throated sparrows, punctuated by the staccato hammering of yellow-bellied sapsuckers. Ruffed grouse drum. Spring unfolds.

We had difficulty understanding why pines were winning here and losing there. Then one winter's day Tom Stephenson provided an explanation that fit our data. Tom's life in the bush fighting fires, marking trees, prescribing management plans, and, most importantly, thinking about what he sees has given him an extraordinary interpretive ability. The Jocko Lake pack had made a kill that required a fifty-kilometre snowmobile trip, and because of the general unreliability of our snowmobile, we asked Tom to accompany us. Late in the day we reached the Jocko territory and churned up a snow-filled logging spur to within two kilometres of the wolves. We stopped on a knoll, put on our snowshoes, and made the last approach in silence.

Around us was a four-year-old, pine-intolerant cut-over typical of most of the Bonnechere Valley and typical, too, in its lack of pine regeneration. The lack of new pines angered Tom.

"Look at the spacing. There's supposed to be a half-crown opening between the pines that they leave. It's about one and a half crowns. They butchered it. Too much light. You can't let this much light into places like this where the soils favour poplars and red maples."

He explained that it is okay to cut at one-and-a-half-crown spacing up in the Petawawa Valley, where it is sandier. Up there the soil is so dry and porous that intolerants have difficulty. But here with more till, the soil is slightly more moist, which is right for them. The pines are outcompeted.

Tom drew circles in the snow to show proper and improper crown spacing and railed against the foresters that marked the trees. "They should have known they would convert this stand to hardwoods."

Soil moisture – that was a key. Different soil types hold more or less water. In sequence, dry to moist, jack pine grow on sandy soils, red pine on slightly coarser sands, white pine on sandy gravels, poplars and red maple on coarser gravels, and tolerant hardwoods on loams. The latter are found only in scattered patches on the east side of the park.

These soil-forest relationships prevail within the broad climate belt that runs across the east side of the Algonquin dome, where annual precipitation is a relatively low seventy-two to seventy-six centimetres per year. West of Algonquin Park, where annual precipitation is greater, even shallow, sandy soils are moist enough to grow tolerant hardwoods.

Within the dictates of soil moisture, shade often is the final arbiter of forest composition. Even on good soils for intolerants, if enough trees are left after logging to provide shade, pines will succeed where intolerants struggle and fail. However, if too few trees are left, the intolerants find both ideal soil moisture and sunlight and will outcompete the pines. Most of the Bonnechere Valley, logged over the previous eight years, intermediate in soil moisture, is coming back to intolerants because the cuts were excessive.

Ironically, despite plenty of sunlight, young pines often line the edges of the logging roads in the Bonnechere Valley like false-front western pioneer towns and fill the log landings where logs were loaded onto trucks. While they create an illusion of good pine regeneration, they present only a façade. The soil in these locations was compacted by heavy machinery, reducing soil moisture and thereby growing pines. But look behind the false front and you see a future deciduous forest.

The AFA is aware of the problem and has sent tree-planting crews out for a few days each spring, but they plant only a small percentage of the cut-overs. Unable to use herbicides in the park, maybe chain saws will be brought in for future "stand improvement." Ecosystem mistakes are not easy to reverse, an argument for establishing parks and leaving them alone.

Moose, deer, and beaver do not share our concerns about the vanishing pines. Just the opposite is true. They quietly go about capitalizing on the increased food the intolerants provide, simultaneously levying their own impact on the forest. Again it took some years for us to recognize their effects. Several years ago, Mary and I were trapping in the Mathews Lake territory and running browse transects up near the Petawawa River. We set up camp in the pines beside an unused logging road. The cold black waters of Lone Creek slipped by into a foam-flecked pool below. As usual a scattering of hermit thrushes and winter wrens were practising their prelude to spring.

As we filled our notebooks with data, we noticed that in the pine cut-overs a greater percentage of regenerating poplars and red maples were browsed than we were used to seeing in the Bonnechere Valley. In some places browsing had been so heavy for so many years that the poplars had died. Without competition, small pines were doing well. Obviously browsing was holding back the poplars and red maples to the advantage of pines. Ironically, since moose do not eat pines, they were working against their own future, but neither natural selection nor moose can forecast the future.

After a week of trapping, we caught a Mathews wolf, so we left for the Bonnechere Valley to confirm our perception that a lower percentage of stems was being browsed there. We were right; in many places regenerating intolerant saplings were so dense you could hardly push your way through, but a lower percentage of them was browsed. Soil and sunlight were so favourable to the intolerants that the ungulate population could not keep all the saplings down. If they missed a red maple leader for three years in a row, it would spring up nine to twelve metres, beyond moose reach.

From this evidence, we realize that very subtle differences in soil moisture and shade can switch the direction of ecosystem control. In the Bonnechere Valley, moose and deer ride forest change, their browsing largely irrelevant; in the Petawawa Valley, however, they drive change by altering the upcoming forest stand. Somewhere between the dry sands and the moister soils, with just the right amount of shade, may be a more equal battlefield where ungulate browsing on the intolerants may balance annual growth.

There, moose and deer, inadvertently, would be practising "sustainable forestry." We have not found such a place; the system is just too dynamic. Ungulates have as much difficulty practising sustainability as we do.

Above the sun visor of our truck, and that of the two vans used by student crews, are file folders marked "Ungulate Observations." On the forms we record every moose and deer we see, with its age and sex, location, and the number of kilometres driven that day or night. All the data, duly entered into the computer, provide an index of their changes in abundance, an important annual checkup.

Our most common view of a moose is from the rear as it thunders down a logging road to get out of our way. Sometimes at night a moose will refuse to leave the road. It will run ahead of us until we feel guilty, stop, and turn off the headlights. When we turn them on again, often the moose is still standing there, or if not, it is just around the next curve waiting to again show us its rear end and flying hooves.

Each summer there is a distinct peak in the number of moose and deer seen per one hundred kilometres driven in June, followed closely by May, but there is a big drop in July and another in August. The same seasonal pattern appears in both daytime and nighttime observations. We suspected that the decline was related to the end of the growing season and a rapid deterioration in food quality. With less to gain from browsing, and the ever-present wolves searching for scent trails, moose and deer may find it advantageous to switch from being energy maximizers feeding all the time to energy conservers.

Many studies have shown that protein, nitrogen, and phosphorus levels are highest in rapidly growing stems and leaves, and that they drop after new growth is complete. As well, unpalatable chemical compounds, plant defences against browsing, accumulate over time especially as the energy required for plant growth declines and can be shunted to their production.

We had a hunch that the growth sequence of the plants was a factor in the changing behaviour of the ungulates. To assess whether this was the case, we had to determine if red maples and poplars stopped growing when deer and moose became scarce at the end of June. We spent a few hours each day measuring new growth, tying red flagging tape to the stems so we could find them again. When we remeasured at the end of August, we found that the red maples had not grown at all since the end of June, the poplars only by 30 per cent.

We repeated the measurements the next summer. Spring was late that year, 1996, and new growth on the red maples was not complete until mid-July. But the sudden drop in ungulate sightings, normally occurring at the end of June, occurred two weeks later too. We felt good; we had one piece of evidence that fit the hypothesis.

Research in Michigan helped us discount a general, weather-induced lethargy in late summer as the reason for less moose and deer activity then. Biologists P. Beier and D. McCullough showed that radio-collared deer increased their activity in August. This increase occurred in the absence of wolves, the one markedly different condition between our studies.

To further examine our hypothesis, we had to find out if wolves were less successful in catching deer and moose after the ungulates became less active. We analysed our collection of wolf scats in the expectation that the proportion of beaver would go up in the last half of the summer to compensate for a decline in deer and moose. Our guess was wrong; beaver in wolf scats peaked in early May, when beaver spend much of their time foraging on land immediately after the snow melts. There was no sudden increase in beaver in the latter half of the summer.

That could have nullified our hypothesis except one day while bumping along a logging road, Mary remarked that many of the wolves we catch in May and June appear to be in better shape than those caught later. We even have had a few cases of wolf starvation in August and September. Perhaps the proportion of each prey species relative to one another does not change in the last half of the summer, but the total food intake drops.

With all our capture data on the computer, that possibility was easy to test. We found that average adult weights fell only slightly in the last half of the summer, not enough to be statistically significant, but we caught both smaller and larger wolves then, especially adult females. Yearling males in July and August, however, were 5.7 kilograms (12.5 pounds) lighter than earlier in the summer, although our sample size was small. So, we concluded that there was some evidence of food stress in Algonquin wolves in the last half of the summer.

The foolproof evidence in support of our hypothesis would be to find that wolves really are less successful in finding moose and deer in July and August. While that just seems reasonable, we have no data to inspect. Here our hypothesis rests, tantalizing us with some supporting evidence but not enough.

There is another intriguing relationship between ungulates and wolves. For years we have carefully noted whether stationary wolves were found in uplands or lowlands. Wolves move through all habitats, but in more than 90 per cent of the locations when we get three good cross-bearings on a stationary wolf, it is in lowlands, usually within fifty to one hundred metres of a lake, stream, or bog.

If wolves are predominantly creatures of the lowlands, you might expect their prey to be more abundant there too. Or, alternatively, natural selection and avoidance might work against deer and moose frequenting lowland areas.

Neither is true. Our data reveal no pattern in deer movements, day or night, early summer or late. Moose tend to be near water more often, but likely for the dual benefits of feeding on aquatic vegetation and cooling their big, black bodies.

Is natural selection on hold? Is there some balance between costs and benefits that we do not know? Is there some long-term cycle – wolves in lowlands, ungulates in uplands, switching to the reverse – that we are unable to recognize with short-term research? Or do wolves kill deer and moose everywhere and just for some reason prefer lowlands for lying around?

Anyone who disassembles and reassembles a machine usually has a few nuts and bolts left over. The machine may work fine without them, or does so until conditions change and the loss makes itself known. *Parelaphostrongylus tenuis*, a tiny roundworm parasite common in deer, is like that, an inconspicuous ecosystem component. Moose and deer both pick it up by accidentally ingesting snails that have crawled over the droppings of infected deer. In the spirit of being a good parasite, *P. tenuis* does not kill its deer host. Such an ideal relationship exemplifies evolutionary accommodation achieved over time.

The larvae show up on deer droppings. We collected them at the height of our interest in *P. tenuis*. One time we emerged from the trees onto a logging road with a plastic bag of droppings just as a pickup truck was going by. The driver jammed on his brakes and backed up. After chatting about the weather for a few minutes, he got to the point. "What have you got in that there bag?"

"Deer shit," I replied.

"Deer shit?" I let him think about it for a few seconds, fully intending to tell him why, but waited a bit too long.

"Well," he broke the silence, "to each his own," and he stepped on the accelerator, leaving us in a cloud of dust.

Had he waited a second more, or had he asked, I would have explained the story of *P. tenuis*. A humble roundworm less than one centimetre long, it lives happily in deer brains. It gains access to them by tunnelling through a deer's stomach to its spinal cord, then travelling up to the brain where it encysts, matures, and lays eggs. The eggs pass through the upper respiratory system, then the digestive tract, and are finally liberated in the deer's droppings. There the eggs hatch into larvae and wait for a snail to ingest them and renew the cycle.

White-tailed deer evolved in North America, presumably with *P. tenuis*. The two creatures worked things out so that *P. tenuis* could live as a free rider, neither harming nor helping the deer. But with moose, this little leftover part of the web takes on significance. Moose evolved in Eurasia and are comparative newcomers to North America. They have no signed agreement with *P. tenuis*. So *P. tenuis* kill moose, committing suicide in the process. Shakespearean tragedy. On the way from its entry point in the spinal cord to the moose's brain, *P. tenuis* destroys nerve cells. Separating mind from body does a moose no good; infected animals run in circles until they die. Unwittingly, *P. tenuis* larvae must realize they are in trouble as the temperature falls around their spinal cord home – bad luck that their snail host was picked up by a moose instead of a deer. The parasites will rot with the moose in the spring.

In Murray Lancaster's parasitology lab at Lakehead University, the droppings we collected were scrutinized microscopically to find the incidence of infection in Algonquin deer. The answer was about 90 per cent, with some uncertainty over identification. Its larval form is practically indistinguishable from other, non-pathogenic members of its genus.

We don't know how many moose carry the parasite. Although we stockpiled moose heads for a time with the view to having them examined, we have observed disoriented moose in our telemetry flights too rarely to justify the cost of analysis.

Maybe something will trigger a *P. tenuis* epidemic some day, such as a greatly increased deer population infecting the range more heavily with larvae. If so, browsing pressure by moose will decline, balsam fir will grow unimpeded, and spruce will lose out for a while in competition with the fir. The web will adjust. Or *P. tenuis* may never rise to prominence and remain an insignificant ecosystem part.

Other seemingly insignificant players in the wolf web live as free riders inside wolves. We have participated in the autopsies of many wolves in the post-mortem room at the University of Guelph's veterinary college, where Ian Barker and his pathologists Doug Campbell or, in the earlier years, Trent Bollinger presided. Many wolves we had come to know well in the wild ended up stretched out on the stainless-steel table with scalpels, scissors, saw, notebook all arranged around their heads. Mary and I, or Graham, usually attended to take measurements and collect the head and small pieces of heart, liver, kidney, and muscle in plastic bags and bring them back to our freezer in the ecology lab. Later the wolf bits and pieces would be shipped to McMaster University for DNA analysis. With the detachment of surgeons, Ian and colleagues made many interesting discoveries.

The intestines of many of our subjects harboured tapeworms, *Taenia* species, often about thirty centimetres long. Living a life of comfort and ease, so long as the wolf was eating, these tapeworms robbed the wolf of some nutrition, but not much. They caused little harm in a friendly if one-sided relationship that the textbooks call commensalism.

In the intestines of approximately one-quarter of the wolves was a tapeworm measuring only a couple of millimetres called *Echinococcus granulosis*. Under a microscope it looked like a slender bag distended with eggs. Usually the eggs were spilled out, crushed by the cover slip on top of the slide. The eggs made us shudder. If a human gets one under a fingernail and takes it in through mouth or eyes, the egg hatches in the host's liver and destroys its functions, which can be dangerous. In moose or deer, however, the maturing egg causes little harm because disease and host have evolved together. A wolf, eating an infected moose or deer, picks up the immature tapeworm and offers it sanctuary for the rest of its life cycle, passing eggs out in its feces.

Even more insidious are viral diseases: rabies, canine distemper, canine parvovirus, and canine hepatitis. Tests were run on blood serum we took from wolves when we collared them. With no refrigeration, we had to drive out to the Pembroke Animal Hospital immediately to have the blood spun. Exposure to viruses is shown by antibodies – defences manufactured by animals – in the serum.

Algonquin wolves have been exposed to canine distemper, canine parvovirus, and canine hepatitis, shown by antibodies in 46, 83, and 76 per cent of animals tested, respectively. These results are not surprising, because all three viruses are common in North

America; most domestic dogs get exposed and develop antibodies too. But the patterns and levels of exposure worked out by Ian and his colleagues revealed something of the viruses' ecology. Canine distemper survives poorly outside a canine animal and, like the common cold, requires nose-to-nose transmission from one animal to another. Our samples showed that an epidemic occurred in 1989 and 1990, abating after that. Its occurrence was high in only a few packs, as expected for a disease that requires animal-to-animal contact. There is logically more contact within than between packs.

The other two viruses can live for years in wolf feces. They may even survive winter temperatures. All it takes is a good sniff by an investigating wolf to get infected. Before a wolf pup is eight weeks old, maternal antibodies to canine parvovirus from the mother's milk will fend off the disease. These antibodies decline, however, leaving the animal susceptible between eight and twelve weeks of age, after which they normally build up enough to protect the young animal again.

Canine parvovirus was unknown before the late 1970s. Mutating from feline parvovirus, it quickly spread among dogs all across North America, possibly killing about 10 per cent of them. By the early 1980s, it was no longer a serious killer in older canines, however, because background, low-level exposure promoted anti-body formation before the virus could kill. Pups exposed to a heavy infection during their susceptible period, though, still may die. Rolf Peterson suspects canine parvovirus caused the wolf population to decline on Isle Royale. Seven out of eight Algonquin pups tested were positive, but these animals, caught late in the summers, were the survivors. We have no way of knowing how many may have died.

Possibly, canine parvovirus is a key player in the web here too, accountable for the unusually low percentage of yearlings in the population. Without capturing and taking blood from very young pups, we will never know, but to attempt such a study would be too disruptive to the wolf population.

These intricacies in the operation of the large mammal component give us plenty to think about up there on the ridge over McDonald Creek, our "ecosystem contemplation place," always to the background music of a red-eyed vireo. Underlying how things shift and change, in 1997 we monitored a different pack, the Zigzag Lake pack, from the same place – there had been a boundary shift. The subtle workings of time re-adjust wolf territories.

Time does more than that. For all living things in Algonquin Park it resets averages, weeds out the weak, selects genes, imposes rhythms based on fire frequencies and wildlife cycles that reverberate right down to the soil.

Tree diseases such as jack pine budworm and white pine blister rust come and go, and the bacterial disease tularemia knocks back the beaver population on occasion. Winter ticks have their variable effect on moose depending on the timing of snowmelt. Climate influences seed production and germination. Snow stresses female ungulates, causing them to abort fetuses or give birth to young that will not live long. Over time, all these things jostle the ecosystem web.

Television hosts often ask us why we are interested in wolves. We know the sort of answer that is expected. "Oh, I fell in love with them when I was a child" – or some such thing. Sometimes a host's eyes glaze over just a bit when we try to explain that the marvel is the whole web and the wolf's place in it, not just the animal itself. Wolves in zoos – isolated, out of context, disconnected – are not as interesting.

But wolves in the web are. Our data do not support a strong top-down wolf influence in Algonquin Park. For that to happen, wolves would have to be changing the numbers of their prey or altering their distribution and movements, which in any major way they do not seem to do.

The ungulate-vegetation link, however, runs both up and down, differing in the Petawawa and Bonnechere valleys. Spruce budworm is a bottom-up strand influencing the forest first, which in turn influences moose, then wolves. Logging is bottom up:

forest, ungulates, wolves. Deer and moose hunting by humans may run up to influence wolves, down to influence the forest. Wolf killing by humans is a top-down effect.

We do an injustice to nature to even search for simple relationships. In any web, every strand plays a part.

FOYS LAKE PACK – SUPRA-ORGANISM

The Best-Fit Group

Scottish biologist V. Wynne-Edwards thrust people interested in ecology and evolution off on a decade-long tangent with his substantial book Animal Dispersal in Relation to Social Behaviour. *I read it as a budding biologist, the book travelling with me as I searched for a suitable Ph.D. thesis topic related to the hot question of how animals regulate the size of their populations, if indeed they do. Jim Bendell, my supervisor at the University of British Columbia, pushed the concept that ideas and principles count in understanding ecology, not species. Species just play them out. He wanted me to find a species to test Wynne-Edwards' ideas.*

The book impressed me then and still does, though Wynne-Edwards eventually backed away from his central premise and others replaced it. Ironically, wolves, and not rock ptarmigan that I studied, have turned out to be better animals for scrutinizing his ideas.

His proposition, simply put, was that natural selection works on groups of animals rather than on individuals. Groups of animals are like supra-organisms. Survival of the best-fit group is the way of things, not only survival of the best-fit individual, as Charles Darwin explained.

Wynne-Edwards bolstered his notion with explanations for a whole range of group social displays, or behavioural rituals that animals perform,

137

that, until then, seemed to have no purpose. So pervasive are such displays in animal societies, he thought, that surely they have some survival value. He proposed that they provide the members of the group with a sort-of self-census that results in social pressure. If the group appears too large for available resources, some animals disperse. These dispersers, the "have-nots," are the losers, sacrificing their individual fitness for the good of the group. They are destined to experience lower-quality habitat or greater susceptibility to predation, resulting in either lower breeding success or death.

Anything even remotely anti-Darwinian is certain to be scrutinized by the scientific community. Natural selection working on the group? The critical evidence, to Wynne-Edwards and others, was self-sacrifice for the good of the group. The evidence gets tangled up, however, with cooperative behaviour.

Nobody doubts that cooperative behaviour conveys advantages, but to whom? To the group, or to the individual in the group? It might be worthwhile for an elk to stand guard as a herd flanker watching for wolves while the herd members graze, if in so-doing that elk also benefits from a better chance of escape. That elk might benefit, at other times, from reciprocal cooperation when others stand guard. If the group is beneficial to an elk, it is worthwhile to invest some effort in its welfare. In that way, cooperative behaviour is universally explained as conveying advantage to individuals in the group.

That sort of cooperative behaviour is abundant but below the level of self-sacrifice. The guard-elk would not stand guard if the price was to be its own death. Unfortunately, self-sacrifice has been seen as the only true test of group as opposed to individual selection, rather than its most dramatic example.

Wynne-Edwards' idea stimulated a concerted search for self-sacrifice among animals — "altruistic behaviour." The result? Not much of it was found. Yet, where found, there were common circumstances. It showed up in kin-related, genetically affiliated groups, especially in maternal behaviour. An example of this is a mother killdeer's broken-wing display to lure a predator away from the nest that holds more than two chicks, so contains more of her genes than she herself possesses. Cases of altruism had to make genetic sense: more genes would remain in the offspring than in the self-sacrificing individual. Such examples resulted in the notion of "kin selection," promoted, in part, in another huge book ten years later called Sociobiology, *by renowned Harvard biologist E. O. Wilson.*

While altruism is a reasonably sure sign of group selection, survival of the best-fit group does not depend on it. All that is necessary is to find groups of cooperating animals working strategically together, especially with some division of labour, whose competitive success against other groups is bound together by one another's skills, and who to some degree share a common fate. Such a group – its pool of genes – is more likely to persist.

It falls to the lot of three groups of people – those studying social mammals, social insects, and human societies – to further consider group selection, thirty-five years after it may have been prematurely rejected.

GRAHAM'S VOICE crackled in over the static of the two-way radio. The Cessna had just cleared a ridge and was in view, crawling along the hazy blue sky looking like one of the dozens of mosquitoes that buzzed around our heads.

"I'm onto Basin 3's signal to the north. I'll be back in a few minutes." The plane banked and inched its way towards the horizon.

Thursday, July 19, 1990, 7 A.M. We were camped in an abandoned, raspberry-choked log landing. An overgrown spur road led out to the hydro line, which cut a wide, ugly swath through the forest. Incongruous in a park, three ranks of steel towers march across hills from the Chalk River dam on the Ottawa River to join the power grid somewhere to the south. Stark brown pine saplings spray-killed by Ontario Hydro stick up through grasses that cover much of the strip. Naked rocks lie obscenely exposed.

Incongruous, too, is the plant diversity the hydro line adds to the east side of the park, attracting foraging deer and moose, providing black bears and pine martens with raspberries, and offering an easy path for wolves. Ignoring many square kilometres of forest, the Foys Lake wolves moved into a bog rendezvous site that extended partway under the wires.

The pack knew we were there, camped a kilometre away. One wolf found us by accident. A summer-day shower had broken the heat, and we were sitting in the truck, doors open, writing up our notes. A bedraggled-looking wolf, head down, walked slowly into the clearing, approaching to within ten metres before the image of the truck caught the corner of its eyes. It looked up, startled. Reflected light on the windshield must have hidden us, because it did not run. Instead, it raised its head and scented the air. In a moment, caution made it turn. Glancing over its shoulder, it walked slowly back the way it had come.

That night a Foys wolf investigated us while we slept; in the morning, big wolf tracks circled our tent.

The plane appeared again and Graham reported, "Basin 3 is up the hydro line six kilometres from the rendezvous site. Foys 3 is back in the logging operation two kilometres southeast of you. Foys 2 and Foys 4 are seven kilometres southwest along the Bonnechere road. Grand 3 has moved four kilometres straight west from last night and now is trespassing in Foys territory. She is beside a bog on a hill. I can't find Foys 1. I'll be back again in four hours."

We spread the topographic map on the hood of the truck and plotted the coordinates for each wolf. After eight consecutive flights, we were getting exciting data. Pack members seemed to be coming and going individually or in small groups, covering their entire territory day and night. Since the previous evening, Basin 3 had moved seven kilometres and Foys 2 eight kilometres to end up twelve kilometres apart. Foys 2 and Foys 4 had left the rendezvous site where they spent the previous night and had also separated.

With five radio-collared wolves in one pack on the air, we had a chance to learn how extensively Algonquin wolves move during the day, whether they travel together or separately, and how long they remain away from the rendezvous site. They also would help us to assess differences in movements of individual wolves. By that time we were pondering the idea that a wolf pack may be acting like a supra-organism and, if so, that there may be some validity in the controversial idea of survival of the best-fit pack – natural selection working not only on the individual, but on the group.

We had booked the Cessna for a week. Volunteer pilot Hank Halliday flew it down to the abandoned Bonnechere airstrip where he and Graham camped in the jack pines beside the runway. They were to fly four times a day while Mary and I camped close to the rendezvous site to monitor movements there. We also planned to check out possible kill sites from map coordinates radioed down to us.

It was a week of relentless sun, flies, and heat except for one morning shower and one violent thunderstorm. Only late at night did it cool off. Some mornings the hills cradled a mist, delaying take-off time. Usually by 9 A.M. the sun cleared away the night-time humidity and heated the tent up enough to fry any sand-flies inside. We lay under a pine at the edge of our unscenic clearing, waiting for the next flight, checking the signals every fifteen minutes. At the abandoned airstrip, Graham and Hank spent their time lying under the wing of the plane waiting for the next flight too. The wolves, however, were much more active.

At 11:30, the second flight of the day, Graham and Hank were back overhead: "Got a lot of wolf movement since this morning. There may be a boundary skirmish going on. Foys 2 and 4 have moved seven and a half kilometres northeast and are less than one kilometre from where Grand 3 was this morning. Grand 3 has cleared out and gone four and a half kilometres southwest, even farther into Foys territory. Basin 3 has moved two kilometres southeast. Foys 3 is near you, just south of the logging area where she was earlier. Foys 1 is up between the Spectacle lakes on the northeast corner of the territory. See you in four hours."

Back in August 1988, Graham and assistant Harry Vogel caught the first two Foys Lake wolves, both big males, not far from the lake whose name Graham bestowed on the pack. Then in May 1989, Graham and Lee caught the next two Foys wolves. In late August 1989, Mary and I caught the fifth wolf, initially called Basin 3 but later Basin 3 Foys, destined to become one of the most valuable wolves of our study. The Basin Depot pack lived immediately east of the Foys Lake pack. Basin 3 Foys was a medium-large, young adult and looked out of a dark face at us from a pile of logs where the trap-hook caught. While collaring her, we noticed that her right hind leg was deformed, and remarked that this wolf would not give us much data. Her tibia-fibula bone, the normally straight "shin bone," was curved like a bow. We could feel no break, nor was there any external lesion. We photographed the leg and recorded it as a birth abnormality, an interpretation later confirmed by X-ray on her dead body.

Mid-afternoon flight, drone of the airplane again. Mary and I roused ourselves from the shade.

"Less movement this time. Basin 3 – same place. Foys 1 – same place. They are eight kilometres apart. Grand 3 – same place. Foys 4 has moved over near Foys 1, about one and a half kilometres apart. Foys 3 has left the logging cut and moved three kilometres across the hydro line. He's near the rendezvous site."

In early December 1989, when the first winter snows sifted among the pines, Graham looked down on eleven Foys wolves walking on the ice of a marsh and three trespassing Basin wolves only two kilometres away. Two days later the packs were together.

That first record of amalgamated packs happened on a piercingly cold day that stripped the sunlight of any vestige of warmth. We drove up a narrow logging road, alert for loaded trucks, and parked in a log landing beside other pickups. From the top of a log pile, Mary picked up the signals of Basin 3 Foys and Foys 2, distant but both on the same bearing.

We packed our carcass kit and started up the skid trail, every few minutes scrambling into the trees while red skidders pulling logs churned by. A group of loggers invited us to stand by their fire, where we chatted about the abundant deer tracks and stayed off the topic of wolves.

The snow was at the awkward depth: too shallow for snowshoes but too deep for easy walking. We made our way down a long two-kilometre ridge and emerged at the McDonald Creek marshes. The signals were still ahead, coming from a spruce- and fir-covered point. Waiting, watching, we spotted a pair of ravens fly by, reach the point, then swerve and drop into the trees. Ravens only do that for a reason.

The wolves had been feeding on a big ten-point buck, having caught it under the shoreline cedars. Most of the meat and entrails had been consumed. According to our reading of the tracks, they jumped the deer and brought it down in only fifteen metres. Its frozen rumen lay nearby, pulled out of the body cavity after the deer had frozen; otherwise, wolf teeth would have ruptured it. Freezing would not have taken long in the -30°C temperatures of the previous night. Often an indication of scavenging, this time it was not, because the bone marrow was creamy with fat.

We chopped off the lower jaw and femur while the pack waited nearby. Long shards of sunlight slanted through the cedars. After we retraced our tracks to the truck, we drove back to Achray.

Two days later we returned to further document this rare amalgamation of packs. It was a Saturday, so the loggers were not at work. Wolf tracks plastered the road. We picked up the signals of the same two wolves as well as Foys 1. The wolves were close when we left the truck, but they moved ahead of us all day. Snow down our necks, near-frozen fingers on the radio dial, glasses steamed up, thick young stands of balsam fir in the way, unseen deadfall – it was a demanding hike. Tracking the wolves to the head of a stream we came to a dead-end canyon where their weak signals deflected from all directions. We climbed up through hardwoods, and as we crested a ridge, the signals suddenly became loud.

Through the conifers we could see the snowy opening of a hilltop bog. We edged closer until it was in full view. A wolf walked out of the trees onto the ice, then another, and a third that sat down. Then out came Basin 3 Foys, closely followed by the two big, collared males and a smaller wolf. Seven wolves, unaware of us, ambled across the bog and into the leatherleaf on the far side.

A few days later, Graham recorded seven tracks from the air where the pack fanned out across a lake. Basin 3 Foys was not among them. Two days after Christmas, he counted fourteen tracks with all three collared wolves present. For the rest of the winter they remained together, their territory covering the combined summer territories of the Basin Depot and Foys Lake packs.

At first we were not sure how to interpret this unusual pack fusion. Both packs had produced pups the previous summer. But then when the two packs stayed together the following summer, and continued to use the combined land of both packs, we realized that in the previous year there must have been two breeding females in just the one pack. Most wolf studies document a low occurrence of multiple litters.

Evening flight, Graham on the radio overhead: "Grand 3 is still living dangerously. She has moved two kilometres to Aurora Lake, even farther into Foys territory. She is almost where Foys 2 and 4 were this morning. Foys 1, 2, and 4 are all close to one another up at the McDonald Creek marshes six kilometres from her. They must have found each other out there. They didn't have time to return to the rendezvous site and meet there. You should be getting both Basin 3 Foys and Foys 3. They're in the rendezvous site."

Clouds were drifting in, heralding a change in the weather. We monitored the signals from our tent. Basin 3 Foys came home at 7:30 P.M. after being away thirty hours. Fifty-five minutes later, Foys 3 returned after an absence of at least fifty-one hours, but he had always been close by and may have come in briefly when we were not there.

The storm hit just before midnight, booming in from the west, illuminating the sky and making the electricity in the hydro wires crackle. No other collared wolves returned. Between 3:05 and 4:50 A.M., Basin 3 Foys left the rendezvous site. By then the storm had faded to a distant rumbling. Foys 3 left too, just as the first strands of daylight were illuminating a wrung-out sky.

As the morning advanced, the clouds stayed draped over the hills, too low for a flight. We sat in the door of the tent and caught up on our notes. A doe came into the clearing and picked nervously at some aspen stems, glancing up every few seconds. Being so near the hub of wolf activity, she was not strategically well placed for a long life.

At noon we drove to the airfield and found Graham and Hank lying listlessly under the wing of the plane. Graham was showing the effects of the motion-sickness pills, and Hank appeared fatigued from the flights. The data we were getting were good though, and we decided to carry on.

By mid-afternoon the ceiling lifted enough for us to fly. Mary and I went along to see the rendezvous site from the air. Beyond our left wing the Bonnechere River snaked through the hills. We flew over the wounded forest behind our camp and could see a pair of bulldozers knocking down trees and a log skidder crawling into a landing. There was the conspicuous hydro line, our tent, and the rendezvous site.

The pack had chosen a system of linked beaver ponds connected by marshes and meadows that were invisible from the ground. Dead standing trees dotted the largest pond, victims of recent beaver flooding. Like other rendezvous sites, this one had its resident beaver. In the early 1970s, we determined from scat analysis that wolf scats collected at such places showed more beaver than those collected on trails and roads elsewhere. Wolves exploit their local resources.

After a few circles we began tracking signals. Like chess players, the Grand and Foys wolves had again made strategic moves relative to each other. All but Foys 2 were absent from the rendezvous site; he had returned after a seventy-two-hour absence.

After the flight, Mary and I drove back to our tent and confirmed from the ground that Foys 2 had indeed come back. A few hours later, on the evening flight, Graham radioed that Foys 4 had moved to the same little hilltop bog where Grand 3 had been the previous morning. It was the same hilltop bog where we had watched the seven Foys wolves the winter before.

That night we sat up late to monitor the rendezvous site. Only Foys 2 was on the air at first, then sometime between 1 and 3 A.M. Basin 3 Foys and Foys 4 returned. At 4:25 A.M. we were woken by a full chorus of howling, the first vocalization in three nights. Voices blended and the air was suddenly filled with sound that reverberated off the hills. When Mary checked the signals, Foys 4 was so close that the receiver picked up his signal even before she plugged in the antenna. He was with Basin 3 Foys on the hydro line less than one hundred metres away. Foys 2 was farther back.

The pack howled at 5 A.M. and again just after 6. We made radio check and found all collared wolves had gone. Something was up. Another pack howl at 6:25, this time initiated by a distant single to the east. The single kept howling after the pack stopped, repeating high-pitched, dropping howls for a few minutes.

After the morning flight, we left to search the hilltop bog for signs of any encounter between Foys wolves and Grand 3. When we climbed out of the canyon and crested the ridge, we heard no signals. No wolf sign – no tracks, scats, broken branches. No carcass. We searched for over an hour. Wolves come and go like phantoms. But trespassing Grand 3 must have left some scent, attracting the attention of the Foys wolves.

Grand 3, a member of the Grand Lake pack to the north, had been collared as a yearling female the previous summer. She had stayed with her natal pack most of that winter, then began pre-dispersal movements to the northwest. Although she returned briefly to her territory in late March, we did not record her with her packmates again. By early summer she had moved southwest and had begun defining a new territory abutting the Basin-Foys pack's land. At times she clearly trespassed, but despite the Basin-Foys pack's large size, it gave ground.

Grand 3 likely was not alone in her search for land, but we cannot be sure. A month after our flights ended, we captured Basin 4 McDonald, the largest collared wolf in our study. He was in the area occupied by Grand 3. After that, these two wolves usually were together and formed the beginnings of the McDonald Creek pack.

At the rendezvous site that night, the Foys Lake wolves gave us five more serenades, and we noticed a correlation with their movements. Every time they howled, either one or more collared wolves had just returned or left. In contrast, every night but the previous one, wolves had entered or left with no howling. This is consistent with our experience with other packs: some nights are silent, others filled with howls. The difference may relate to hunting success, or to a decision to change rendezvous sites, or to trespass, or some wolf social event.

The series of flights ended the next day, but Mary and I stayed at our camp. By early August we were locating the wolves more commonly to the east. We began a second block of flying, and Graham pinpointed a new rendezvous site in a boggy hollow so close to a logging road that the dust from the logging trucks at times must have reached them. Each evening after the loggers left, the wolves would leave their footprints on the tire tracks and around the skidders parked for the night.

What had attracted the pack to such a place? Probably deer, themselves attracted to the good browse provided by the crowns of the felled trees.

On calm nights we tape-recorded the pack whenever it howled. The Foys wolves were beautiful howlers with deep, resonant voices, high, dropping voices, sonatas, concertos, full orchestras. As August wore on, their howling increased.

The pack was still there by the logging road late in the month when we had to break camp and end the field season. By then we had much of the information we wanted.

These data indicate that for four days the pack was feeding on a moose at a bog edge ten kilometres from the rendezvous site. Foys 2 and Foys 4 were in on the carcass first, stayed there for fifty-two hours, then left to alert other pack members. Foys 4 met Foys 1 four kilometres to the north and led him to the carcass. Foys 2 returned to the rendezvous site, where he met Basin 3 Foys and led her there too. All four collared wolves stayed at the carcass another twenty-four hours when our block flying ended. Foys 2 and Foys 4, instead of hogging it all for themselves, which would maximize their individual fitness, gave up some food for the good of the group.

That type of cooperative behaviour is explainable as "reciprocal altruism": you scratch my back and I'll scratch yours. It is worth sharing my kill with you if sometime later you share yours with me. The pack seemed to be operating to maximize its chances of making kills. Never were all five collared wolves together during our monitoring. Instead, they hunted in three loose parties. Occasionally, individuals moved from one party to another.

The pups waiting back in the rendezvous site for food would approve of what the adults were doing. Three parties were out hunting, not just one, and they were searching their entire territory. In one-quarter of our recorded fixes, the collared wolves were between twelve and eighteen kilometres apart, much of the diameter of the territory. Maybe they were having to work hard to find prey, or maybe wolf mobility is so great that they cover their whole territory with ease. Nevertheless, because of their hunting tactics, most of the deer, moose, and beaver in the territory were liable to be found every day. The pack seemed to be operating as a cooperative team.

At the same time, pups would be glad that the adults were keeping an eye on them. Collared wolves were in the rendezvous site for 19 per cent of the seventy-eight fixes. The baby-sitting task was shared; all wolves were there on occasion. Basin 3 Foys and Foys 3 stayed closest to the rendezvous site. Foys 3 was especially attentive to the young. His average distance away was only 4.1 kilometres, and even that is an inflated value because of one brief trip seven kilometres to the west.

Later, genetics showed that Foys 3 was the grandfather of the pups. Basin 3 Foys was his daughter, and she was, as expected, the mother of the pups.

Different wolves appeared to be playing different roles in the pack. Foys 2 and Foys 4 were more closely associated as wide-ranging hunting partners, although near the end of our monitoring session Foys 3 and Foys 2 made a short trip together. Foys 1 associated with the other wolves only at the moose kill and on one visit to the rendezvous site. He appeared to be more of a boundary patroller, averaging 8.1 kilometres from the rendezvous site, greatest of them all. He moved more than other wolves too, averaging 4.5 kilometres between fixes compared with the least active wolf,

Foys 3 at 2.5 kilometres. Oddly, despite Foys 1's apparently limited interest in the pups, genetics showed that he was their father.

Division of labour is a hallmark of advanced societies. So is reciprocal altruism expressed by food sharing and cooperative care of the young. So is group hunting, the social characteristic that best defines wolves. The Foys Lake pack showed them all.

When we look through our winter data, all the collared Foys wolves were together for half the recorded fixes. Several wolves can subdue adult ungulates more effectively than one or two. Similarly, when coyotes turn to larger prey, they tend to hunt in groups, as observed in Yellowstone National Park, where, without wolves present, coyotes broadened their prey base to include adult female elk. Coyotes, or coyote/wolf hybrids, form packs in the New England states and Maritime provinces too, where in winter they prey on white-tailed deer.

Mary, Graham, and I followed the Foys Lake pack one December day, with only a few centimetres of snow on the ground. The wolves travelled in single file through dense lowland conifer, then along a narrow stream running between cattails to a bog where they finally fanned out. Thirteen tracks arched over to a beaver lodge. Some wolves climbed up and dug at the breathing hole, but a lodge cemented with frozen mud is wolf-proof.

The Foys Lake pack was travelling as a unit too, on February 22, 1990, when Graham spotted twelve of them from the air. That was at 8:50 A.M., only two hours after we had seen them from the Achray parking lot trespassing on the ice of Grand Lake. They had travelled up a chain of small lakes along their northern boundary, covering approximately nine kilometres at four and a half kilometres per hour in deep snow.

The entire pack was together on a February afternoon as we followed their signals along the Bonnechere River. In successive survey flights, Graham had picked up Foys radio signals coming from the same patch of spruces along a nameless little creek. We struggled through snow-catching conifers, one wolf howling ahead of us, another to the right. More joined in – one behind, one ahead – tuning up for a two-hour concert among the best in our experience. Theirs were long, expressive howls, rising and falling in uneven steps. At dusk we reached the carcass they were feeding on. The usual black avian cloud lifted off to reveal an almost entirely consumed moose.

While we hacked off the bones we needed, wolves kept howling from all sides, long, beautiful, deep-throated howls. We started back, able to follow our snowshoe tracks without a flash-light. For more than an hour we shuffled along, the temperature dropping, pinpricks of starlight shining through the branches overhead. The wolves escorted us all the way, howling every few minutes, never close enough to hear in the brush, often half a kilo-metre or more away.

The remaining half of our winter fixes showed the Foys Lake wolves travelling as singles or in small groups. But if their move-ments were coordinated, this can be interpreted as group hunting too. Packs split into several hunting groups will detect more prey. As long as groups can locate each other, as they seem able to do, splitting up may represent a more efficient hunting strategy. Even when wolves seem to be alone, they may not be out of touch, like two people shopping together in a grocery store who go down separate aisles but know they can find each other easily. Hunting wolves may be a few kilometres apart, but their paths cross period-ically so that they are really hunting together. The wolves' world of scent and their mobility may make a grocery store out of a seem-ingly extensive landscape.

Reviewing winter movements, travel as a pack may be neces-sary when deep snow increases the energetic costs of wolf travel, although we recorded it in shallow snow as well. Elsewhere, where prey are more sparse and wolf territories larger, wolves may have a more difficult time relocating one another, causing them to travel as a pack more often. Or, when hunting caribou on the tundra or elk on grasslands, whole packs may be strategically more successful than individuals in chasing, flanking, and cutting off prey, although small groups have been shown to do well too. Or, if prey is difficult to kill, it might be best hunted by packs; small wolves in an already small subspecies such as the Algonquin wolf may benefit from numerical strength to subdue a healthy moose, one unencumbered by snow.

The best test of pack coordination, even when wolves are spread across a landscape, is whether they all find and feed at each other's kills. While we have yet to calculate an exact percentage, all collared pack members have been present at most of the one hundred or more prey carcasses we have located. That they find each other is convincing evidence that they are cooperating in the hunt even when seemingly apart. That describes a supra-organism.

If survival of the most fit pack is a valid idea, what constitutes pack fitness? A "most fit" individual, in purely biological terms, leaves the most offspring to survive and reproduce. A "most fit" pack will do the same. An obvious requirement for both is plenty of food.

The Foys Lake wolves claimed the largest territory in our study, approximately 275 square kilometres, probably larger if we had located them more often. If prey are distributed evenly across the landscape, more land means more prey. The Foys Lake pack held title to most of the broad Bonnechere Valley inside the park. Flanking packs – Ryan Lake to the south, Redpole Lake to the west, Grand Lake to the north, McDonald Creek to the northeast and east – gave it room, willingly or otherwise.

Probably not a coincidence, the Foys Lake pack also was the largest pack. Larger packs will have more hunters searching more places. A large pack also increases the possibility that especially skilled hunters may be among its members. However, more wolves in a pack means more mouths to feed, so a larger territory may not necessarily result in more food per wolf. We, like others, have not had continuous contact long enough or often enough with packs of different sizes to be able to compare their kill rates.

Large packs may not be more fit if the reason they are large is simply a lack of opportunity to disperse, such as on an island like Isle Royale. Nor do large packs necessarily reflect greater fitness if they only result from more room to feed around larger prey, as sometimes suggested, such as around the carcasses of the large subspecies of moose in northwestern North America or bison in and around Wood Buffalo National Park.

Large wolf packs are not analogous to large packs of African wild dogs and spotted hyaenas, which can contain up to fifty animals. These species have a problem that wolves do not: they must defend their kills against other species of predators, especially lions. Even lions have large prides to overcome the problem of displacement at carcasses.

The reason that the Foys Lake pack was so large may have been simply that there were two breeding females. Only in one other pack have we recorded more than one breeding female. Dave Mech in Minnesota describes roughly a 15 per cent incidence, higher than in our study. Normally, social hierarchy works against multiple breeding.

Large packs, then, may or may not signal greater fitness. We assessed the idea, but it comes out inconclusive.

Evidence of competition between packs – staking out and holding land that other packs want – supports the idea of supra-organism and survival of the best-fit pack. We witnessed passive competition in the delayed boundary skirmishes between the Foys Lake wolves and the newly forming McDonald Creek pack represented that summer by Grand 3. That winter, Grand 3 and Basin 4 McDonald were usually together right on Foys Lake pack's northeastern flank. They had succeeded in taking over about twenty square kilometres of land that the Foys pack had occupied the winter before. How two wolves managed to wrest land from twelve wolves is unclear, but the shift in boundaries did occur. Maybe Grand 3 or Basin 4 McDonald were related to other Foys wolves that were not collared and so escaped our genetic analysis. If so, the territory adjustment may have been made with consent. The McDonald Creek wolves expanded their new territory later, only after the Foys Lake pack was killed.

We have other evidence of passive competition between packs. In the summer of 1996, a collared wolf trespassing just inside the Jocko Lake pack's territory was stationary by a bog while a wolf from the resident pack approached on a trajectory that would bring them into close proximity. The approaching wolf was still one and a half kilometres from the stationary wolf when the stationary animal suddenly moved off and within minutes was out of signal range. Nineteen minutes later, when the approaching wolf was exactly one kilometre from where the stationary wolf had been, it swerved abruptly and went to that exact spot. The incident suggests that detection may have taken place more than one kilometre away. Here was a possible case of avoidance on a territorial boundary, passive defence.

More dramatic, of course, are other examples of trespass resulting in killing, such as the Nahma wolf, Travers 8, probably Pretty 6, and, later in the story, Pretty 7. One must conclude that wolf packs live in a situation-specific world that embraces mutual acceptance, avoidance, competition, and vigorous defence.

Being fit ultimately did nothing to prevent the demise of the Foys Lake wolves. Natural selection had tuned them up to survive in nature, not for what occurred.

Events began to turn against them on November 15, 1990. Foys 2 was shot by an archer less than one kilometre from the park's eastern boundary. Basin 3 Foys died the following March – one bullet straight through the heart in a woodlot outside the park.

Only a few weeks later we tracked Foys 3 on mortality mode to a bare spot of ground beneath a large spruce. His trail was unusual; he had been dragging his hindquarters in the snow. Branches and sticks lay broken around his body. He tested positive for rabies. So did Foys 4, picked up two weeks later by Lee and Tom.

That summer we could find no evidence of a Basin-Foys pack. Foys 1 seems to have been a lone wolf in August when Jenny and Carolyn recollared him. He was alone in early December on Graham's flights.

On December 18, Mary and I went to check on him near the junction of the hydro line and the Bonnechere road. It was dusk as we set out, shuffling through twenty centimetres of snow. We followed his signal off a side hill and into a lowland spruce-alder tangle where tracks of deer and snowshoe hare were plentiful. As we proceeded with flashlights, the signal became louder. In places the brush was so thick we had to crawl. Soon the signal was very loud, too loud; we were closer than wolves ever allow. As we aimed our flashlight into the thicket, we knew the wolf was within a few metres of us. Then the flashlight beam hit him. He was lying on his side on a patch of bare ground under low spruce limbs, legs spread as if he were running, dead. He had died so recently that his body was still unfrozen and his collar not yet on mortality mode. He had dug out a hollow in the spruce needles, curled up there for a while, then moved a metre where he stretched out for the last time.

I hoisted his emaciated body across my shoulders and we made our way back. A three-quarter moon illuminated the forest and stars ornamented the sky on this funeral march with the last of the Foys wolves.

Later autopsy at the University of Guelph showed five broken ribs, one of which had not healed, and a broken leg that had fused crooked from an injury long ago. A stick had lodged between his upper carnassial teeth against the pallet of his mouth. It had been there a long time as shown by the adjustment of his gums. The stick suggested rabies, but results came back negative. Body worn out, he had starved in the midst of plenty.

We had learned from the Foys Lake pack that a wolf exists at two biological levels: individual and pack – and claim that our observations support those who believe that natural selection operates on them both. There is general agreement that nature selects the best from functional, biological units, defined as living systems that work synchronously and share a common fate. In an individual, cells, genes, tissues, and organs function together, with mutual interdependence. The better fit the individual, the more successful it will be in leaving genes to future generations.

At another level, however, individual wolves are imbedded in packs where they also function together, with mutual interdependence. The genes of all the individuals form a pool. Pack members work synchronously, displaying cooperation in group hunting;

reciprocal altruism in sharing kills made by various pack members; and division of labour in caring for young, in hunting, and possibly in boundary patrolling.

Individual wolves compete within a pack for dominance with attendant rights to breed and feed. Similarly, packs compete with one another for land and resources. If the pack includes animals that are good at finding and dispatching prey and caring for pups, then as an amalgam of individuals, it will be more fit — be a more successful competitor in land-claim negotiations with other packs, and leave more offspring than other packs with fewer skills.

Wolf — individual. Wolf pack — supra-organism.

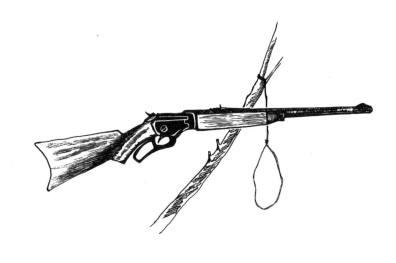

WINTERS OF DEATH

THE WOLF evolved primarily as a hunter. Its low reproductive rate offset its low mortality. The survival of only a few young each year was enough to maintain populations. A conservative strategy, it served the wolf well throughout its evolutionary history – until the wolf itself became hunted. After that, over much of its range, the strategy failed.

Despite similar human persecution, the faster-breeding, eat-almost-anything coyote has managed to persist. Though millions of coyotes have been killed, more may live in North America now than ever before. Coyotes compensate better than wolves for their losses. No complex social structure limits breeding, and they can breed at a younger age than wolves. While wolves compensate too, their ability to do so is more limited. The wolf, hunter-turned-hunted, is biologically set up to be victimized by humans.

The war on wolves has been well chronicled both by the bounty hunters of old and the writers of today. Chronicled, but except for the famous "last of the loners" such as the "Custer Wolf," not personalized. Few trappers know anything about the individual wolves they kill. Most acquaintances are brief, made down the barrel of a gun or at the end of a snare wire, ending in death.

Mary, the student crews, and I see wolf killing differently because, for us, wolves are not just impersonal quarry, but subjects of great interest. Their histories personalized them – where they were likely to be on a star-filled night, where they dug their dens and their pups played, where they liked to hunt and with whom they hunted. The social carnivores and primates, especially, show personality, emotion, variation in behaviour, freedom of choice. To know how these traits have shaped the lives of individual wolves develops empathy, respect, compassion.

Lace curtains framing the farmhouse window slid aside and a head appeared. A man at his woodpile behind the house stopped chopping. We felt conspicuous out there in the open, standing on a concession road between two farmhouses. We were being watched. Normally we take bearings on wolves from the seclusion of the Algonquin Park forest. But with this fix made on Jack Pine 1 on January 26, 1991, all that changed. The bearing lined up with a dilapidated outhouse, the wolf somewhere in the forest beyond. It seemed incredulous to be tracking Algonquin Park wolves in the farmlands, but we would have been more amazed had we known the new direction our research was about to take.

The new direction, in retrospect, had been apparent five days earlier when Graham flew a telemetry survey that ended over the southeast side of the park. To get back to the Pembroke airport meant flying beyond the park boundary north of the town of Wilno, then over the village of Round Lake Centre and the cluster of houses at Bonnechere. Out there, farm fields make up about 20 per cent of the landscape scattered among pine plantations and mixed forests. Long ago an ancient Bonnechere River flowing off the Algonquin Highlands deposited delta soils onto the floor of an expanded Round Lake, providing the substratum for marginal farmlands today.

As he flew over this partly settled land, Graham idly dialled up a few wolves listed as missing and got a shock. He heard the signals of two wolves on mortality mode and another wolf still alive. The live one, Lavieille 5, held a territory in the centre of the park sixty kilometres away. An adult female, she had been missing since summer.

Until then, we had recorded a few instances of park wolves that had been killed out in what we had labelled "the farmlands." Their radio-collars had been turned in to the MNR. Graham had talked to the people who had shot, snared, or trapped them, and although he had identified some anti-wolf sentiment, we thought little about it. We had listed those dead wolves as dispersers, young animals looking for land of their own. Even a large park cannot be expected to contain all long-distance dispersers.

Looking back now, I count six radio-collared wolves that died in the farmlands near Round Lake Centre before Graham's memorable flight and our outhouse fix. Three of them had been identified by the field crews as yearlings and therefore good candidates for dispersal, but three had been classed as adults.

In those years, we were aware of the annual deer migration to the Round Lake area twenty kilometres beyond the park, but we did not know its magnitude. In 1990, Lee Swanson had begun her master's research on the environmental stimuli that triggered this migration. Early each winter, deer previously scattered across the eastern twenty-seven-hundred square kilometres of Algonquin Park migrate up to fifty kilometres to the vicinity of Round Lake. They seek shelter and shallow snow provided by lowland conifers and, to get it, concentrate into approximately two hundred square kilometres of this semi-agricultural landscape. Some deer continue another ten kilometres beyond Round Lake to farmlands near the village of Germanicus, and a small number migrate from the northeast corner of the park to the vicinity of the town of Petawawa. In some winters a few deer stay in lowland pockets inside the park, as Graham's aerial observations showed.

Despite the deer migration, wolves in the park still had plenty of moose as prey. Packs stayed mostly on territory, and Graham succeeded in finding almost all the radio-collared wolves on most flights. The idea that wolf packs would abandon their territories to follow migratory deer did not occur to us. No other study had reported that.

So we envisioned Lee's work as adding to our general knowledge about the large mammal system and did not closely connect the wolf and deer studies until that January day. In my notebook I wrote: "Could wolves other than dispersers be following the deer out of the park, and if so, what are the consequences?" We soon found out.

February 21, 1991. I answered my telephone at the university to a man who said he knew someone who had shot a radio-collared wolf near Round Lake Centre. If we wanted its carcass, he would get it for us. Mary and I drove up the next day.

His farm buildings were clustered on the snowy flats southeast of Round Lake, a green pickup parked by a two-storey square house. In the back of the truck lay the dead wolf. A tall man came out, introduced himself, and watched while Mary turned on the receiver and scanned the frequencies. The wolf had a dark face and a bowed hind leg; we knew who she was even before the receiver cycled to her signal – Basin 3 Foys, alpha-female of the Foys pack, the wolf we had come to know so well.

The man invited us in, and we sat in his kitchen. His father came over from next door and explained that he had poisoned wolves in the past. Before long, the son admitted shooting the wolf himself. When we described in sympathetic terms what we knew of her life, he seemed surprised. He explained that when his friends shot collared wolves, the standard procedure was to smash their collars. Unlike them, however, he was concerned that the wolf was important to somebody's research. He had been away to university and had come back to take up farming on land next to his father's.

We drove with him to his woodlot where he told us that he had heard wolf howls late one afternoon while chopping wood. Grabbing a rifle from his truck, he walked a short distance before encountering the Foys Lake pack. His shot had gone straight through Basin 3 Foys' heart.

It had never occurred to him to do anything else, he said. All his friends, everyone around there, would have done the same thing. We walked on and he showed us where deer tracks pummelled the snow in a cedar stand he was cutting for fence posts. No shortage of deer. After he felled a cedar, he told us, deer would be there feeding on the top in only an hour. In a few days everything green on the tree would be eaten.

By the end of the afternoon, he admitted that wolves had never done either him or his father any harm. Deer were plentiful. Why not live in peace? His mind was more open than many others we would encounter.

The upshot, though, was that Basin 3 Foys now lay dead and frozen stiff in the back of our truck. We thought about her rendezvous site at the hydro line, and the ten-point buck in the cedars beside McDonald Creek, and her deep howl intertwined with those of her pack on the quiet August evenings. Making her loss even more poignant, the next day we discovered that the pack was still in the same woods, moving slowly away from the scene of their tragedy.

All that day we trailed them through the shallow snow over hardwood hills into the next concession and beyond. Foys 1, 3, 4 – the pack was heading back to the park. We stayed far enough behind not to disturb them, yet were close enough to hear the repeated howls of one wolf – long, forlorn notes breaking downward in melancholy intervals. From past experiences we recognized the howl as one we had come to call the "mourning howl." We have heard it both in the wild and in captivity when a packmate has been injured or killed. Sorrow and grief are not just human emotions, as people who own dogs know.

The very idea of a park with its purpose of wildlife protection was tarnished, diminished, made hollow by the senseless death of Basin 3 Foys. It should not have happened. But similar deaths kept happening. Travers 1 and Mathews 5 both were shot near Round Lake Centre; Annie Bay 2 disappeared near the town of Wilno; Grand 5 went missing. In day-to-day contacts with local people at gas stations and grocery stores, an unsavoury picture began to emerge. Conservation officer Pat Sloan, not a wolf lover but dedicated to upholding the game laws, recounted the story of periodic wolf roundups. Snowmobiles were used to drive wolves to concession roads where hunters lined up to shoot them. We learned the names of locally famous wolf killers such as Max Lepinski, reputed to have killed more wolves than anyone in the district. He baited them with carcasses just outside his kitchen window and shot from there. As proof, he turned in the radio-collar of Travers 1, a big adult male killed that way on March 13, 1991. Travers 1 had been the second wolf radio-collared in our study back in 1987, but we had lost track of him in 1989 after his collar had gone dead.

By the end of March 1991, 61 per cent of the twenty radio-collared wolves that were alive the previous summer had died, a few to rabies, others to humans, maybe more that we didn't know about with smashed collars. Whenever a biologist has more than 10 per cent of a population marked, as we did, it is fair to conclude that the sample represents the entire population. We interpreted our 61 per cent as indicating a loss of approximately fifty to sixty wolves from the eastern half of Algonquin Park, at least half killed by humans.

That winter of death, in contrast to previous winters, most of the packs moved back and forth between their territories and the farmlands. Something different from the earlier years was happening to precipitate so much wolf migration, and we began to reconsider a possible connection with the migratory deer.

According to local people, deer had migrated to the vicinity of Round Lake for years although they used to stay closer to the park where logging was the heaviest. In the late 1960s when the density of deer in the park was close to ten times its 1990 level, the drainage area for deer migrating to Round Lake was much smaller. Most deer travelled instead to other heavily used wintering areas throughout the park. The park's first master plan drawn up in 1975 identified ten such areas. Doug Pimlott calculated that back then 90 per cent of the diet of park wolves in winter was deer.

The deer population collapsed in the late 1970s and early 1980s. Winters of heavy snowfall, lack of suitable conifer cover, and less early successional forests took their toll. To bolster the remnant herd, the MNR began distributing hay to landowners in the Round Lake area. Both deer and local people developed traditions difficult to break.

The years just before our study were ones of slow, steady deer recovery despite one setback in 1983, according to the MNR, when the deer migrated out of the park early during the rifle season. Throughout the 1980s, deer benefited from a decade of low snowfall all across the northeastern portion of their North American range. As our study progressed, we documented their gradual expansion in the park as more of them appeared each summer farther west towards the height of land. We speculated that as their population increased, the area occupied by deer accustomed to migrate to Round Lake would increase as well.

At some point in this modest deer increase, the wolves apparently began to key in on this migration, possibly when the drainage area reached some threshold size. Or perhaps it occurred when the deer population reached some threshold density, or the migration reached some threshold degree of completeness. Whatever the reason, for the wolves, following the deer more closely than in previous years had disastrous consequences.

We began field work earlier the next winter, 1991–92, anxious to see if the wolves would follow the deer again. Lee and Graham arranged with the superintendent of tiny Bonnechere Provincial Park to use the gatehouse just off Highway 62 as occasional winter quarters. Mary and I stayed there too, all sleeping on the gatehouse floor.

On December 5, the nighttime temperature dropped to -26°C, and just like the previous winter, within forty-eight hours the deer came pouring out of the park. With infra-red trail monitors set up on six runways, Lee counted 1,822 deer entering the winter yard within a few days. Snow was only twenty centimetres deep, and the temperature, after the cold spell, hovered near freezing.

When Mary and I arrived on December 16, no park wolves had travelled down to the Round Lake deer yard, but each of Graham's flights held surprises: Travers wolves in Mathews territory;

Pretty wolves in part of old Foys territory; Jack Pine wolves in McDonald Creek territory. As the deer vacated the central part of the park, the wolf packs did too, trespassing on each other's territories with abandon, even poaching deer along the way.

On December 17, the Pretty Lake pack of five travelled twenty kilometres off territory and killed a deer on Feely Lake while the resident pair was fifteen kilometres away feeding on its own deer. The following day, cold and sunny, Mary and I drove to within a couple of kilometres of Feely Lake on a one-lane logging road. We announced our presence to approaching logging trucks over our CB radio every half-kilometre, and pulled off quickly into the snowbank if a trucker answered. Because of their limited ability to slow down, we granted them the right of way. Eventually we parked at a ploughed pull-off and hiked from there.

Out on the ice of Feely Lake, a few scraps of the deer lay in the centre of a converging lattice of wolf tracks. The deer pelt lay among red pines on a nearby point, everted and skinned just as neatly as if done with a knife. Pretty 1's signal came in distantly to the northwest as the pack headed back to its own land. It had left its territory, made the kill, consumed it, and was heading back home all in twenty-six hours.

Wolf movements were perplexingly erratic, and we asked ourselves whether the previous winter's heavy mortality could have fractured their system of land tenure. In late December, the Grand Lake West pack of four came down to the deer yard, then two days later returned to its territory. During much of December both the Jack Pine and Travers packs were split. A pair, or possibly trio, of Travers wolves moved east to the boundary of the park, then northwest almost to the Ottawa River thirty kilometres away, an unusual movement well off territory. Meanwhile, the other Travers trio took an excursion through the territories of three different packs and finally stopped at a dead bull moose frozen on its brisket in starvation position under some red pines.

Mary and I tracked them to their carcass. The moose's bone marrow was bright crimson and jelly-like from fat depletion. Hair was missing from its belly and flanks where the skin had been hemorrhaging, but we found no ticks and were unable to determine the cause of death. We monitored the site from the air and ground for a few days, and as far as we know the other Travers wolves never showed up. Nor did the landowners who were six kilometres away at Feely Lake, where no doubt they found the deer hide and rumen left by the poaching Pretty pack.

Complicating our interpretation of these tangled movements was a new source of food for the wolves – moose and deer shot in the park by native people. With the stroke of a political pen, a new predator entered Algonquin Park or, more accurately, a predator re-emerged with much-enhanced hunting efficiency, after an absence of one hundred years since the park's creation.

There was a new scavenger too. As we drove through the town of Round Lake Centre one day, we spotted a highway-killed deer up on a snowbank. Wanting to see how quickly an off-territory pack can discover a carcass, we loaded it into the back of the truck and drove to the end of a nearby concession road close to the Grand Lake West pack's temporary location. We met Graham, who helped us unload the deer and drag it along a snowmobile trail into the woods. On the way back we kicked snow over the drag marks to conceal our experiment from snowmobilers. Just as we reached our trucks, an ancient-looking snowmobile approached and a very old, toothless man dismounted. After an awkward silence, Graham explained that we were listening for wolves. The man got back on his snowmobile and drove on down his lane.

The next morning when we returned, ravens were circling and wolf tracks plastered the trail. The carcass, however, was gone. Over our trail ran fresh human tracks and a new drag mark. Judging from the raven droppings and wolf scats littering the snow, the old man must have had some well-seasoned meat.

By mid-January all the packs had come down to the deer yard. From a big, blue highway sign high on a hill advertising "Wilno Body Shop," we could dial most of them up almost any time. Once, standing at a deer kill in a red pine plantation, we could hear the signals of four wolves from three different packs. We broke that record from a snowy hardwood ridge when we picked up seven wolves from five packs. Throughout February we tracked wolves across farm fields and found deer kills out behind barns. One cold, calm night we howled the entire deer yard and heard five packs, a record, three of them from one place – and many farm dogs.

Then, by mid-March, all but one pack returned home. We howled the deer yard again on the night of March 17; only the Grand Lake West wolves responded – and again many dogs. The Grand West wolves were on a deer they had killed recently. We were surprised that the wolves would leave, because the deep snow hung on and the deer stayed for almost another month. The wolves may have had something else on their minds; it was late in the breeding season, time to think about den sites and property boundaries.

Known mortality was comparatively light that winter at 18 per cent. We were missing other wolves and suspected some smashed collars, but we could count only known deaths. The next winter, however, was more disastrous.

Acting on a tip in late November 1992, I telephoned an employee of the Chalk River Atomic Energy Centre just north of the park who told me his brother had recently shot a collared wolf. It turned out to be Pretty 2, a yearling female collared that summer. During the conversation he recounted how he had overheard a maintenance man in the coffee room explain that he, too, had shot a radio-collared wolf. My informant described the man as an old fellow from the town of Barry's Bay, a wolf hater who would not divulge where he shot the wolf because he did not want other people to know where he hunts. When Graham phoned him, the man vaguely mentioned White Mountain a few kilometres behind Round Lake Centre but refused to be more precise. He must have smashed the collar, because we could get no signal on mortality mode either around White Mountain or over the town. Missing and never accounted for was Foys 7 Ryan, likely his victim.

By the end of November, even before our winter field season had begun, two wolves had been killed and another was missing. Snow was light and temperatures mild until just before Christmas. Then, on December 22, deer began pouring out of the park and pack territories broke down again. Both the Jack Pine and Travers packs moved onto land claimed by the Jocko Lake pack while the deer were passing through. The McDonald Creek wolves, following the leading edge of the migration, came out to the periphery of the deer yard.

On December 28, student Stephan Beauregard flew over the Pretty and Travers packs, both close together on a plateau at the top of White Mountain. Because the packs were near each other, Mary, Jenny, Michelle, and I investigated. We drove a snowmobile trail along the south side of the Bonnechere River until, at an overflow, we could go no farther. From there we hiked up an old road that climbed the south slope of the mountain and soon came to a trail of wolf tracks that turned off at a bog. Ravens circled the trees on the far side. We spread out and, after a brief search, Jenny found the carcass, an almost completely consumed deer.

Remarkable about that kill was that while we stood there, we could dial up Pretty 1, Travers 1, Travers 4, and Travers 5 all within three hundred metres. After examining tracks, we concluded that the Pretty Lake pack had made the kill but the Travers pack had arrived and either displaced the Pretty Lake pack, or was allowed to feed, or was staying close hoping to feed. Anyhow, with wolves from two packs so close to a carcass, this was a case of extreme tolerance.

The next day, Travers 5, with three other wolves, left this carcass and moved down the mountain, across the ice of the Bonnechere River, and killed a deer six kilometres away. They consumed it completely and left while one of their packmates was still up on White Mountain and another had travelled more than ten kilometres to the north. Here was another case where they were not hunting or even feeding as a cooperative group.

By early January when we left the field, three radio-collared wolves had been confirmed shot and one more was suspected. Unfortunately, that was only the beginning; numbers rose by the time we returned in February. Conservation officer Blake Simpson met us at a gas station with Grand 6 in the back of his truck. This was a wolf we had known for nearly three years.

Grand 6 was born in the spring of 1989 at the den dug into a balsam-covered esker that lined a fast-flowing creek. That was before the Grand Lake pack separated. After it did, he stayed around the west end of the lake in the general vicinity of the den. Possibly he matured to be the breeding male in his last year of life.

Often on hot summer evenings we had listened to his howls tangled up with those of his pack, floating across Grand Lake and adjacent Clemow Lake. Twice the previous winter he had come down to the deer yard with his pack and returned. On one of these trips they killed a deer close enough to the Round Lake School that when we investigated the site we could hear children playing in the schoolyard.

Once, he and his pack chased some wintering deer that had bedded in an aspen stand on a series of knolls where visibility was good. Despite plentiful prey, the pack had been unsuccessful. That led us to wonder whether in areas of high deer density the wolves create a deerless zone around themselves as they travel, the fleeing deer causing others to flee, emptying the area in a domino effect.

Grand 6 had made a fatal mistake. In broad daylight he stood near a mailbox on the Bonnechere road long enough for the owner to spot him through the window, grab his gun, go outside and shoot. We were sorry to lose him.

Mortality mode was becoming unpleasantly familiar on our receivers. A few days later, Stephan heard Pretty 3 from the air on mortality mode just beyond the northern border of the park. When radio-collared the previous summer, she had been the lactating female of the Pretty Lake pack. We spent one long day in a February thaw and heavy rain, assisted by Tom Stephenson, trying to retrieve her. By snowmobile and snowshoe we managed to get close to her burial place under the snow, but her signal was deflecting from steep hills, confounding our efforts to figure out where to dig. With approaching darkness, the temperature dropped suddenly, and the possibility of hypothermia from wet clothes forced us to abandon the search. While Pretty 3's cause of death remains unknown, her remoteness rules out humans.

One cold, brittle evening a few nights later, when stars were brilliant, we picked up the signal of Travers 5 on mortality mode just south of town. The signal seemed to come from a farmhouse whose light we could see through shadowy pines. Leaving the truck by the road, we walked up the dark laneway. A yard light lit up a pickup parked by the door. I was almost certain the collar was in the house but wanted to be sure. Mary and Joy Cook stayed back in the shadows, and by the time I reached the farmhouse, the signal was very loud. Standing midway between house and shed I tuned the receiver down and realized the collar was not in the house but the shed.

Suddenly a curtain moved and a head appeared. The porch light went on and a man yelled through the window, "What do you want?" For a moment I did not know what to say, so I yelled back, "You have a wolf collar. I'd like to get it."

"Eh?" he called.

I said it again, this time gesturing to my neck, "Collar, a wolf collar."

"No, no," he called. "Go away." But then his wife's face appeared at the window so I tried again. "We're doing research on wolves and you killed a wolf with a collar. I want to get it." I heard the wife tell him, "Let him in," but to me she called out, "Do you know how many deer these wolves have killed?" Then she said, "Go around to the back door."

I struggled in, tripping over my antenna, and said that my wife and student were out in the lane. She motioned that they could come in too. Things were a bit tense for a few moments, then both of them started talking about all the deer the wolves had killed. We learned later that they routinely fed the deer beside their barn, effectively baiting the wolves as well. Either they did not make the connection or were deliberately attracting wolves to kill them. To defuse the situation I explained that we were studying wolves to see if we could find out how much they killed, and no matter what a person's attitudes, it seemed best to have some accurate information. That seemed to change the atmosphere, and they offered us chairs.

Joe Mask is a small man with rugged, weathered features, recently retired from a labour job with the MNR. Once, he helped build logging roads in the park, and only a decade before was employed by the MNR to kill wolves. Gradually it emerged that he had shot three wolves the previous Saturday (upon autopsy we learned that they had been snared, then shot) back in the bush behind the barn, and that there had been, and still were, many more around. They were very bold, he said.

Joe's wife explained how disgusted she was by their cruelty. The wolves were so bold that she feared for her husband when he went out to shoot them. Emphasizing their fearlessness, she told of a wolf encounter that had taken place just the previous week. A neighbour was snowmobiling close to their farm when a wolf jumped right up onto the back of the machine behind him. The driver rushed to their house and was so upset he fell to the kitchen floor. They thought he had suffered a heart attack.

Joe explained how one wolf had turned and snarled at him back in the bush, and he motioned to his face for emphasis. "Oh! He was vicious." Undoubtedly the wolf was in a snare.

Finally Joe got up and went out to the shed for the collar. He returned saying, "Those darn wolves are howling now." From the doorway we heard a pack in full chorus, likely the McDonald Creek wolves who only an hour earlier had been just behind the school, but we did not take the receiver out to check. As we left, Joe agreed to recover the carcass of Travers 5 the following morning.

The next day we were back and saw the farm in daylight – log barn with a couple of steers in the barnyard, a few pines scattered around a clapboard house, a small field rolling to the forest beyond. Three deer – good animals – were feeding on hay beside the barn. Joe was out shovelling snow in the yard. Travers 5 lay at the door of the shed with its frozen feet in the air. A rope that Joe had used to drag him behind his snowmobile was tied around the wolf's neck.

Joe was in a snarly mood. "What good are they?" and he quickly answered his question with "no good. Just cause a lot of trouble. Cause trouble everywhere. I shot lots of wolves, last winter. Collared ones too. And I'll shoot any more I see."

We lifted Travers 5 into the back of our truck. Mary tried to persuade Joe to recover the other two wolves he said he had killed, but he refused. "Darn deer killers. Not as many deer around as there was a few years ago." Behind him the wall of his shed was covered with deer skulls, trophies of his own hunts.

We thought that maybe there were no more wolves for Joe to retrieve, but when we phoned again a few days later, he had retrieved another wolf. When we drove up, it also lay by the shed door, its frozen feet in the air. Mrs. Mask unexpectedly invited us in, and again we sat on the kitchen chairs. The previous evening, CBC Television had shown "Cry Wolf" on the series "The Nature of Things." They had watched it, and rather than fan the flames of their animosity, it seemed to have done just the opposite. We talked about the film for a while, then as we left, Joe said almost under his breath, "I understand more now." He had obviously been giving wolves a lot of thought. We were quietly elated, and that night I wrote in my notebook: "Who knows if he will kill more wolves? Maybe his recent experiences will make him reconsider." They did not, as we would learn a year later.

The following summer, there was no Travers pack, nor the next year, nor the next. The work of one man had silenced wolf voices from the pineries around Lake Travers and washed out the wolf tracks from the sandy places along its shore. Single wolves travelled through the area but moved on. For a few years, the land lay vacant.

Different from the Masks are younger, macho types who kill wolves for ego gratification. They are fearless men held in awe at the local pub or mill. We encountered several of them, among them Richard, who killed most of the East Gate pack and was proud of it. We were at the MNR workyard at the park's east gate to pick up a snowmobile when Richard expressed his annoyance with Graham, who, the previous year, had come to pick up the carcasses. Richard interpreted Graham's remarks as agreement to go out trapping with him and show him our techniques. Graham laughs about it, as if he would instruct the man who killed the East Gate pack.

Eugene appeared to be in it for ego too. He bragged that he

had killed thirteen coyotes down near Bancroft and had outwitted a wolf that was hanging around. Both he and Richard work for the MNR.

Such men are different from professional trappers, many of whom neither feel animosity towards wolves nor use them for ego enhancement. They are making a living. Animate things are no different from inanimate. Most of the McDonald pack succumbed to a commercial trapper who felt neither hate nor pleasure when he killed them.

Eulogy for Basin 4 McDonald

Basin 4 McDonald died in a neck snare on Saturday, March 6, 1993. At the same time, 300 metres away, a packmate died the same way. Four days later, within 150 metres, a third wolf died.

Other members of the pack were at the snare sites, possibly watching the death struggles. Wolves have deep social ties. They are loyal. Most of them paid for staying around by getting snared too.

The destruction of the McDonald Creek pack occurred in Hagarty Township within two kilometres of Round Lake Centre. A trapper had laced the deer trails there with snares. Unsuspecting, the pack of twelve entered the death zone. It was reduced to three.

The previous August, the McDonald Creek pack had selected a complex of small ponds and bogs as a home site. There they hunted beaver and came and went on distant forays for deer or moose. Each night their howls rang through the forest – like the Foys Lake pack who owned this land before them, they were good howlers. We camped nearby, staying quiet so not to disturb them as they went about their business. Later we returned when the red maples flared and the bracken had browned, but they had gone, following secret forest pathways to some other place.

Basin 4 McDonald was born in the spring of 1985 (confirmed by tooth ageing) and died in his eighth year, an old wolf by the standards of the persecuted Algonquin Park wolf population. He had distinguished himself as the largest wolf in our study. When radio-collared in late August 1990, he recovered from the drug so quickly and ran over the nearby ridge so fast that we mistakenly thought his radio had failed. He was recaptured the next summer and his collar replaced. Often he hunted by himself along a favoured system of forest trails. He held a position of dominance in his pack and left several offspring – two daughters that we know of: Basin 9 McDonald and McDonald 5, confirmed by DNA evidence.

Basin 4 McDonald must have known tragedy in his life. When we first saw his big tracks, he was a five-year-old male, alone without a pack. At that age he should have been surrounded by family. That was the summer he met Grand 3, who had dispersed in March 1990 as a young female from the Grand Lake pack immediately to the north. After they met, in thirty-eight of fifty-two fixes from then until his death, they were together. That first winter they spent most of their time in and around the McDonald Creek marshes, often leaving the imprints of their tracks in the snows along Carcajou and McDonald creeks.

The following summer, 1991, they successfully raised a litter of five pups. Now as a pack of seven they often travelled the chain of lakes between Carcajou Bay of Grand Lake to Carcajou Lake lying ten kilometres to the west. That was the old travel route of the late Foys Lake pack. Late that winter they travelled out of the park to the Round Lake deer yard in search of food.

In the summer of 1992, they again raised a litter of five pups and as a pack of twelve again returned to winter in the Round Lake deer yard.

Graham discovered that Basin 4 McDonald was dead on March 13, 1993, while radio-tracking from the air. Hearing the wolf's radio signal on mortality mode, he was drawn farther east than Algonquin Park wolves normally go. The signal came from a row of houses along the shore of a lake. Later that day, Mary and I drove there and by walking up the road with the receiver picked out the house. We rang the door bell, but nobody was home. Behind the house was a pile of dead wolves, some skinned, others not. Some had bloodied heads where they had been clubbed. On the pile was Basin 4 McDonald, identifiable by his size. His collar and pelt had been removed.

When the trapper returned, he invited us in and explained where and when he had caught the wolves. He conveyed no animosity towards either wolves or us, and was interested in our study. He showed us wolf pelts with colour variation and we discussed whether coyote genes might be present. He was the first resident of the area to show an interest in wolves, and he has offered us his assistance since then.

Autopsy was performed at the University of Guelph by veterinarians Karrie Rose and Dale Smith on March 26, 1993. Lack of edema around the neck showed that he had not been in the snare long, just long enough for some fluid accumulation in his lungs, when the trapper arrived and clubbed him over the head, crushing his skull. On the autopsy report is the comment that he carried a "moderate to marked number of cestodes (tapeworms) in the duodenum and jejunum," not uncommon for Algonquin Park wolves and not disabling.

Nine days later, Graham radio-located the three surviving wolves, all females, back on territory in the park. Like the Travers territory, their land became packless. Grand 3 went off the air in the spring, possibly a battery failure. Basin 9 showed up on territory periodically that summer, then dispersed northwest into vacant Grand Lake West territory. She was alive and back in the deer yard early the following winter, but then she vanished for good. For two years we collared single, transient wolves as they passed through the old McDonald Creek territory, but they all moved on. Only McDonald 5 stayed to carry on the lineage. She is alive as I write, recollared by helicopter netting on Grand Lake in January 1998.

We lost the Grand Lake East pack that winter too. That pack consisted of eight wolves including radio-collared female Grand 2, on the air since summer 1988, giving us almost five years of data. She may have been the architect of the split in the Grand Lake pack. After she lost her mate the year before, she had restaked a territory at the east end of Grand Lake, abandoning her den in the esker by the fast creek.

The pack gave us an off-territory winter's day of tracking in late February 1993, close to Highway 62, north of the town of Killaloe. This was to be the last time Mary and I tracked them. We parked our truck on the shoulder of the highway and snowshoed into a woodlot. Eight wolves had bedded in a hollow only thirty metres from the road. They had no deer carcass, so it appeared that the pack was just resting.

The next day they moved closer to the town of Killaloe, not suspecting the snares strung in a brushy fenceline along a snowy road. Periodically the trapper had made an opening in the brush, an invitation for any wolf travelling along to leave the road for the fields behind. A few days later, Graham found five of the snares and pulled them; on a road allowance they were illegal. But it was too late for most of the pack. After that, Grand 2 was with only one other wolf, and then she was alone.

She stayed near the spot where her pack had died for two more days; we were learning that such behaviour was typical. She was in heat judging by the spots of blood in her bedding sites. A wolf in heat is rarely alone. A few days later her collar fell silent.

Never the following year did we find wolf tracks or hear howls in the hills around and beyond the east end of Grand Lake, despite much time spent in the area. As I write, five years later, there is still a wolfless hole in the western quarter of the Grand Lake East pack's land. Wilderness violated.

Jocko 2 was a large yearling male that Mary and I collared on the west-central part of the old Foys Lake pack's territory in the summer of 1992. We named him Jocko because a new pack was forming near the lake with that name. After collaring, however, he never associated with the Jocko pair or its first set of pups. He must have been a disperser from another pack. We could not identify him from genetic affinities.

After the capture he moved east, then for a time the forest swallowed him up. We listed him as missing but still had him programmed into our receivers in case he ever showed up. He did early one morning near the end of the summer, twenty kilometres east at Basin Lake. When the sun was just up, he and his pack-mates walked along the road, then stopped and howled. He was ensconced in a new pack that we later learned lived to the south, outside the park.

There are other gaps in our data for this wolf, likely because we were not flying far enough south, but periodically he appeared in the deer yard. Then, on March 15, 1993, halfway between the villages of Round Lake Centre and Killaloe, he put his head through a noose. We did not know that, however, when Graham located him from the air and reported that his collar was giving a regular signal.

Late that afternoon Mary and I tracked him. At first his signal was weak but strengthened as we snowshoed over a series of hills. We picked our way through cedar woods heavily trampled by deer, then across a small bog, and a larger one. Ahead we heard the sound of branches breaking that initially we thought was caused by a bounding deer. Through the trees we saw something moving, then Mary recognized it as a wolf. With our hearts pounding, we snowshoed towards him until we could see him clearly. He lunged repeatedly, sprang into the air, and fell back into the snow. As we approached, we saw the wire noose attached to a dead tree that gave him about twenty centimetres of play. We thought each leap would be his last. The ratchet on a neck snare moves only one way – tighter – and locks, an ingenious little contrivance, an icon of human cruelty. The wire threatened to slice the skin of his neck and cut his trachea. We remembered the Billy Lake wolf from several years previously, its neck one-third severed.

As we watched him struggle we felt helpless. We had no syringe, drugs, poke stick, or other equipment to handle a wolf. Because there were no human tracks around, we concluded he had been snared elsewhere, had broken the wire, and had become hung up on the tree. He had pounded a pit in the snow on the side where the snare had tangled. A spattering of blood lay crimson on the snow. About five metres beyond were the body imprints of two of his packmates who had been lying beside him while he fought for his life.

Suddenly he stopped struggling and lay still. His back was towards us; the snare did not give him enough slack to turn around.

At first we thought he was dead, but then he moved his head and tried to face us. We approached very slowly, and I gently placed one snowshoe along his back. He did not move. I applied more pressure in case he lunged, but he lay still. I knelt down, gradually inching my hand forward until I could grasp his radio-collar. We knew we could save him.

Mary eased her way in front of him and knelt in the snow to hold his attention. Feeling along the collar my hand came to the taught steel cable-wire and I followed it to his throat. Pressing, I managed to get my fingers into the noose, but the wire was so taut I could not enlarge it. Taking the risk that the wolf would lunge, I lifted my snowshoe off his back and, holding his collar, pulled him towards me. His body was limp, his attention focused on Mary, who by this time was taking pictures.

I eased my hand back to the snare and this time was able to open it. The wire had caught across the radio-pack on the lower side of the collar, and that had saved his life. In one swift movement before he had time to react, I pulled the noose over his face. He lay there in shock.

He let us examine him as if he had been drugged. We felt all around his neck; only a small amount of blood came away on my fingers. The skin on his right hind leg, however, was cut all the way around as if someone had used a knife. During the struggle, the wire had become wrapped around his leg but only briefly. The same thing had happened to the Billy Lake wolf, that time the wire cutting through flesh and bone leaving the leg dangling from a thin piece of skin. Fortunately, while Jocko 2's Achilles tendon was completely exposed, it was not severed. Mary photographed the glazed look of despair in his eyes, the resignation. Then we drew away, giving him room to run, but he just lay still seemingly too stunned to move, not realizing he was free. I poked him in the back with my snowshoe, but still he did not move. I did it again. No reaction, so I reached down, put my arms under him, and flipped him over. He looked up at me then and suddenly he understood. Bounding to his feet, he ran away.

As we snowshoed back to the truck, we talked about wolf snarers who lived nearby and might have done it. But what did that matter? Snaring is legal in Ontario. It is illegal, considered inhumane, in most of the United States and even parts of Africa, but not in Ontario. Fair game. Mostly we talked about the real culprits, the office-insulated park and wildlife officials whom we had informed about the inordinate amount of killing but who refused to act.

The next day Graham located Jocko 2 from the air four kilometres from the snare site, and that night we heard his signal from a road nearby. Mary howled, and sure enough he was with his pack. They gave us a serenade of joy, or at least that is how we interpreted it.

We could not find Jocko 2 at the beginning of the spring field season and speculated that he may not have survived the winter. But the following January he showed up with his pack in the deer yard again. We tracked him to the carcass of a big buck out behind a farmer's barn. He was on the air until early March when either his collar failed or he was killed. He had lived at least another full year; that was worthwhile.

We lost 55 per cent of the wolf population that winter, all but one to human killing. Between 1988 and 1993, the wolf population on the east side of Algonquin Park had dropped 43 per cent. Lost were entire packs: Travers, Grand Lake East, Grand Lake West, Foys Lake, McDonald Creek. Where they had lived, there were now only gaping, wolfless holes.

BUREAUCRATS, BIOPOLITICS, AND THE WOLF-KILLING BAN

NOT ONLY data accumulate in any good study, so does animosity. Although not as neatly recorded on data sheets or organized in computer files, ill will invariably piles up like manure in a barnyard. If it doesn't, you are not addressing real environmental issues. Somebody or some department, division, branch, or organization always has a vested interest in keeping things the way they are.

While it seems noble to attempt compromise with those who hold different opinions, often beneath the surface are totally different world views, different perspectives on the central purpose of nature. Are we owners or tenants, proprietors or lessees?

Early in the research we aroused the hostility of the Ontario Federation of Anglers and Hunters (OFAH). We did not intend to; after all, many of its members champion the outdoors and some are sensitive to nature. As well, we struck the tender nerve endings of some tourist operators who cater to non-Canadian hunters coming here to live out their frontier fantasy.

People who kill wildlife for sport, meat, profit, ego enhancement, or hate have almost all of Canada to do it in. While there

ON THE MOVE
Above: The Jack Pine pack, March 1998.
(Photo by Michelle Theberge)

WOLF PREY

Above left: White-tailed deer are the preferred prey species of Algonquin wolves.

Above right: Moose are hunted successfully by Algonquin wolves in all seasons.

Below: Michelle examines a moose carcass, February 1998. Two different packs, both trespassing, fed on this moose within one day.

Top: Colin Fabian digs into the ice to recover the femur of a moose that froze into a lake and was being fed upon by the Zigzag Lake pack.
Above: John drags a deer kill off thin ice covering Basin Lake.

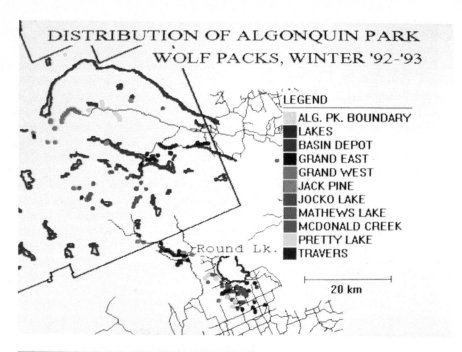

DISTRIBUTION OF ALGONQUIN PARK WOLF PACKS, WINTER '92-'93

LEGEND

ALG. PK. BOUNDARY
LAKES
BASIN DEPOT
GRAND EAST
GRAND WEST
JACK PINE
JOCKO LAKE
MATHEWS LAKE
MCDONALD CREEK
PRETTY LAKE
TRAVERS

Round Lk.

20 km

Above: Typical winter distribution showing wolf migration outside park. We make computer-generated maps like this on a regular basis.
Left: Tracks in the snow on Feely Lake, made by the trespassing Pretty Lake pack, lead to a deer carcass, December 1991.

THE DEER YARD

Above: Farm near Round Lake, immediately southeast of Algonquin Park, where deer and wolves migrate each winter.

Below: Local residents frequently put out food for deer in winter, a practice no longer favoured by the Ministry of Natural Resources.

Above left: McDonald 4, killed in
defiance of the wolf-killing ban, in March 1994.
This act of violence marked a turning point in
community attitudes.

Top right: Jocko 8, killed by strychnine poison
just outside the town of Round Lake Centre,
February 1996.

Above right: Jocko 2, found alive in a snare and
successfully released, March 1993.

Above: Not all wolf deaths are caused by humans:
Foys 3 dead from rabies in March 1991.
Below: Grand Lake 5, Travers 5, and another wolf
snared near Round Lake in the "winter of death,"
1992–93.

Above: Camp among the red pines.

may be justifiable debate about whether people living in an urban society should be killing wildlife, there can be no argument about this imbalance. Almost all provincial, federal, and territorial Crown land is open to hunting and trapping, and that makes up more than 80 per cent of Canada. Wilderness parks, in contrast, encompass less than 6 per cent, far less than in many other countries of the world, far below the internationally accepted target of 12 per cent. Even much of Canada's "protected" land is hunted, including more than half the national parks. Game laws do not reflect public attitudes nearly as well as they do an exploitive past and inertia.

We attracted public attention in the fall of 1988 and again in the spring of 1989 because of the Little Branch wolves, one snared inside the park and left to rot, the other shot by a bear hunter from a tree stand just outside the park. After Graham met with the chief conservation officer, showing him photos of the dangling neck snare and the pile of wolf fur beneath it, the MNR felt obligated to comply with its own policies, which forbid wolf trapping and snaring inside the park. This development was not well received by local trappers. Nor were Graham's comments to a large public meeting in Toronto in June 1990. He said that so many park wolves were being killed outside the boundaries of the park that a buffer "no-kill" zone for wolves might be necessary if such deaths were to be prevented. Significantly, as it turned out later, the MNR's Algonquin regional director, Al Stewart, was in the audience.

These two events caused a flurry of correspondence within the MNR that was leaked to us later. Confidential correspondence in a government file can be like a time bomb waiting to explode.

Jack O'Dette, a secretary treasurer of the OFAH, wrote to Algonquin Park superintendent Ernie Martelle, with a scattering of carbon copies, on September 4, 1990: "The work of Dr. John Theberge and his wife with some assistance from Graham Forbes was not well planned and probably would not stand up to good scientific analysis and as such would have limited value. It was also our understanding that there was the possibility of a seven mile buffer zone being requested around the park. We know of Theberge's anti-use leanings and would suspect that this might just be an attempt to expand the no-hunting or no-trapping zones and we would strongly object to this."

In reply, to his credit, Martelle explained that no one had approached him about a buffer zone, but that "if in the future my staff biologists determined that the wolf packs were in trouble in that part of the District outside Algonquin Park and needed protection we would take the moves necessary to protect them as we would any other species." He added, ironically, "I'm sure your organization would support such a move," then, "One of the purposes of Theberges' research is to hopefully educate people about wolves and their role in the ecosystem."

Taking a lead from its parent organization, the president of the Whitney Fish and Game Club, Doug Harper, wrote to Al Stewart, referring to "the questionable conclusions of a study on wolves in Algonquin that led to the end of trapping in the southern part of the park," and, he went on, "there does not seem to be a scientific balance to the harvest of renewable resources viewpoint expressed by Graham Forbes." Then Harper, whom we have never met, disconnected his brain from his pen and wrote: "It appears to be quite possible, even likely, that 'research' information is being massaged to support the pre-determined personal viewpoints of these government funded anti-use advocates." Like O'Dette's letter, carbon copies were distributed within the MNR, making both of these letters dangerously libellous. Again, a copy was leaked to us.

There are some who say with good reason that the OFAH exerts an overrepresentative influence on MNR wildlife policy, even though less than 10 per cent of Ontario residents of hunting age actually hunt. So, these letters were disturbing. Al Stewart, instead of objecting to this sort of letter, wrote an appeasing reply. He stated that the MNR had just put our research under review, and that had led to "total restructuring of Mr. Theberge's and Mr. Forbes' wolf research activities. The new experimental design will focus on two discreet pack territories. . . ."

It was true. Only a month after Graham's public address in which he made his comment about a buffer wolf protection zone,

Mary and I were out of the park one day for gas when we received a note from the MNR asking for a meeting. We had no idea why. Innocently, we did not make the connection with Graham's presentation. We closed up our field work and drove to Huntsville.

It was a hot summer day, and the windowless MNR boardroom was stuffy. Brought in from the research branch was the MNR's wolf biologist, George Kolenosky, who had stopped field work on wolves and switched to black bears many years before. Selected members of regional and district staff were also present. Only a few minutes into the meeting, we realized that we were under attack. Kolenosky affronted us by advising us to get on snowshoes and track the wolves, as if we never had. Director Al Stewart shocked us with the statement that one condition of our continuance was that we stop causing the MNR problems. He must have been thinking about the hemlock embarrassment and the unenforced trapping ban in the southern part of the park. He made it clear that our funding would be withdrawn if we did not immediately refocus our research to study just two packs. His viewpoint was seconded by all the MNR officials present. They were not bothered by our objections that doing so would destroy the design of Graham's Ph.D. research based upon a comparison of packs with and without deer throughout the park, with its two years of field work already complete. They gave us a week to change everything. We had no choice but to drive home to Waterloo and do it.

In retrospect, their motive was transparent, but at the time we were mystified. We had not yet seen the letters. By studying only two packs, we would have no data on the wolf population as a whole that could be used to comment upon the adequacy or inadequacy of the park to protect wolves.

We remembered Doug Pimlott's prediction years before when he handed us the wolf research. He told us that "they will throw endless barriers in your way." His prophecy was coming true. We were learning that although some MNR people supported our research, others, in particular the politically sensitive senior managers, were looking at us askance for raising difficult issues. Issue-avoiders rather than issue-solvers often taint government departments, especially at senior levels. These are people who see their job primarily as "protecting their minister." Wolf management invariably becomes a hot political issue that many politicians, and therefore senior managers, would just as soon avoid. Better to get rid of the individuals raising the problems than to solve them.

MNR personnel were familiar with our research because we had to apply for an annual permit. They also knew it because we made the unfortunate tactical mistake in those early years of offering to do research cooperatively. Perpetually short of money, we applied to a government-funded program for university research called the Ontario Renewable Resource Research Grant (ORRRG) and were successful for a while. The government, however, acted as if its contribution to our research, which is largely funded by World Wildlife Fund Canada, implied control.

So, over the course of a few frustrating, hot summer days we sat on our deck at home and rewrote a research outline to focus on two packs. MNR biologist Dennis Voigt provided telephone guidance. When completed, the MNR approved of our now-innocuous research – "good science" – and we drove back to the park. The time lost in the field had cost us some important continuity in our data.

After the meeting in Huntsville, we became an excuse for a couple of delegated watchdogs to get out of the office periodically "on inspection." Our student crews were visited in the field by these people who were seemingly just passing through, although often our camps were remote, not in the sort of places you get to just by chance.

There were more meetings, never as openly hostile as the first but obviously intended to find some reason to discredit our data or us. We even learned of a mid-level employee in the Huntsville office who was told that "we have been trying to close them down for three years" and then was directed to "try to get something on them." Instead of complying, he told a member of our research group.

By then the script was becoming obvious, and MNR senior managers played it out without flaw. Confrontations such as this between researchers and bureaucrats occur often enough that they are discussed and joked about in a bitter way in university faculty lounges across the continent. They represent government's usual reaction to those whose research points to needed but politically difficult changes in policy. Knowing the expected train of events removed any element of surprise. In the first act, research objectives are questioned and criticized as either not worthwhile or not justifying the funds. In the next act, the researchers typically find themselves faced with a mountain of administrative trivia, followed by threats of closure for non-compliance over a host of minor logistic procedures. The third act features efforts to refute the research findings. The bureaucrats raise technical issues related to sample sizes, research design, and related topics. The last act, in plays that go on that long, is the dramatic finale: attempts are made to discredit the researchers themselves.

I know of a university scientist whose career in Ontario was ruined because he was among the first to find compelling evidence that acid rain was a serious problem. At a large gathering of scientists a decade later, the Environment Minister publicly acknowledged both the problem and the attempted, and for a long time successful, cover-up.

After the first winter of death, 1990–91, the need for a buffer zone to protect wolves outside the park became even more apparent. As we published technical papers and wrote memos for the MNR documenting the increasing wolf deaths, we sensed the MNR's heightening determination to thwart us. Some of our friends in the MNR, field people who were interested in Algonquin Park, began to keep their distance.

The following summer and fall, Mary contracted a serious illness that for a time caused us to put aside any thoughts about research. She ate an improperly cooked hamburger at a fast-food outlet the day we began our 1991 summer field work and consequently spent six weeks in an Ottawa hospital, two of them in intensive care. "Hamburger disease" is fatal in many cases and causes permanent kidney failure in most others. Taken by ambulance at top speed to Ottawa, she had a very close brush with both.

In the Ottawa hospital, as she recovered, we had many long days and evenings to reflect on the situation: people were killing park wolves, the government was refusing to stop them and, worse, appeared to be intent on avoiding the problem by getting rid of us. For a time we thought about closing up, going part-time at the university, and taking trips to see the wildlife spectacles of the world. We resolved to see the migrating wildebeests and their interactions with the big cats in Kenya, the wintering masses of monarch butterflies in the highlands of central Mexico, the humpback whales in the Bay of Fundy, the harp seals on sea-ice off Prince Edward Island, the muskoxen of the western high arctic, and the steaming tropical rain forests of Costa Rica.

We have acted on that resolve. The periodic trips to far-off places have provided necessary release from the increasingly frustrating aspects of our research. But after coming so close to the end, we viewed the research in a new light, as one of the best wildlife studies anywhere.

In late August we drove back to the park with renewed respect and love for its wildness and new dedication not to let the MNR beat us. Mary was still too weak to hike, so we just camped in a few favourite places and bathed a few nights in the howls of our radio-collared packs – Jack Pine and Basin Depot.

Then came the second winter of wolf deaths, not as severe, but following the same pattern of deer and wolf migration and vulnerability. By spring we were willing to face whatever the MNR dealt us to end the wolf killing. Graham had collected sufficient data for his Ph.D. and we had protected him long enough. While we had complied with the MNR and redesigned our research to study two packs, we had made that only a minor add-on. The entire study had continued with only minor modification, as before. My university obligation did not allow me to be manipulated into abandoning a Ph.D. student with an approved research design partway through his degree.

In the summer of 1992, we were camped north of Basin Lake when Monte Hummel, president of World Wildlife Fund Canada, and his wife, Sherry Pettigrew, came to visit. They came each summer, partly to be sure WWF research dollars were being wisely spent but more because they wanted to get away from the city to the park and its wolves. They have been two solid supporters, buoying us up at crucial times. Monte is universally cheerful.

For most of their visit we sat in the truck and watched it rain. Their trip was turning into a disaster. In hopes of salvaging it, we proposed an afternoon and night canoe trip down the chain of Turcotte, Guthrie, and Clover lakes to see which of two packs was using an interface area there. At the portage, as we unloaded the canoes in the downpour, Sherry asked if we would be doing this even if they were not there. "Oh sure," Mary replied with obvious overenthusiasm. We started off, hoping the rain might eventually stop and we would be rewarded by hearing a signal or a pack howl after dark. Instead, the sky stayed grey from horizon to horizon, without a break. At Clover Lake we built a huge pine-stump bonfire to ward off hypothermia and huddled around it. Finally in a premature dusk, we climbed into the canoes and paddled back, rain in our face the whole way.

At our campsite, the more we talked the more we realized that our efforts to reason things out in meetings with the MNR had failed. It was time to open the issue up for wider public scrutiny. Conservation victories are won out in the open with public exposure. It has always been that way; in a democracy, it should be.

We also talked of the added danger that going public posed to our research. There is a shameful history of university or independent scientists being closed down by governments over their public opposition to existing policy or recommended change. I think of the pioneering grizzly bear researchers of Yellowstone National Park; the biologist who conducted the first major North American study of wolves, in Alaska's Denali National Park; a biologist who watched a government research team move in and begin studying the same packs he was already studying; all suffered a similar fate. Then, right at home, Doug Pimlott was closed out of Algonquin Park by the same government that now was trying to do the same to us.

We knew the Pimlott story well. Doug believed that attitudes about wolves would change only if he tackled them in public. By doing so he raised debate over government policy. Doug also

repeatedly, publicly criticized the government over its misman-
agement of parks. One day, without any warning, he was advised
that he could work in Algonquin no longer. At the time he had
a master's student halfway through his field work. The president
of the University of Toronto, where Doug worked, wrote the
premier of Ontario that the government had no right to interfere
with university research and gave the premier a deadline to change
the decision by midnight on a certain date. At 11 P.M. on that day,
Doug received a telephone call and was granted permission to continue. He predicted, however, that endless roadblocks would be
thrown in his way. So he decided to move on to other things and
handed the Algonquin research over to us.

Our intent was to give broad public exposure to the excessive
killing of park wolves and the failure of the MNR to live up to its
own wildlife and park conservation mandate. A ban was needed on
wolf killing in the townships adjacent to the park. We hoped that
public criticism would be more effective than our attempts at reasoning with MNR officials, and that the minister would be embarrassed into taking action.

We began late in the summer of 1992 with a request to talk
with the MNR staff in Pembroke. To a room unexpectedly full of
people, Mary and I explained our data and advised that we were
going to the public with it. Later, in a leaked confidential memo,
district manager Ray Bonenberg reported our intentions to director Al Stewart. In his conclusion, Bonenberg swung his support
behind us: "We support in principle that society should not be
hunting down and killing an excessive number of wolves due to
cultural or social biases." He had been superintendent of another
large provincial park and understood the validity of wildlife protection. Without his decision to support us, we may have accomplished little.

It was a good start, but our hopes for a quick success were dashed
when we advised MNR head office in Toronto of our plans. Chief
of wildlife, Jim MacLean, inhabited a typical glass tower in north
Toronto. He knew all about the issue and us, but explained that he
could not do anything because MNR biologists – George Kolenosky

and Dennis Voigt from the research branch and Algonquin Park's chief interpreter, Dan Strickland – were saying that additional protection for park wolves was unnecessary.

They claimed that we had not documented a decline in the wolf population. They ignored the evidence in the scientific literature that the level of annual mortality we were finding clearly is not sustainable by wolf populations. They stated that the wolves had been migrating out of the park for many years and the population had managed to survive, ignoring Doug Pimlott's evidence collected in the 1960s to the contrary. They said that it does not matter if park wolves are killed by humans because a certain number have to die anyway. They paid no attention to our appeal to consider the fractured social system we were documenting.

We are by no means alone in insisting that wolves and other social carnivores are much more than numbers. Wolf packs are ecological teams; individuals play different roles; skills develop through experience. Alaskan biologist Gordon Haber has argued that the loss of particular individuals, especially the experienced elders in a pack, is equivalent to a basketball team trading away its stars because it can recruit just as many rookies from the minors to replace them and so keep the team the same size. Fitness in a wolf population depends upon the persistence of its social order, and that is impaired when experienced elders are lost.

We asked Jim MacLean to consider the possibility that he was being given poor advice and to respond officially to our upcoming press release. He said that we would hear from him within ten days. Seven months later we were still waiting. We waited all through the third winter of death, 1992–93, through the loss of the Travers, Grand Lake East, Grand Lake West, and McDonald Creek packs. As we picked up dead wolves week after week, we saw the faces of these men, who to our way of thinking were as much responsible for killing those Algonquin Park wolves as the individuals who set the snares.

On September 15, 1992, a few days after the MacLean meeting, Graham, Mary, and I drove up from Waterloo, and Monte came from Toronto, to address the Hagarty-Richards Township Council.

These townships make up most of the Round Lake deer yard. Because we booked this meeting well in advance, we expected a room packed with people, but only the council and one visitor were there. We also had offered to address the Barry's Bay Rod and Gun Club, but its president wrote back that "the membership feels that no useful purpose would be served by your attendance." Later, we were castigated in the media for not consulting with local people.

The council members listened politely to our presentation. After we finished, the mayor explained that she and others feared to let their children out of the house because there were so many wolves around. One councillor asked a familiar question: "What good is a wolf anyway?" The meeting adjourned and we knew we had accomplished nothing.

Monte headed back to Toronto, and Mary and I drove into the park to collect scats in a rendezvous site used a few weeks before. We put our tent up in the headlights of the truck. The next day among the flaming red maples and yellow poplars, we mulled over the gulf between the two world views and talked about how you can ever answer a question such as the one put to us so often: "What good is a wolf?"

The WWF press release came out three days later. It called for an "upgrade of provincial wolf conservation policies, as Ontario still allows wolves to be killed all year round with no limit, and with no reporting of the number killed." The release drew attention to the unwarranted killing of Algonquin wolves. It received a modest flurry of media attention, but did not usurp as much space from the usual topics in the front sections of newspapers as we later would.

Still, we waited for an MNR response, all the time picking up dead wolves, our anger mounting. The director of parks, Norm Richards, who should have been concerned, declined to answer our letters. Dan Strickland wrote a defence for doing nothing in the Barry's Bay newspaper, emphasizing that because many pups are born every year, many adult wolves have to die anyway. Renfrew County petitioned the Minister of Natural Resources for permission to reinstate the bounty that was lifted in Ontario in 1972.

Finally on March 22, 1993, wildlife chief Jim MacLean responded with good news and bad. Good was that the MNR intended to grant our first request, a review and revision of provincial wolf-management policy. That was easy for him to do. Such reviews often are used to shield inertia. They can, and this one did, drag on for years. Today, more than five years later, the completed review is still "at the printers." The bad news was that "I do not foresee a closure of wolf hunting or trapping in the Round Lake and Whitney areas as you request."

Monte answered that "I'm afraid your response has not met our concerns. . . ." Mary and I replied, "You are violating your wildlife management policy, your parks policy, your general purpose MNR statement. And for what possible reason – to support a wanton slaughter of animals? Why do you back these people and what they are doing? We were patient to the extreme to wait six months for you to answer our last letter, all the while picking up dead wolves as a result of your inaction."

We accompanied our letter with a "Report on Extensive Movements and Mortality of Algonquin Park Wolves, Winter 1992-93" to give the MNR an opportunity to reconsider. Then we prepared a more headline-catching media release describing the killing and MNR indifference, and contacted members of the provincial Opposition party to arrange for the minister to be questioned in the legislature.

Then, unexpectedly, the MNR phoned to request a meeting in Huntsville. We complied, ready for yet another confrontation, our adrenalin levels high. Director Al Stewart was absent, though the meeting was held in the room next to his office. We wondered why. Only later did we find out that because the outcome of the meeting had been pre-determined, he did not need to come.

Again we presented graphs, showed slides, explained our results. When we stopped talking, in contrast to every other meeting with MNR officials, we were not immediately put on the defensive. On the contrary, we watched in amazement while the MNR people nodded in accord. They said they should do something to stop this killing, as if they had never known about it before. They discussed among themselves various strategies including appealing to local people or drafting a new game regulation, and decided on the latter. Then they turned to us and asked directly, "What is your bottom line?" We had to think fast, and replied that we wanted closure to wolf hunting and trapping in Hagarty, Richard, and Burns townships while the Algonquin Park wolves normally use that area, December 15 until March 31. To our complete amazement, they agreed.

Although their decision was made for immediate reasons, it had broad, even international, significance. The scientific literature in conservation biology is full of examples of the need to do a better job protecting large carnivores in all large parks, worldwide. Transboundary movement and killing are global problems, not just for wolves, but for wild dogs, lions, tigers, cheetahs, grizzlies. As human populations make increasing demands on the available space, and parks become isolated fragments of nature in a sea of urbanization and agriculture, without added protection these species will lose ground even in parks.

Yet nowhere that I know of, certainly not in North America, has any government extended special protection for a park population of carnivores beyond park borders. The three-township success may seem small, but it is huge – precedent setting.

We speculated about what had happened to cause this unexpected turn of events and, with time, pieced together the answer. At the meeting were two MNR people strong enough to operate from their own convictions. John Johnson, MNR area manager for the townships in question, had made up his mind that he would not accept the mindless slaughter of any species in the area where he was in charge of wildlife management. It was a courageous decision. Ray Bonenberg, his supervisor, backed him. When people like them with a high level of integrity act on their convictions, governments do things right.

But what had caused this sudden about-face only two weeks after Jim MacLean had written that the MNR would not act? In due time, another leaked memo provided the answer. It was written by director Al Stewart to an internal "Distribution List," and it read: "We are receiving a number of signals that John Theberge is gearing up for a major press conference around wolves. . . . Most of his claims are accurate and we are vulnerable. Everywhere the wolf thing raises its head anywhere in Canada or the U.S. it becomes a major issue. . . . We need to ban trapping these creatures (at least around Algonquin Park). It will upset some rural municipalities, but for the most part there is no farming bordering the Park, the pelts have no value, and there is certainly no shortage of natural prey species. We will prepare a note as soon as possible to get this proposal into the system."

The decision to protect wolves, in other words, had been made even before the meeting. Anyway, we had accomplished partial protection outside the park, so at the time we did not care how it happened.

As weeks went on, however, despite our success, the more we thought about the meeting, the more we felt that we had been manipulated into giving them a "bottom line," the minimum area to protect. Al Stewart's memo indicated that the MNR had been prepared to protect wolves all the way around the park. Our mortality data were most convincing for those three townships, but even back then, many wolves had been killed elsewhere. By 1998, just as many wolves have died in other townships, and those numbers continue to mount. We especially regret not having included Airy Township, with the town of Whitney in it, to prevent the MNR's own employees from ever again slaughtering the East Gate pack. Airy Township was a poignant omission too, when the following winter a trapper snared Annie Bay 3 and a wolf travelling with her. When we went to pick up their carcasses, we felt like we had betrayed them. It was also a mistake not to include Alice and Fraser townships near Pembroke, and we can only say sorry to Mathews 7, who went missing there, and Mathews 8, who died a bloody mess all over the snow in a neck snare. It was a mistake not to include all the townships around the park: sorry to Basin 7 – shot; McDonald Creek 6 – shot; Pretty 8 – shot; Travers 7 – shot. However, all we can say is that we were taken off guard, and the wolf deaths in the winter deer yard provided our most convincing numerical data. We intend to rectify that.

The ban order was written as an amendment to the game regulations in the Huntsville office of the MNR and was to be sent to Toronto for Minister Howard Hampton's signature. It was early December and the order needed to be signed by December 15 to go into force that year. Just before the deadline, somewhere between Huntsville and Toronto, the order "got lost," as it was explained to me over the telephone. Nobody could do anything about it. Very unfortunate. Sorry.

I telephoned an ally who worked as an adviser in the minister's office. "Don't worry," he said. "I'll see that the minister signs it."

He did.

WINTER OF HATE

Just the thought of wolves works an evil alchemy in the minds of some people that penetrates deeply into the psyche, locks on to hidden fears and frustrations, and magnifies emotion. Maybe subliminally we remember when the competition was more equal, ancient struggles before humans took command. Maybe because we do not condone overt racial discrimination, some people need something to master and condemn.

Perhaps it is simpler than that. A hunter goes hunting for moose or deer and comes back empty-handed. A farmer loses a sheep – or worries that his flock is in danger. Parents raised on fairy tales and myths fear for the safety of their children. All blame wolves. Whatever the reason, the wolf-killing ban did not bring out the best in many people living in the Round Lake area. If the wolf holds up a mirror, what it reflected was ugly.

Consider these headlines from local newspapers such as the Eganville *Leader*, Barry's Bay *This Week*, and the Pembroke *Observer*:

"Wolves Spark Feud In Ontario Park."

"Big Bad Wolf."

"Wolf Killing Ban Annoys Council."

"Residents Angry Over Ban On Wolf Trapping And Hunting In Local Townships."

"Wolves Mangle Deer In Residential Area."

"Something Has To Be Done About The Wolf Ban."

"Tell Us The Whole Story, Professor Theberge."

The writers of these newspaper articles expressed frustration over outsiders "telling local people what they can and cannot do." Local Member of the Provincial Parliament Sean Conway encouraged this complaint at a meeting of the Barry's Bay Fish and Game Club, where he was quoted saying, "You elect me, you don't elect John Theberge to make decisions and I am, quite frankly, just getting more and more ticked off." And, he continued, "the minister and his senior advisers accepted the advice of Dr. Theberge without any input from anyone else, particularly people familiar with the wildlife situation in the Round Lake area. Part of my frustration in this particular issue is that Dr. Theberge isn't here."

The club's president obviously had not told Mr. Conway that he had turned down our offer to make a presentation. Conway, an Opposition party member, went on to criticize the government for its continual interference with local people. Other examples he gave included the proposed new wilderness zone for the east side of Algonquin Park, and the nearby Madawaska Highlands Land Use Plan that threatened to restrict what people could do on their own land. He could have cited other issues that were receiving media coverage in his riding, such as the unpopular pickerel quotas, or the proposed regulations that would require woodlot owners to employ the services of a government tree marker before they logged their land. The wolf-killing ban, he said, was the last straw. The club presented him with a thousand-name petition against the ban.

Some students of democracy say that the current shift to decentralized decision-making and power to the local people has its strong points, that it provides a greater sense of control, and that is an important antidote to alienation in our increasingly globalized world. Any apparent gains at the local level, however, may be offset by losses at the provincial or national levels in being able to act on broadly held standards or ideals that may be embodied, for example, in a system of parks or wildlife preserves. Can local people be expected to make decisions that they do not perceive as immediately good for them or that restrict their freedoms, in the interests of broader societal objectives?

The MNR made a tactical decision: they chose public explanation over public consultation. The public goes to meetings labelled consultation in the expectation that their opinions will be weighed into the outcome. Explanation, however, is based upon a decision that has already been made. Explanation is normally the route followed for annual changes in game regulations.

In the weeks before the ban, MNR officials met with township councils and local people to explain the decision. The combined townships of Sherwood, Jones, and Burns immediately wrote the minister complaining that the decision was based on only one researcher's results and therefore was invalid. They petitioned the MNR to remove the ban, based on the prediction "that there will be a total decimation of the deer population in this area and possibly a dramatic increase in the loss of livestock due to wolves." I was sent a copy of the petition and asked to attend the next meeting "to enlighten us on your studies of wolves in Algonquin Park." The council apparently did not recognize the transparency of its motives by acting first and requesting information later. They wanted an argument, not information, so I declined.

Most vitriolic was one large public gathering at Round Lake ironically held in the basement of the Catholic church. Area manager John Johnson thought it was best that we not attend, thinking that our presence would only provoke greater controversy. Instead, he asked us for a set of slides and graphs of our data. To some extent, government officials are experienced at taking public abuse, and at that meeting they took a lot. One member of the audience asked what the MNR would do if they caught somebody breaking the law. When John answered that they would charge him, the person responded that he was going to do it anyway. The crowd applauded. One person was quoted saying, "If I see a wolf, I'll squeeze the trigger, because I didn't get to shoot a deer this year."

Another person pleased the audience by saying, "I'll tell you right now, any that I see I'll kill them. You can charge me, you can do anything."

It was just the kind of public meeting that has characterized wolf conservation efforts everywhere – Alaska, British Columbia, Yukon, Montana, Wyoming, North Carolina. Supporters of wolf conservation in all those places have the same stories to tell. They hear the same arguments against the wolf, the same refusals to obey the law, the same out-of-control anger.

In Pembroke, John Johnson faced another loud and abusive crowd, and after that he encountered a hostile Alice and Fraser Township Council. Through it all, he maintained that wasted and useless killing of wolves was unacceptable in his jurisdiction. He explained at these meetings that even he had taken part in wolf-control programs in the past, but times and attitudes had changed, and the viability of a park wolf population, not just any wolves, was at stake. The public criticism bothered him though, as it did us. Later, however, in summarizing his experiences, John staunchly retorted, "That's my job," and left it at that. He deserves much praise. Supporting him and present at all the meetings was his supervisor, Ray Bonenberg.

Oblivious to the storm of controversy around them, the wolves went about their biological business. December 1993 was mild with little snow. The deer drifted more slowly than usual towards their Round Lake wintering area, hanging back on oak ridges along the way. That was the year of a bumper acorn crop; never had we seen anything like it. Walking down an oak slope was like walking on ball bearings. Deer pawed for acorns as the snow became deeper and bedded among the high oaks. There they had the advantages not only of food, but of detecting wolves more easily and running from them downhill.

For a while most of the wolf packs stayed on territory hunting the deer that remained. One wolf from the Jocko Lake pack made a foray down to the edge of the deer yard, possibly to check out the prey situation there, and returned. The Basin Depot pack killed a deer on Basin Lake, where they shared it with a red fox and a bald eagle. We watched for some long, cold hours at daybreak from our truck parked in the pines nearby.

Soon the Jocko Lake pack came out of the park, but instead of entering the yard as in the previous year, it remained in the snowy hills on the periphery with the deer. The single remaining McDonald Creek female, having dispersed to the Grand West territory during the summer, came down with two other wolves and killed a big deer at the edge of a bog.

By early January, the time-tested deer trails were grooved with fresh tracks. While many deer entered the core of the yard, others stayed back, still feeding on acorns. Local people, seeing fewer deer around their houses, were quoted in the newspapers as saying that the deer population had crashed and the wolf ban was to blame. Conservation officer Blake Simpson spent a day with us back in the park where we knew there were still plenty of deer, so in his dealings with the local people he would have some observations to counter their speculation.

We were beset by newspaper reporters attracted by the demonstrative people speaking out against us in local newspapers. We prepared a full explanation of our research results showing the need for the ban, and it was featured in the Eganville *Leader*. Instead of setting the record straight, our article fuelled more controversy, eliciting heated comments about bleeding-heart environmentalists and our failure to "get the facts straight." The "facts" included such things as the increased danger to human safety, and a belief that in one year there would be "no more deer." In a frightening miscalculation, a local medical doctor and long-time anti-wolf advocate explained that "a timber wolf in captivity will devour one deer a week." In fact, this is a metabolic impossibility: a wolf that maintained that level of consumption – more than 6.8 kilograms (15 pounds) a day – over a period of weeks would be in danger of exploding. Wild wolves normally consume between one-third and one-half that amount.

Occasionally we would see a newspaper letter expressing support: "If I went outside on a cold, clear winter night knowing I would never again hear a wolf howl, it would make the world for me a lesser place to live"; "Canada's wolves deserve better"; and "live and let live." A nearby township, North Algona, even went on record as supporting the ban. One councillor said, "A lot of wolves are blamed for things they do not do" and "I'd like to see them do more study."

When Brian McAndrew, the environmental reporter for the *Toronto Star*, phoned us, we saw a chance to explain the need for the ban to a larger audience, so we agreed to a three-day visit along with photographer Dick Loek. Some people who spend time with us luck into good wolf experiences, others come away with a blank. Brian and Dick were lucky. The first morning we tracked Basin 9 McDonald to a ten-point buck with the largest antlers we had seen. Its remains lay scattered under a big balsam fir where tree limbs had been broken during its final struggle. Later that day we tracked the Jocko Lake pack across LaFleur Lake into a tangle of alders where they had also killed a ten-point buck. While we were photographing the kill, two or three wolves howled from down the lake, their serenade softened by the wind. The next day we located the Mathews Lake wolves on a half-consumed deer in a little clearing close to a concession road.

Dick was keen to set up a blind to photograph the Mathews Lake wolves, so we strung up two large, blue plastic tarps on a knoll in the conifers about thirty metres from the carcass. Behind the tarps we put a deck chair for Dick to sit on with his big 600-mm lens sticking out. At 5:30 A.M. on a blistering cold morning, we drove to the concession road and walked quietly by flashlight to the blind. There we sat, Mary and I on our knees in the snow, while first our hands and feet, then our legs and arms grew numb. Our face muscles stiffened, and our blood seemed to congeal. Unprotected from any wolf eyes behind or to the side of us, we could not make a move.

Ever so slowly daylight roughed out the fir trees and outlined the clearing. The carcass had been dragged a few metres during the night, but no wolves were visible. One or two blue jays called as they flew over. A few ravens, unsure about making a final descent, circled before settling into the trees. After a while the first rays of sunlight struck the treetops and inched their way down, missing us with their weak warmth. Just when the sunlight reached the clearing and illuminated the carcass, a wolf stepped out from the shadows. Head up, scenting the air, it walked directly to the carcass. Dick hunched over his Nikon camera, then swore softly. The shutter was frozen. Like any good photographer though, he had a second camera in a bag at his feet. He twisted the camera off the tripod, and suddenly the telephoto lens fell forward, rustling the crisp plastic tarp. The wolf looked up and was gone.

Reporter Kelly Egan and photographer Wayne Cunningham of the *Ottawa Citizen* spent a cold, sunny day with us radio-tracking a Vireo Lake wolf. The subsequent article and a colour photograph appeared on the front page of the *Citizen* with the headline "The Rising Howl Over Wolves."

These articles were generally well received. There was some counter-argument in local newspapers, such as, "He's supposed to be a professor of some kind but I wouldn't send my child to him."

Pretty 4, a yearling female, seemed to live a charmed life, bent, as she appeared to be, on testing the wolf-killing ban. Unlike the Jocko Lake pack, the Pretty Lake pack wandered widely throughout the deer yard during the last half of the winter. We tracked them by day as they walked ahead of us on concession roads and listened to their howls at night. Most unwise was their use of Joe Mask's property. Joy and her assistant, Andrew Hawke, got cross-bearings on Pretty 4 and asked Joe for permission to track her. Joe refused, saying, "There's no place for wolves on my land."

We were surprised by his reaction, remembering the apparent softening in his attitude the winter before, so Mary and I drove to his farm. Mrs. Mask answered the door and invited us into the kitchen. Joe appeared, hesitated when he saw us, and, without offering his hand, asked us what we wanted. His eyes hardened and we knew our hopes for him had been wrong. We made our request and suggested he accompany us, but he refused and started in about wolves being no good and that he killed them in the past and always would. Mary pointed out that we were only trying to learn what the wolves are doing, so people have some facts to go on. We explained that we were trying to find out the condition of the deer they killed, but he said, "The fewer wolves and the farther away the better" and "We don't want any university professors around here." He went on to say that it was the intention of local people to stop our research. This was a reference to a campaign mentioned in a newspaper spearheaded by a local logger to get enough no-trespassing signs up that we would be stymied. Mrs. Mask asked and answered the familiar question, "What good is a wolf anyway? They're no good to anybody."

It was useless. Neither facts nor reason were relevant. Their minds were closed. Joe was almost speechless as we left. He mumbled, "They're no good. I'll kill them. No good." His eyes glistened with the fervour of hate.

After that day, Pretty 4's signal was never heard again.

At a sideroad one snowy day, we were getting a bearing on a collared wolf when a short, round-faced man drove up in a Jeep. He got out, aware of what we were doing, and was quick to make his opinions known. He had no use for wolves or for us. In an aggressive manner he explained how he had seen wolves get into a bunch of deer and kill the whole lot and just leave. When I asked where and when that had happened, he responded, "Oh, over in Quebec a few years ago." This observation served as convincing evidence that wolves are wanton killers, whether accurate in itself or not. I asked him how often he had seen this sort of thing, and rather than answer he began to raise his voice. Mary tried to explain that what he saw was an extremely rare event, but he got more and more worked up, so finally we got back in the truck and drove away. During the exchange he had revealed that he was a retired schoolteacher, a frightening admission considering the way his emotions overrode any ability to weight evidence.

Friends of the Wolf is an activist organization with chapters in Ontario, British Columbia, and the Yukon whose volunteers, according to its newsletter, "have logged thousands of unpaid hours, travelled thousands of kilometres, and faced very real danger in defence of the Wolf Nation. Arrests, death-threats, job-loss, frost-bite, and the glare of publicity are all part of the job description." For its members, civil disobedience is a legitimate weapon for policy change. It brings assured media attention and at times is effective. But daily, international news portrays the consequence of not abiding by laws, so, despite our appreciation for the organization's concern over the plight of Algonquin wolves, we distanced ourselves from it.

The public perception did not notice the distance. Anybody who speaks for the wolf is, as a township reeve told me, "a wolf lover or a Greenpeace guy." So when Friends of the Wolf angered local people, we were blamed. Anger them it did with a flyer posted on bulletin boards in grocery stores, nailed up on telephone poles, and put in rural mailboxes. Below a picture of a wolf was written in bold capital letters "HOW DARE YOU!!" and then: "On behalf of this and other citizens of the Wolf Nation, Friends of the Wolf hereby order human citizens to immediately cease and desist on all attacks and plans of attack on the Algonquin and all other Wolves. Any further violence against wolves in these areas will be met with prolonged and diverse resistance."

I telephoned the president, Bill Hipwell, to point out that so far most residents appeared to be respecting the wolf-killing ban. The poster, instead of doing any good, was bound to infuriate people.

Then, on March 12, 1993, an event occurred that changed the whole temper of the wolf controversy. Unwittingly involved was adult male McDonald Creek 4, radio-collared the previous July. He had disappeared the day after capture. In October, Quebec student Stephan Beauregard learned from the Montreal office of Ministère du Loisir de la Chasse et de la Pêche that someone had seen a radio-collared wolf on the east side of Gatineau Park, beyond Ottawa. Stephan knew the frequencies of our wolves, having worked for us the summer previously, and he borrowed a receiver from the Quebec government. He located the wolf, McDonald 4, 170 kilometres southeast of his capture site. The wolf had crossed the wide

Ottawa River before freeze-up either by swimming or crossing the one long bridge at Pembroke.

By mid-December, McDonald 4 surprised us by turning up again, this time on the periphery of the deer yard. Then he went missing until mid-January when he showed up again in the Bonnechere Valley just outside the park. He seemed to be alone, travelling back into his home territory in early February, then back out to the periphery of the deer yard. Our last fix for him was on February 16.

On Saturday, March 12, his severed head appeared, with radio-collar underneath, mounted on a telephone pole at the main intersection in Round Lake Centre just across from the church. Above his head was one of Friends of the Wolf's posters, and below in large letters on a board was painted "DO NOT DARE US." A reporter from the Barry's Bay newspaper was telephoned at 6:30 A.M. The township reeve was there an hour later, and so was the parish priest and conservation officer Blake Simpson. A photograph of McDonald 4's head was featured on the newspaper's front page.

Our winter funding had just run out so none of us were there. I was telephoned about the incident and later sent a colour photograph and newspaper clippings. MNR area manager John Johnson was quoted saying, "This incident portrays a sadistic image of Round Lake residents that is a real shame."

The barbarism of the event shocked the community and made many people take stock. For a while it seemed to cause such a revulsion that people just wanted to forget it, forget wolves, concentrate on other issues. For some months, even a year, we could not gauge its impact, but in retrospect, it was a turning point in public attitudes. Gradually, press coverage declined.

As months went by, an acceptance of wolves seemed to grow. Some people befriended us, even tried to help us understand their neighbours or relatives who see the wolf as evil. Beside a field one day, the landowner pointed to a crew stacking bales of hay on a wagon behind the baler and said, "You see that fellow on top of the load? He's my brother-in-law and he hates wolves. But he's never lived away from here. That other fellow lived down south for a while and has come back, like me. He can live with them." A local newspaper editor told us that a silent majority either valued the wolf or did not care.

Something had happened to the psyche of the community. People started thinking about their environment, so easily taken for granted, and why they lived there. In our subsequent newspaper articles designed to keep people informed of our results, we referred to the accumulating evidence that wolves and people could live in peace. Despite the ban, there were still deer in the hills, no livestock had been lost, no humans endangered. In our daily contacts we often asked people why they did not live in Ottawa or Toronto? They did not have to answer; they knew why. There is a peaceful wildness to the forest-farm interface, one you can sense when the moonlight floods the fields and outlines the distant trees, one that is richer because of the presence of wolves. What the wolf issue did was force people to face themselves.

Once, an anonymous person phoned the MNR to say he had killed a wolf in the ban area with an ice pick and thrown away the collar. As well, Blake Simpson was told about a collared wolf shot beside a road, and he shovelled in the ditch to find it. But, in the end, almost everybody obeyed the ban.

Looking back now, community hostilities towards us seem to be over, notwithstanding some continued illegal killing and the occasional newspaper article to the contrary. The MNR did the right thing, for wolves, for conservation, for Algonquin Park, and for people with a sensitivity towards nature both close to and distant from Algonquin Park. It was not enough – Ontario still has the most disgracefully exploitive wolf policy in Canada – but it was something. We had hopes that the park population could rebound.

STRUGGLING REOCCUPANTS OF
THE BONNECHERE VALLEY

A FRACTURED wolf society is memory-impaired, order-attenuated, adrift like a hockey team that has traded its veterans and fired its coach. What remains is only what has been coded in genes, still the essence of the species and its way of doing things, but without the same synergy, cohesion, or breadth of learned skills.

The Bonnechere Valley greened up in the May sunshine, and the passerine birds flooded back. The songs of white-throated sparrows rang through the forest at daybreak, and the fluted hymns of the veeries softened the gathering dusk. Olive-sided flycatchers swooped from spruce spire to spire, and woodcocks danced in the clearings. In the years after the wolf killings nothing seemed different, but that was an illusion. The population of the summit predator was in disarray. Gone were the wolf footprints that once had sutured the high hills in the upper end of the valley to the plateaulands lower down. Instead, gaping, wolfless wounds separated the tracks of one pack from another. Silence replaced wolf howls that normally reverberated from the dark hills as pack members sought each other for direction and solace.

Foys Lake supra-organism might have come and gone without human notice except for the five radio-collars we put on pack members. But human notice is no requisite for relevance. The land knew them well – the ridges and game trails they followed, the beaver dams they crossed, the granite outcrops where their pups had played. The McDonald Creek supra-organism, too, might have lived out its days in anonymity centred on the wide McDonald Creek marshes where few canoeists ever go – not much water over the mud – and departed, unknown by any humans. But the forest, without wolf influence on its herbivores, would have written a different signature across the land.

The Foys Lake pack had occupied most of the Bonnechere Valley, where, like a firefly, it glowed for a moment – three years in our data – and went out. Then, up in the void of the valley's north-eastern corner, the McDonald Creek pack blinked on and off over the course of another three years. In a more appropriate evolution-ary time scale, difficult to discern even with a "long-term" study such as ours, this transitory nature of wolf packs may be natural, but not at that rate. Pack turnover, like species extinction, is a normal process. The impact of humans is speeding it up.

In the summer of 1993, we continued working the McDonald Creek area to be sure the pack no longer existed. We lurched over the haulroads and skid trails, the man-made venous system used over the preceding few years to drain the lifeblood of pine from the land and transform some of the most noble stands into "shelter-wood" skeletons.

Ironically, logging improved the habitat for chestnut-sided warblers, magnolia warblers, black-throated blue warblers, redstarts, all birds of second growth. Each June morning as we bounced along, windows open, we recorded the number of singing males per kilo-metre: white-throated sparrows, hermit thrushes, winter wrens, pounding sapsuckers, drumming grouse, all part of, and responding to, one of the most dramatic pulses of productivity on Earth. Farther south in warmer climates, the pulse of spring growth is diffused over a longer time; farther north, productivity is limited by short growing seasons and permafrost. But here in the middle, the energy machine reaches a late-May and June six-week high. In logged-over forests, the pulse beats strongest.

That summer of 1993 the McDonald Creek pack's territory was not wolfless, just packless. Two of the wolves we radio-tracked stayed in the vicinity, others wandered widely, and still others were just passing through, unfettered by bonds to the land. Still threading the same forest pathways, remembering, was dark-faced Basin 9 McDonald, who Mary and I had collared by the same patch of sweet fern where we had collared her now-dead father the summer before. In June, the student crew caught a medium-sized adult male, McDonald 1, genetically unrelated to any former residents. Occasionally over the following nine months we located him with Basin 9 McDonald, but the association was infrequent, and by the following summer they had separated. That winter, Basin 9 McDonald picked up at least two other wolves in the "singles bar" down in the deer yard and then shifted her range northwest into the old Grand Lake West territory. McDonald 1 left too, carving out a new territory in former Mathews land.

Other wolves caught in the McDonald Creek area showed even weaker bonds. McDonald 4, for example, whose head ended up on the post at Round Lake Centre, had wandered across the Ottawa River to Quebec and back before he was killed. Skinny little McDonald 2, a twenty-kilogram (forty-five-pound) yearling male, left the park within two weeks of capture and showed up in the farmlands south of the town of Wilno, his home turf for the next four years.

We came to think of the McDonald Creek area as a social wasteland for wolves. There were just too many unpredictable wolf movements, temporary alliances, and weak territory associations. We found an uncommon number of landless refugees, not just young dispersers looking for new land and a mate, but adults. A lone, wandering, middle-aged wolf implies something has gone wrong. Basin 4 McDonald, the biggest wolf in our study, had been one of those when he was joined by Grand 3 in the summer of 1990.

Similar cases were McDonald 4, McDonald 1 Hardwood, Basin 9 McDonald, McDonald 8.

Elsewhere in other persecuted packs we found the same thing: Mathews 11; Travers 8; Redpole 5; Pretty 6; Jack Pine 7 after she lost her entire pack one year and her new mate the next. The land across eastern Algonquin Park lacked beautiful, coordinated wolf supra-organisms like it had when Foys Lake, McDonald Creek, Jack Pine, Grand Lake, and other packs had practised their synchronized magic there. The contrast was disturbing, making us talk a lot about pack integrity, not just numbers.

A lanky young female we named McDonald 5 finally administered first aid to the wolf-impaired McDonald Creek lands. Students Joy Cook and Mark Hebblewhite collared her first in May 1994. Just as we found elsewhere, recovery here centred on one or two key wolves possibly with survival skills, or social skills, or tenacity that exceeded others. Good news emerged after we caught and collared McDonald 5; genetic analysis showed that she was the granddaughter of Foys 3, the medium-sized male who had died of rabies in March 1991, so at least the Foys Lake lineage lived on.

Initially she showed erratic movements, like the others. For a time in 1994, she associated with Basin 9 McDonald in that wolf's new territory to the northwest, even travelling back and forth with her to the deer yard occasionally from the early snows of December until the cold of late January. Then they separated permanently, McDonald 5 embarking on a month-long excursion north of the Petawawa River, where, from the air, we found her with a former Petty Lake wolf who had dispersed to form a new pack there. Then she turned southwest into the new territory of the Hardwood Lake pack, where, again from the air, we found her with a probable past associate that lived there. Finally, after her "fling," she returned and settled for good in her old McDonald Creek territory.

Mary and I recaught her on a May day in 1995, when the hazel was still in red brushcut flower. Unexpectedly, she was with three other wolves of unknown origin, all who left big footprints in the sand up the road. Singles bar shenanigans?

One of the wolves with her was McDonald 8, caught a few days later, a handsome, dark wolf with black rings around his eyes. He was destined to become her mate, but not that year. Although a full adult, he wandered even more widely than McDonald 5. We dubbed him a "wild card," one of three such wolves in 1995, because he seemed free to trespass in any pack's territory – either that or he was stealthy and never caught.

McDonald 5 centred her activity at an extensive bog south of the Spectacle lakes, as shown by aerial tracking. Later that summer of 1995, we took a three-day canoe trip to reach the bog. She had moved again, but we found the tracks of pups along its muddy edge. That winter the pack consisted of eight or nine wolves, an abnormally high pup production and survival unless unknown older wolves immigrated into the new pack.

After a year of wandering, McDonald 8 began to centre his movement back in the McDonald Creek territory and was with McDonald 5 more frequently. From the spring of 1996 on, he became her constant companion. In August 1996 again we canoed to the Spectacle lakes. Hot days forced us to lay over rather than make the long portages in this region of the park where few people go. On the way back, as the wind blew us down Lower Spectacle Lake, we picked up the signals of both wolves. We circled back for cross-bearings, blew back down the lake again, and made camp in the pines behind a rocky outcrop that sloped to the water. While waiting for dusk, we cooled off with a swim.

The signals showed that the wolves were southeast in the McDonald Creek marshes. As the sun left the water, we canoed across the foot of the lake and paddled through a high-walled rocky channel that connects to the slow-moving creek. Rounding a point, McDonald 5's signal became much louder, too loud, so we stopped paddling and let the canoe float back. We pulled up in a little arrowhead-choked cove surrounded by high grasses to wait for dark and whatever the wolves would tell us. Soon, a howl broke the evening hush. It was McDonald 5, confirmed by the bearing on the signal. She howled half a dozen times, her voice echoing off the hills to the west, hanging over the marsh for a moment, then fading like the mist.

At dusk we slipped past her, paddling silently, tracing the stream's convolutions through the marshland, and putting her signal behind us. Suddenly we heard a splash and the sloshing of running feet and caught a fleeting glimpse of a wolf. It must have been hunting beaver or muskrat along the water's edge. Around another bend where the stream wound close to a hillside, another wolf shattered the stillness with a series of short howls. Maybe it mistook the noise of our paddles for a packmate. We heard it enter the water and splash towards us, then at twenty metres pause, realize its mistake, and plunge back to the forest. Seconds later, a full pack responded from off in the distance. We sat quietly in the canoe and listened, pleased that for the second consecutive year there were pups and the land was again well stocked with wolves.

But it wasn't for long; something happened to the McDonald Creek pack – again. We do not know what. In the winter of 1996–97, both collared wolves, McDonald 5 and McDonald 8, spent much of the early months in the Round Lake deer yard close to the highway and people. Our tracking consistently failed to show them with a pack. In February they returned to the park, and on repeated flights John Pisapio reported either seeing them alone or just their two sets of tracks. At first we hoped that they were only temporarily separated from their pack, but as time went on, that possibility became less likely, and by the end of the winter we were forced to conclude that tragedy of some form had struck again.

In the summer of 1997, we confirmed that there were only these two adults, but again they produced pups – we heard them howl. Maybe this time the pack will persist, learn the land, avoid its dangers, stay out of the deer yard, survive. ·

Southwest of the McDonald Creek pack's lands, other wolves struggled to rebuild wolfness across a large sector of the former Foys Lake pack's land, empty after the winter of 1990–91. We could sense the Foys Lake pack's loss in the summer of 1991 as we drove through this incomplete domain from kilometre 14 to 40 on the Bonnechere road, or up the nearby logging roads. We never saw wolf scats or tracks, and our nightly howling excursions were uneventful. When we hiked the overgrown roads or portages, we felt the emptiness.

In the fall of 1991, a young male from the Jack Pine pack initially named Basin 6 dispersed to the southwest and found this vacant tract. Later we learned that he was only on a foray away from home and really was born a Jack Pine wolf, son of Jack Pine 3. By early December he had found a mate. We called them the Jocko Lake wolves (and Basin 6 became Basin 6 Jocko) after the lake at the centre of their movements.

Soon after they met, one December evening just at dusk we heard them perform a magnificent duet. Rapidly dropping temperature had caused cold air to settle over an expansive snowy bog. The cold pressed even the gentle, whispered forest sounds into silence. We stood on a logging road where the signal came in best, talking softly because the wolves were close. Suddenly one deep voice, then another, cracked the stillness, so close you could hold the howls in your hands. The two wolves, destined to found a new pack dynasty, sang on and on with the vigour of youth, their howls resonating from the hills across the bog. Bracketing each howl, making each a work of music, was the counter-point of complete silence, leaving the forest, and us, in breathless anticipation. This was their land now, and their howls an ode to joy.

That winter the newly formed Jocko Lake pair spent much of its time down in the deer yard. As with the McDonald Creek wolves, when they returned in the spring we counted four sets of tracks where there only should have been two.

From the time the spring peepers tuned up until the green frogs took over, we camped under the pines where Feely Lake lapped at the leatherleaf and bog laurel in front of our tent, a place that became a favourite in years to come. Often Basin 6 Jocko's signal was audible from across the lake. He and another wolf, likely his mate, serenaded us morning and night, sometimes stimulating a resident pair of loons to join in and together make the hills radiant with sound.

Besides the wolves nearby, that camp was memorable because of an abundant crop of oyster mushrooms that we ate with eggs in the morning, cheese at noon, and spaghetti or anything else at night. The mushrooms, growing on dead trees, came complete with their own little food web – pleasing fungus beetles with their red-brown thorax and squirmy rove beetles; we managed to pick most of them out, and the rest added protein.

The night of June 22, 1992, was marked by a severe late frost that left its beauty mark on the hills for the entire summer. The soft, vulnerable, expanding leaves of red maples turned a crimson red, their chloroplasts permanently out of order. The afternoon of the frost, Mary, Michelle, and I canoed a string of lakes and howled our way back after dark. When we set out, the air was still and the afternoon sunlight translucent. In a picturesque bay, a feeding moose raised her head, mouth full of dripping potamogeton, and watched us paddle by. A pair of ring-necked ducks splashed off the water and beat their way to the far end of the lake.

We reached our destination, Wenda Lake, by dusk, and sat under the shore pines to wait for dark. Slowly the temperature slid below the blackfly threshold, then the mosquito and spring peeper line; it was strangely quiet. When the stars were all lit we put out onto the lake, watching the dark shoreline slide along our port side. Subdued northern lights played across the horizon. Somewhere in one of the string of ponds we went wrong, and Michelle climbed ashore to find the portage. A thin mist rising off the water shortened the flashlight beam. She crashed around in the bush for a while and then called out to "backtrack"; we had come up the wrong channel. Eventually we poked our way through.

When we were back at the first lake, ice was forming on the gunwales, and it was warmer to dip your hand in the water at each paddle stroke than to keep it out. We reached the truck at 1:30 A.M. to find it covered with frost. No wolves had howled, but an hour later as we crawled into the tent back at our Feely Lake camp, the Jocko Lake pair gave us a brief, conciliatory chorus.

In early July we caught Basin 6 Jocko's mate and named her Jocko 3 – a sharp-featured, dark-faced lactating female. Later genetic analysis showed that she was the daughter of Annie Bay 3 and had dispersed some thirty kilometres from her natal pack across one other existing territory, about the same distance Basin 6 Jocko had come from his natal pack. Over the following year and a half, rarely were these two wolves more than one hundred metres apart. Theirs was one of the close alliances we have often recorded between mated pairs.

We also caught what must have been the other two wolves that had come back with the Jocko Lake pair from the farmlands. Both were transient yearlings, possibly orphans or dispersers from other packs, who soon left the Jocko Lake territory. Both these wolves lived charmed lives, after a fashion. One was the wolf we later extracted alive from the snare in the deer yard. The other one, dubbed the "Jesus Christ" wolf, arose from the dead. On a telemetry flight with volunteer pilot Hank Halliday, I heard the fast pulse rate of mortality mode and located it down below, but, a few hours later when Mary flew with Hank, the wolf, still "dead," was a few kilometres away. The next day he was even farther away, and we realized his collar had slipped onto mortality mode. Soon the collar failed completely.

Lying in our sun-speckled tent one morning we heard the tiny, weak voices of pups and knew that this part of the Bonnechere Valley was beginning to heal. By midsummer we were able to confirm that the Jocko Lake pair had three pups. The pack spent much of its time in a large complex of bogs tied together by a beaver-impeded little stream that wound its way through the hills east of Loonskin Lake.

Tragedy struck the new pack, as it did so many packs, down in the farmlands that winter of 1992–93. When the Jocko Lake pair returned to the park in spring of 1993, only one pup was left. That pup, eventually collared as Jocko 10, would eventually take over as the alpha-male.

That summer they produced another litter destined to die. It was Jocko 3's last litter. On a grey mid-December day in the heart of her territory, Mary and I were disappointed to hear her signal on mortality mode. She was just a skeleton when we found her, lying on top of sodden leaves. Her fur lay in a pile a metre or so away, not under her skeleton, showing that her body had been disturbed. Strangely, the radio-collar, still bolted up, lay another metre away, not around her neck, although her skull was still attached to her vertebral column. It seemed unlikely that a small animal could have pulled the collar off because pulling on one side would lodge it sideways and prevent it from going over her head. All we could surmise was that a bear had skinned her by everting her pelt over her head, removing the radio-collar in the process.

Basin 6 Jocko was without a mate until early January. Then we discovered that Mathews 6 had joined the pack. Rarely after that were these two wolves apart.

Mathews 6 Jocko (last name now added) had been collared the summer before, two territories to the north. Her adoption into the Jocko Lake pack may have been simple because Basin 6 Jocko was the only mature wolf; the others in the pack were pups of the previous summer, plus one immature yearling.

She was destined to make a heroic and eventually successful effort to stabilize the Jocko Lake pack. She produced pups every summer from 1994 through 1997. We saw her 1995 pups, three of them, one day as they wandered unconcerned along the hydro-line road in front of our truck. The largest pup, very reddish behind its ears, picked up a flat, run-over frog and threw it up in the air a couple of times. The pack had chosen an extensive system of bogs for its rendezvous site.

Each year she denned in a different place, twice in different uncut forest patches surrounding a rock fault or a bog. Both these places were remnants in logged-over shambles where half the trees had been cut the previous year. Both places showed the dramatic environmental alteration that wolves can accept.

While she was tolerant of logging effects, she was not tolerant of humans near her den. In early May 1996, an Algonquin Forest Authority supervisor phoned to ask if there were any dens they should avoid. Pleased by the AFA's concern, we drove to Pembroke and showed them the location of the den on a map. The supervisor tentatively agreed to keep their tree-planting crew out of the area, but wanted to check with the MNR. Unfortunately, an MNR biologist in Whitney advised them that one kilometre was excessive, and that a few hundred metres would be enough. (In other parks the distance, established by policy, varies from two to fifteen kilometres).

The morning the tree planters arrived, John Pisapio flew at 6:30 and found Mathews 6 Jocko a few hundred metres from the den. He dropped us a note from the airplane where we were camped twenty kilometres away, and we quickly drove to the site. When we arrived we found the branches hauled off the road and the tree-planting crew spread out through the forest, calling to one another, within three hundred metres of the den. When the AFA supervisor showed up, he explained what had happened, but by then it was too late. The signal told us that Mathews 6 Jocko was at the den, but she stayed only a half-hour. Then she abandoned it.

For some weeks we could not determine the fate of her pups. She centred her activities three kilometres away along an alder-choked stream, but often we found her elsewhere. Finally, when we were camped on the edge of a large bog-marsh at the foot of Jocko Lake, we heard the pups howl and so confirmed that she had moved some or all of them successfully.

It was there we saw her for the first time after listening to her signals for more than two years. One sunny afternoon as we sat in the truck overlooking the bog-marsh, her signal became louder and suddenly she trotted out of the trees, a big light-tan wolf. She slipped down into the sedges, not slackening her pace despite the difficult footing, crossed a small beaver dam and loped up a bank into a stand of red pines. For a few metres she paralleled the stream, then turned in and was gone. She appeared to be intent upon some task, probably bringing food back to the pups.

Many nights we set the antenna on top of our dome tent, pointed it towards the wolves, threaded the coaxial cable in through the door and plugged up the small gap around the cable with a sock to keep the mosquitoes out. We had three wolves collared. Periodically we would wake up and scan to see which of the collared wolves were there. We never howled at them, just listened as is our practice when camped near a rendezvous site. Some nights they howled a lot, all duly noted. Other nights they were completely silent although their signals showed that at least some of them were present.

Despite the wolf-killing ban, the Jocko Lake pack suffered its share of losses. In the winter of 1995–96, we tracked the mortality-mode signal of a young male collared the previous summer to the fenceline of one of Round Lake's most bitter wolf critics, a man we know only from his repeated exhortations in local newspapers to ignore the wolf-killing ban. We went in the long way to avoid trespass and found the wolf stretched out full length, frozen stiff, on a knoll in a recent maple-birch cut-over. No blood, no obvious injury, no human tracks, no signs of a struggle, but the wolf's face wore the contorted death mask of pain we were used to seeing on wolves who had strangled in snares.

We tied a rope around his legs and dragged him the kilometre back to the truck, and he was delivered to the post-mortem room at the University of Guelph. Doug Campbell, who performed the autopsy, could find no obvious cause of death. The wolf had plenty of body fat, no sign of disease, no abrasions, and by elimi-nation he had to consider poison. Tissue was sent to the University of Michigan because of a strike that closed the provincial toxicology lab. Diagnosis – strychnine.

Conservation officer Blake Simpson interviewed the prime suspect as well as others he considered capable of such an act, but the case was never solved. The Jocko Lake pack, like others after losing a family member, returned a few days later to the park.

In the spring of 1997, the Jocko Lake pack consisted of six wolves, despite the deaths of various yearlings and adults, rising slowly from a founding pair in 1992. Recovery had been slow and, reviewing our data, one of the main reasons was loss of pups in their first year: all the 1992 crop, all but one of the 1993 crop, all but one of the 1994 crop, all but two of the 1995 crop. Finally three pups survived to yearling age in 1997 to bring the pack up to six.

When we succeeded in collaring these three yearlings, we found that we could examine their surprisingly complete paternal lineage from a cross-confirmation of field evidence and genetic analysis: father Jocko 10, grandfather Basin 6 Jocko, grandmother Jocko 3, great-grandmothers Jack Pine 3 and Annie Bay 3. Mother Mathews 6 Jocko. They were great-nieces and -nephews of Jack Pine 7, Jack Pine 6 Zigzag, and Acorn 1, and second cousins of McDonald 9, McDonald 10, and Jack Pine 12. Their relations lived in four packs.

Over the recovery years, both founding alpha wolves died and were replaced, the female by an immigrant, the male usurped and expelled by his son. Two members of the pack were killed illegally and one killed legally in the ban area.

In the winter of 1997–98, for unknown reasons, the pack dropped to just four.

In the lower Bonnechere Valley, the Basin Depot pack gave us a workout over the years, right back to the first wolf collared by Graham and Jenny in 1988. Part of the pack's territory was accessible along the Bonnechere and Basin Lake roads, and we often heard howls from the vicinity of a restored log cabin that in the mid-1800s had been part of a thriving logging camp and depot farm. The rest of the pack's territory, however, was difficult to reach, lying across the Bonnechere River in a roadless area a long hike from anywhere. Boundaries shifted over the years, but much of its territory was in forested land outside the park, which is probably one of the reasons for the high turnover it experienced.

We worked the Basin Depot pack from a beautiful campsite in a slowly healing log landing beside fast-flowing Basin Creek. Head-height pines obscured the edges of the clearing, thinning to a grassy eye in its centre. In early spring, overwintering mourning cloak and anglewing butterflies danced through the clearing on their way to find the oozing sap from holes made by yellow-bellied sapsuckers. By early summer, yellow and orange hawkweed brightened the clearing, taken over later by goldenrod and asters. Hermit thrushes were common there, singing from the forest around, and red-breasted nuthatches cranked out their repetitive calls.

We never slept late at that campsite no matter how long we worked the night before. The morning sun slanted into the clearing and soon our tent heated up like an oven. The heat always drove Mary out first; I would hear her starting breakfast on the tailgate of the truck and talking to the dog.

The Basin Depot pack originated as an offshoot of the Foys Lake pack, the two packs amalgamating each winter to form a large hunting unit of twelve to fourteen wolves. In the early years, we radio-collared three Basin Depot wolves. One was hit by a car only a few months after capture, one integrated with the Foys pack to become the alpha-female, and the third, a scrawny little three-year-old weighing only eighteen kilograms (forty pounds), provided our first record of starvation. Since then we have recorded four other starved wolves, all in late summer or early fall. That may be a stressful time, with hungry, growing pups, and with young deer and moose fast on the hoof and beavers rarely on land.

With the demise of the Foys Lake pack in the winter of 1990–91 came the demise of the Basin Depot pack for a time, although genetic evidence later told us that one breeding wolf with no mate and one yearling had survived. The summer after the killing, 1991, the territory was packless, and just as in other such territories, we caught wandering dispersers. One wolf never found again after collaring was shot more than two years later beyond the west side of the park, 125 kilometres from its capture site.

After only one summer of vacancy, however, the remaining adult found a new mate and a new Basin Depot pack became re-established in 1992. Between then and 1997, it struggled to survive. Both alpha animals changed, the new alpha-male coming from within the pack and the new alpha-female an immigrant, just as in the Jocko Lake pack. Like the Jocko Lake pack, human-caused and natural mortality were barely offset by pup production because of low pup numbers by the end of each summer and heavy pup losses in their first winter. Pup survival to yearling age was only two in 1992, possibly four in 1993, none in 1994, two in 1995, none in 1996, and three in 1997. (We know of another five pups that vanished before they were ten months old; presumably they died.)

In addition to these eleven pups that reached yearling age, we know of three immigrants. One of them was a tiny but feisty sixteen-kilogram (thirty-five-pound) animal with a narrow, coyote-like nose. Its genetics showed no affiliation with any Basin Depot wolves, so it was an immigrant. Here, yet again, was an example of a coyote-like animal invading the park and coming into a vacant or fractured pack territory.

Two wolves collared the summer of 1993, sisters, paid the price of territorial overlap with the park border. Much of the time the pack used a rendezvous site south of the Bonnechere River, barely beyond the protection of the park. From two sources we learned that hunters shot them. The hunters must have smashed the collars although the November hunting season preceded the annual wolf-killing ban.

Another female showing signs of false pregnancy was in poor condition, extremely skinny when she was caught in early August. After capture she travelled to the north part of her territory, then returned to the rendezvous site, where she died. Concerned that their handling had been involved, John Pisapio and Mark Hebblewhite hiked into the rendezvous site, normally something we never do, to collect her carcass. Upon autopsy, Doug Campbell found severely atrophied muscles and concluded she had been starving for at least three weeks before capture.

Known pups surviving to yearling age over those years totalled fourteen. Known losses include four dispersers, six yearlings or adults dead, and one vanished, for a total of eleven. During the winter of 1997–98, the pack consisted of four wolves: the alpha-male and three pups. His mate had died of unknown causes the previous August.

Genetics showed that long-lived Redpole 4, who lived two territories distant to the west, had made an important contribution to the Basin Depot pack. He was the grandfather of three Basin Depot wolves and the great-grandfather of three more. His descendants, however, are spread through five different packs.

Recovery of a wolf population is an uneven process. Even though the ban reduced wolf killing, wolves continued to die, just enough to keep disrupting continuity and erasing gains. The population struggled, with life expectancy remaining low, dispersal exceeding immigration in the Bonnechere Valley, and low numbers of pups making it to yearling age. In 1996–97, mortality was 36 per cent and the population of our entire study area declined again by 28 per cent. Human killing in townships outside the ban area accounted for 75 per cent of these losses. In 1997–98, the population remained stable and low.

Until the Basin Depot pack expanded its territory to the west to meet the eastern boundary of the Jocko Lake pack in the summer of 1995, a big, packless piece of land about ten kilometres in diameter remained between them. That was not the only persistent wolfless hole. To the north in the Petawawa drainage, the territory of the Travers pack took two years to refill. North of Grand Lake a fifteen-kilometre hole between the Pretty Lake pack and the newly formed Hardwood Lake pack took three years to fill, and still there is a gap.

Just when the landscape seemed mended and the population had patched most of its holes, new ones appeared, the consequence of the 1996–97 decline. After we lost two radio-collared Pretty Lake wolves, both dying north of the park, the Pretty Lake territory remained vacant throughout the summer of 1997. A crew worked there for six weeks and only found evidence of wandering singles. Then in January 1998 the adjacent Jack Pine pack claimed the western part of the land. Something happened, as well, to the land lying north of Grand Lake – it was packless again.

As they resettled the land, the struggling reoccupants carved out largely different territories than those held by their predecessors, making it obvious that topography does not define boundaries. Grand Lake may always separate packs, as may the Petawawa River in summer, although wolves can swim both. Other than these two features, territorial boundaries must exist in the minds of individuals. They may fall where wolves first turn around because they are too far from a den or rendezvous site or other pack members, or where they encounter the scent of unknown wolves, and those places are remembered, retraced, and remarked over time.

In an exploited population, boundaries may be forgotten. Survivors may have no memory of den sites, rendezvous sites, ambush sites, or easy travel routes along esker ridges and across beaver dams, leaving the population less fit. The relationship between animals and ecosystem is fractured. A pack – especially a small, reforming one – may need all the subtle advantages it can get to bring enough pups through. The inexperience of breeding animals may contribute to the low number of young that reach yearling age that typifies the Algonquin population.

Up to a point, a wolf population has the biological capacity to offset its human-caused losses. A numerical balance between births and deaths may be acceptable today as a conservation objective over much wolf-occupied land.

Someday, however, we may re-evaluate our place in nature and decide that it is no more acceptable to kill wolves than it is to kill lions or cheetahs or other big cats. And, even today, is the mere maintenance of such a balance between births and deaths good enough for special places we call parks – supposed holding places of biological treasures? Should wolf populations even there be continually chipped away at, their adaptations driven by human influence? Can't we allow nature to run anything any more – just on principle, just out of humility?

Unless officials that control policy in the MNR come to see parks as places to provide this ecosystem-sensitive level of protection and complete the task of boundary protection all around Algonquin Park, the wolf population there, as in so many other places, will never heal. At best it will only persist.

SPACE GAMES AND
WOLF-DEER RELATIONSHIPS

COLD CLOAKS the snowy Algonquin landscape, and a deep quiet settles into the hills. Tourists have departed. Pine-softened wind sometimes brings the distant call of ravens, or a jay. Up in the hardwoods a downy woodpecker hammers, or some siskins with their questioning calls dip by. Even these quiet sounds cease as shadows swallow the day. Winter Algonquin is a place of snow-filled silences.

Wolves can find "peopleless" sanctuary there, can concentrate on being predator, not prey. Across vast stretches of the park, no human tracks disturb the snow. No threat of a bullet in the open places, no risk of a snare along the trails or strychnine in a chunk of meat. Just wind, cloud, ice, snow, moose – the wild harmony of winter.

Yet many wolves choose to leave the park and go where they daily encounter snowmobiles, cars, trucks, people, dogs, houses, barns. There they wait in ditches for vehicles to pass – at least the cautious ones do. They circle open fields and avoid barking dogs. They feed on deer behind the store at Bonnechere or the public school in Round Lake Centre. They die in traps and snares and on roads – less than before the ban, but it still happens.

An evolutionary irony, wolves are only partially adapted to shun humans. They would fare much better if the first hint of human presence triggered greater fear, if they always associated snowmobiles and cars with danger. But they hedge their bets and often lose.

They don't need to leave the park. In the park's northwest sector, despite a near-absence of deer year-round, the wolves have managed just fine. Their only adjustments are slightly larger territories and an increase in snowshoe hare in winter diets to about 10 per cent. Yet in the east, the wolves follow the deer out of the park even though moose and beaver are just as abundant as in the west. Apparently deer are so highly preferred that the wolves are willing to risk exposure to people to follow them. This deer storehouse may be just too attractive for their predatory genes to ignore.

Up to fifty-eight wolves, our highest one-time estimate, or about twenty to thirty on average, concentrate in one hundred to two hundred square kilometres of deer yard. This constitutes an almost unprecedented density, more than ten times greater than in the park. Normal wolf spacing is temporarily on hold, and so is aggression. Never have we recorded a wolf-killed wolf in the deer yard.

The events of one late February afternoon should have erupted into wolf violence. Instead, what we found was a dramatic example of tolerance. The big radio-collared Vireo male had travelled west of his usual location into high hills on the periphery of the deer yard. We took a bearing on his signal and crossed a snowy field to a stone fence where we picked up his tracks. Following them downhill into the trees we saw where he was joined by packmates eventually making four sets of footprints. Then, to our amazement, even more tracks appeared, exceeding the number of wolves in his pack. The tracks were strung out along a small creek. Soon we came to deer hair and a little farther found a vertebral column and skull. The wolves had pulled the deer down under spruce trees, where the snow was blood-stained and packed into ice. A typical, skinned-out deer pelt lay nearby, along with the pelvic girdle and two hind legs.

The Vireo wolf had moved off the carcass and was about one hundred metres to the south. While Mary unpacked our carcass kit, for no distinct reason I flipped the receiver to scan. At four-second intervals it switched from one frequency to the next and suddenly another signal came crackling in. Unbelievably, McDonald 1 was there too.

Just then a wolf howled not more than fifty metres behind us, deep, throaty howls that reverberated in the quiet woods, each emphasized by a few seconds of expectant silence. I pointed the antenna towards the wolf and scanned through the frequencies, but it was uncollared. So was a treble wolf who howled equally close to us from the creek.

Never had we found two packs at the same kill simultaneously, breaking all wolf rules. In summer, these packs were separated by one pack between. Yet there they were together.

We moved back along the creek, and still the Vireo and McDonald wolves shared the same bearing. Then we returned to the carcass and moved off in another direction, taking a third bearing with the same result. These two wolves and likely others were together, silent but near us, probably anxious to return. At the kill again, we hacked off the femur and mandibles, then in the fading daylight backtracked out of the wolf-filled woods.

Nobody has described wolves concentrating like this in response to the movements of deer. A wolf pack with a deer yard in part of its territory may centre its activities there, as François Potvin found in Quebec and Dave Mech in Minnesota. What we found was different: a migratory wolf population. Similar are cases of wolf concentrations around migratory caribou in Alaska reported by Warren Ballard, Bob Stephenson, and co-workers, and in the Northwest Territories by Gerry Parker. Wolves also have been found to concentrate around bison at Wood Buffalo National Park by Lu Carbyn and associates. In none of these instances, however, have the social and spacing dynamics been described.

We wanted to describe them here and in the process re-examine territorial behaviour. Were the wolves setting up and defending mini-territories in the deer yard, or were they roaming freely? If they set up territories, did packs return to the same ones each winter? Did packs avoid one another? Was wolf spacing a response to the distribution of deer, or to human disturbance, or to interactions among packs? Were wolves scavenging or killing deer, and were the deer they killed in poor shape, ready to die anyway? Why wasn't the deer population increasing? After expanding moderately in the early years of the study, deer numbers had fluctuated erratically.

Among the possible explanations for the lack of aggression and resulting concentration of wolf packs is a superabundance of food. While not explaining why only the Algonquin wolves are migratory, the difference between our study and the ones with non-migratory wolves in Minnesota and Quebec may be only a matter of scale – ours features a complete or near-complete deer exodus over a very large area.

Alternatively, the high level of genetic relatedness among packs we found may turn off aggression and allow wolves to concentrate. Heavy human exploitation and consequent dispersal to vacant lands probably drove up this relatedness, although heavily exploited and highly dispersed wolf populations in both Minnesota and Quebec did not concentrate.

A third hypothesis is that on a range-edge for wolves, there are no defending wolf packs in the farmlands to repel migratory wolves. From the howls we heard in summer, we had an idea that only coyotes lived in the Round Lake area.

Whatever the cause, what we were seeing did not happen thirty-five years previously. Then, with many small winter deer yards scattered throughout the park, Doug Pimlott found that packs stayed on territory. Deer numbers were about ten times as great and snow was deeper. The system had changed, as systems always do.

Two master's and two bachelor's theses based upon five winters of data helped answer these questions. Each December after term exams we would head north, stopping to check for signals from the blue body-shop sign on the big Wilno hill. Looking over the flat extent of deer yard, we always wondered what new twists the wolf-deer system would take, as it invariably did. I arranged my lecture schedule to allow us at least one month in the field between early

December and the end of March. We lived periodically for two winters in a small MNR staff house on the edge of the highway near Bonnechere Park, the first year dodging scaffolding as the house was being renovated. Then we rented various small cottages to fit our budget. One of them, the most comfortable, came with a wood stove and an outhouse.

We had funds for sixty to seventy hours of aerial radio-tracking each winter, which worked out to one three-hour flight every few days. On flight days we followed the same routine: a graduate student made early airborne reconnaissance, then Mary and I tracked to whatever kills were reasonably close. Often we arrived back at our lodgings long after dark. Occasionally we would howl the deer yard, but infrequently to avoid raising the ire of people and dogs. Saturday evenings during "Hockey Night in Canada" attracted the least attention.

As data accumulated, what we saw was almost patternless. While each winter we came to expect certain packs in certain areas, they rarely stayed for long. All packs shifted, some more frequently than others. Some stayed in the deer yard and never returned to the park all winter; others made up to eight return trips. Packs whose park territories lay closest to the deer yard travelled back and forth most often. When packs returned to the yard, sometimes they would go to the same area they had left, but other times they would centre their activities elsewhere. Each winter, a few packs did not come to the deer yard at all, or they went to the smaller Black Bay deer yard near the Ottawa River.

Some packs occupied only a few square kilometres in the deer yard; others travelled more widely. Joy Cook calculated that an average area covered by a pack over the period of one month was less than forty square kilometres. Some wolf movements were random, others clumped, others scattered. Single wolves without packs wandered everywhere.

We were seeing a maximum variety of responses to packs presented with the same environmental situation and stimuli, resulting in maximum unpredictability. That must have been confusing to the deer who could do nothing to reduce their exposure to wolves. From the wolves' standpoint, it seemed almost planned, although a deliberate strategy for an entire population is impossible. Members of one pack can communicate frequently enough to act strategically. A whole population cannot.

We should have expected the wolves to display the unpredictable movements considering their circumstances of having no land to defend, hunting deer that were shifting in response to snow conditions and food availability, and trying to avoid other packs and human activity. Adding to the unpredictability were individual differences in experience, memory, social position, age, and pack size.

Yet, except for two instances when packs temporarily amalgamated, they were never in the same place at once. Close encounters were common, such as two or three packs only a few hundred metres apart in the same county forest, for example, or two packs heading towards one another but one turning aside. Occasionally, one pack was on a kill with other packs nearby.

Examining the data, Joy found that packs were deliberately avoiding each other. Close range, spatial-temporal avoidance was a principal conclusion in her master's thesis. Ryan Norris, applying Joy's analytical approaches to the previous two winters of data, found the same thing.

Still, it seemed improbable that avoidance could be so perfectly executed for such long periods each winter. At times avoidance did fail, as shown by the two-pack incidents at deer kills. As well, there was the singles bar phenomenon. Late winter is the breeding season and some wolves undoubtedly were looking for new alliances and opportunities. We know some packs went back to the park with extra members, or some single wolves associated with packs in the deer yard for a while.

Jack Pine 7, for example, joined a pack in a county forest in February 1997. Alone after losing her mate in the park, we found her bedded down in a young cut-over forest with four other wolves. Because she had been there for a few days, we expected to find a deer carcass. The snow was deep enough for snowshoes, but packed from a thaw. With us was Bob Chambers, a biologist from New

York State interested in the ability of canids with different-sized feet to handle deep snow. He speculates that coyotes, with their small feet, can live in the Adirondacks, where snow is even deeper than in Algonquin, because periodic thaws condense the snow. By his reasoning, long periods of deep snow may help keep coyotes out of Algonquin Park.

Jack Pine 7 and her new associates had bedded in the open on snowy knolls, typically good vantage points. After counting the sites, we made a large circle, noting every wolf track going in or out. The next day we returned and followed the pack a few kilometres as it skirted fields and travelled through forest patches. This was a temporary alliance; by spring Jack Pine 7 was alone again.

The other three instances of wolf concentration, in the Northwest Territories and Alaska, took place at caribou or bison aggregations. Similarly, grizzly bears leave their territories to come together at salmon runs in British Columbia, Yukon, and Alaska. Both grizzlies and black bears are well known to converge at garbage dumps. Spotted hyenas and silver-backed jackals take advantage of migratory herbivores on the Serengeti Plains. Coyotes come together to scavenge winter-killed elk in Wyoming and were reported foraging at a cattle-feed yard in Arizona. Once, Mary and I studied radio-collared red foxes that showed the same territorial breakdown we were seeing here by gathering each winter at a dump along the Alaska Highway. Local abundance of food induces many predators to leave their territories and congregate without displaying obvious aggression to one another. With abundant prey, there is simply no reason to pick a fight.

Was prey abundant for wolves in the Round Lake deer yard? While deer were plentiful, they may have been difficult to catch. Some biologists, most notably Mike Nelson and Dave Mech in Minnesota, concluded that deer yarding evolved particularly as a defence against predators. Encumbered by deep snow, lone deer are vulnerable, but in groups, an individual may benefit as it does in all herd species, by earlier detection of predators and lowered odds that it will be the one singled out for pursuit. If deer yarding reduces predation, then the apparent abundance may be only an illusion.

Occasionally, wolves have responded to prey that are concentrated and vulnerable by killing more than they need – surplus killing. They reportedly did this when encountering snow-disadvantaged caribou in northern Saskatchewan, and again among wolf-naïve elk that had no experience fending off predators after wolf reintroduction into Yellowstone National Park. Biologist Doug Smith explained that the Yellowstone killing in 1997 happened with the highest elk density of the century near the end of the most severe winter of the century. In both Saskatchewan and Yellowstone, surplus killing was transitory.

We did not find surplus killing. While the kill rate was difficult to ascertain because the wolves were often on private property and moved so rapidly, we found that packs of four to six wolves appeared, on average, to kill a deer every four to six days. The wolves indicated that periodicity when, occasionally after killing and consuming a deer, they would go back to their territories in the park. We found that at times we could predict when they would return for another deer – unless they obtained food on territory.

That frequency of predation is somewhat longer than Doug Pimlott's estimated three days. Deer were much more plentiful thirty-five years ago, however, when he did his study, and average pack sizes slightly larger. Many carnivores, including wolves, respond to more prey by increasing their consumption and end up in better condition. Wisconsin biologist Lloyd Keith reviewed various wolf studies and described a three-fold difference in consumption per wolf depending upon the density of prey. Our lower consumption may indicate some difficulty in obtaining prey compared to thirty-five years ago, but not so great to represent a food shortage when translated into pounds of meat per day per wolf and compared to reported requirements.

All but two of the deer carcasses we examined were completely consumed, either when we found them or before the pack left. The two exceptions were revisited and consumed a few days later. Typically, only hide and blood remained, or a thoroughly chewed skull, or a femur, or part of a vertebral column. Consumption took between eighteen and thirty-two hours, during which the wolves typically stayed close to their carcass, possibly concerned about losing it to other wolves. After that, they would wander around but normally not hunt immediately, because kills in close succession were so rare. Ravens and foxes shared the feast, but most meat ended up in wolf stomachs.

Even though we found no surplus killing, food could still be abundant enough to turn off aggression. Surplus killing is aberrant behaviour not favoured by natural selection because it may result in a lack of food later. So we had to look for other evidence that the deer in the yard were easily available. We hoped it would come from our pool of descriptive events – anything that showed how well deer or wolves succeeded or failed in the prey-predator drama, especially how well or poorly the migration and yarding phenomenon served them both.

Colin Fabian, living near Bonnechere, has been an observer of this deer migration for many years. His map, showing all the trails used by deer, looks like a stretched-out spider web with strands funnelling into a distorted centre. Once, Colin killed wolves, but he says they are too interesting. Now he prefers to track their movements as he does the deer. He has witnessed changes in deer distribution and movements over the years. Originally, the deer concentrated in a recently logged area just outside the park ten kilometres to the west, but they adjusted as browse declined. Also stimulating their move was the feeding of hay promoted by the MNR as part of a province-wide program to avoid winter deer starvation. The hay brought the deer right into the towns of Round Lake Centre and Bonnechere. People enjoyed watching them, like watching birds at a feeder.

Years ago, the deer migration drained a much smaller area. Other deer yards were used throughout Algonquin Park. Then deer numbers crashed. As the population began recovering through the 1980s, the area draining into the Round Lake yard increased to cover most of the eastern side of the park. In 1991, the MNR stopped providing hay, a wise reversal of policy, and attempted through posters and meetings to explain why. Artificial feeding promotes local overbrowsing. As well, deer become dependant on the hay even though they have difficulty breaking it down in their digestive tracts.

Each winter, two or three packs always position themselves on the main deer runways leading into the Round Lake yard. Other packs do the same for runways into the auxiliary "Germanicus" yard separated from the Round Lake yard by Round Lake itself. Their runway kills, together with kills made earlier in the migration, show that migratory deer are especially vulnerable to wolves. This conclusion supports a similar one based on limited evidence from radio-collared deer in Minnesota. The time wolves normally spend searching for prey is reduced by the concentration of deer in one place. It seems a stupid strategy for deer to set themselves up in this way, but they appear to be intent on reaching the yard and willing to run the wolf gauntlet to get there.

Wolves undoubtedly remember from experience where to position themselves to intercept these converging deer, but, as well, have an ability to find them almost immediately. Whatever the deer do differently, the wolves quickly detect. In 1993 and again in 1997 when acorns were plentiful and the deer hung up longer in the hills, so did the wolves.

To understand the risks of migration to deer better, we wanted to contrast their survival with those who stayed in the park. Small pockets of deer normally stayed in, especially when the migration was late. Sometimes we would track a pack to a deer carcass even when we could find no trace of any deer from air or ground.

That happened one blustery day on Sec Lake. We were anxious to find this kill because the Sec Lake pack has never visited the deer yard. It has been the only pack not to, although its territory is only one pack-distance away. The wind-driven snow fast-froze our faces as we headed out on the lake by snowmobile. On our list of items to buy are plastic visors for our snowmobile helmets.

Rounding a point, we came upon the partially drifted-over skeletal remains of a deer. The wolves had jumped it in the pines on the point and pursued it about two hundred metres from shore before bringing it down.

On another excursion, the Hardwood Lake pack had attacked a moose on the ice of Lone Creek, leaving slush-frozen tracks and broken branches along the shore. The moose escaped, but only fifty metres away, surprisingly, was a dismembered deer.

From these and similar experiences we concluded that the wolves selectively hunt deer wintering in the park over moose, making these deer especially vulnerable. These non-migratory deer may be inadvertently gambling on low snow all winter, or may have been caught by deep snow and forced to stay. Whatever the reason, their vulnerability may help perpetuate the migration tradition. Few of the deer that stay may survive to build up a sub-population of non-migratory deer.

After the migration subsides, the deer gradually shift into the lowland, conifer-dominated core of the Round Lake yard. German student Doerte Poszig constructed computer maps based upon intensive tracking in 1996–97, and they illustrated this shift. The maps also showed an accompanying shift in most of the wolf locations. Over the winter, most deer were killed by wolves in areas with the highest deer concentration. Doerte used the information for a bachelor's thesis at the University of Marburg.

Her observations run counter to those of Steve Fritts and Dave Mech in Minnesota, who found more wolf-killed deer in areas of low deer density. Their findings had made us speculate about a "domino effect," where deer at high density running away from wolves cause other deer to run, leaving wolves perpetually in a deer void. At times we did track wolves into dense pockets of deer that simply scattered, but wolves still were successful often enough.

Occasionally we could read a snow story that explained the wolves' success. Most commonly one or two wolves would run right behind a deer, while other wolves acted as flankers. Sometimes the deer would turn to avoid deadfall and encounter a flanker; other times the deer would pause at heavy brush, or a fence, and wolf tracks would converge there.

The deer might have had a better chance of escape had they stayed on their well-established trails, particularly when the snow was deep, but they didn't. They simply bounded off anywhere in a panic. That observation contradicted one of the supposed benefits of yarding to deer.

Other benefits speculated upon by various biologists were not apparent either, most notably the "dilution factor." In other studies, wolf packs stayed on their summer territories, allowing deer to reduce the predator-prey ratio by migrating. The Algonquin wolves kept the ratio up by migrating too.

Nor did individual deer benefit greatly from the anonymity of being part of a tightly formed group. Many species form flocks or herds because individuals try to obtain an internal position and by that means reduce their chances of being the ones selected for pursuit. The predator, whether a hawk flying into a flock of swallows or a grey whale swimming into a school of herring, benefits from a "sure" meal. Even though predation is made easier, often resulting in more prey being killed, that does not matter to the individual prey animal as long as the meal isn't it.

In comparison with these tight groupings, even in yards, deer are scattered mostly in small groups of twos or threes over many square kilometres – except where they are being artificially fed. Not only is anonymity limited, but so is any potential benefit from earlier detection of wolves.

Yarding, like migration, does, however, reduce search time for wolves, setting them up for more frequent encounters with deer. Similar predator "set-ups" resulted in increased predation in central Labrador, where, with a previous graduate student, Kent Brown, we found caribou aggregated because of deep, soft snow. On Vancouver Island, wolves reportedly benefit where black-tailed deer are concentrated by a patchy pattern of logging.

If yarding reduces search time and does not benefit deer greatly through the "domino effect," or enhanced escape along established trails, or predator dilution, or earlier prey detection, or anonymity, how might it have evolved as a predator defence? The answer has to involve snow, because snow, not the presence of wolves, causes deer to yard. Deer do not yard on red wolf range in North Carolina and Tennessee. In Minnesota, deer were shown to concentrate less in winters of low snow. Yarding occurs only where snow is deep enough to make moving around energetically costly, with or without wolves.

Yarding still could have evolved as an anti-predator strategy as well. There may be dual benefits for deer. You have to see it from the individual deer's perspective. Being running-impaired in deep snow, and so stripped of its major defence against wolves, individual deer head for places where the snow is shallower, as it is in conifer-dominated deer yards. Whatever deer choose to do, detection may be inevitable, not only in the yard but even if they had stayed on territory — wolves on territory course their lands repeatedly. An ability to run may be the key to an individual deer's survival.

Nevertheless, more deer appear to end up in wolf stomachs because of yarding. Supporting that conclusion, in Minnesota, Mike Nelson and Dave Mech found that wolf predation was lower in the low snowfall winters when the deer stayed more dispersed.

It seems contradictory that individual deer would benefit by yarding at the expense of the population. However, like all tight groupings of prey, decisions are made by individuals for their own welfare, and the population as a whole simply takes the consequences.

We concluded that because we found no underutilized carcasses, deer were not so abundant and easy to obtain that the situation overcame the biological wolf taboo on overkilling. But, because of reduced search time on migration and in the yard, deer were sufficiently easy to catch to explain the high level of tolerance among packs. Possibly the high degree of genetic relatedness may have helped too, but knowing the genetic make-up of only part of the population, we could not fully work out its significance.

We wondered if the Algonquin Park wolves were allowed to concentrate in the Round Lake deer yard because no resident wolves lived there. In the summers of 1995 and 1996, John Pisapio and various partners radio-collared twelve resident canids in four packs. To our surprise, these wolves varied considerably in size. Smallest were two sharp-muzzled, coyote-like, 14.5-kilogram (32-pound) animals, smaller than anything we had collared in the park. The largest were thirty and thirty-six kilograms (sixty-seven to eighty pounds) – typical Algonquin Park wolves.

The southern portion of the deer yard was occupied by the Byers Creek pack, with a twenty-kilogram (forty-four-pound) lactating female. To the north near the village of Bonnechere was the Cybulski pack, and extending beyond the northern fringe of the yard, the Acorn Lake pack. The two coyotes ranged to the east.

Possibly some of these animals were wolf-coyote hybrids, with even a mixture of genotypes within packs. Summer territories of the Byers Creek and Cybulski packs covered less than sixty square kilometres, more typical of coyotes than wolves. Also coyote-like were the howls of the Byers Creek female we recorded late one warm summer night along a concession road.

With coyote-like animals present, we wondered if they would get out of the way when the migratory park wolves appeared. Canadian Wildlife Service biologist Lu Carbyn found that coyotes avoided wolves at Riding Mountain National Park in Manitoba; some that didn't were killed. The same thing happened in Yellowstone National Park after wolves were reintroduced there.

Starting the winter field work in 1995–96, we found the signal of one of the coyote-like animals coming from a pond beside the highway where someone had thrown the collar. This was a significant loss because much of that winter the migratory Travers pack was resident in the woods where it had lived.

Over that winter, both the Byers Creek and Cybulski packs reduced their summer territories by one-third. The Cybulski and Acorn Lake packs were well positioned to take advantage of the migrating deer and, after that, benefited from pockets of deer that stayed in their territories the rest of the winter. The Byers Creek pack did not move to intercept the migrating deer, but because it was well situated in the core of the deer yard, it shifted within its territory to stay with the greatest concentration of deer.

After the deer migration, the migratory wolf packs seemed to avoid the resident packs, except single collared wolves that moved everywhere just as they do in the park. Between the Byers Creek and Cybulski packs was a gap of about two kilometres, and there most of the fixes of the migratory packs fell. Use of this gap was even more striking the following winter when the Byers Creek pack consisted of only three wolves. They drew back from the northeastern segment of their territory next to the gap, and it was used like the gap itself by most of the migratory packs.

Notably apparent in the maps is the more limited use of the core of the deer yard by the migratory packs in recent winters than in the previous winters of heavy wolf killing. In those earlier years, any resident packs may have been fractured or annihilated too. The obvious conclusion, in hindsight, is that in the earlier winters without these resident packs, the deer yard was not being defended, or was defended less, and so was open for more complete wolf migration. The presence of more migratory wolves back then, the result of people killing resident wolves, probably resulted in more dead deer.

With the enhanced susceptibility of the yarded deer to wolf predation, we wanted to compare the importance of predation with other possible causes of deer death. Tracking wolves to more than a hundred deer carcasses over the years, we found only one deer that had died of malnutrition. Bone marrow for all but that one was typically fat-rich, even in late March, the only exception being a pinkish tinge in big bucks, expected because male deer suffer greater energy stress during the rut.

The one starved deer was discovered by the Travers pack. The deer was frozen on its brisket just like the many moose we found over the years being scavenged by wolves. Its bone marrow was bright red. It had died in a large cedar swamp, a type of forest rare in the park but the preferred habitat for wintering deer in our study area. Cedar swamps are dark places under dense tree crowns that hold the calm, cold winter air as if it were delicate. The sound of just a coat sleeve brushing on a twig carries a long way; these are silent places too, with few birds. Every green cedar-twig was browsed to deer height.

We came upon that starved deer in midwinter 1995–96, a year when the deer travelled to the yard early because of mid-November snows. The finding was a forewarning of possible starvation ahead. MNR biologist Dennis Voigt found that more deer died of malnutrition in a variety of Ontario deer yards when deer entered the yard early. However, shortly after we found the starved deer, a big thaw bared the fields, and the deer took immediate advantage of the exposed forage. We watched dozens of deer grazing out in the open. The vegetation had been fast-frozen in the fall so was likely highly nutritious. They made out fine after that.

Reducing the effects of any overbrowsing at Round Lake, too, has been a shift in the yard. In 1996–97, the yard expanded southeast into an area unused before, and more deer went to Germanicus. The whole region has the same requisites of a good yard – low snowfall, abundant conifer cover, cedar swamps, and hardwood browse – so undoubtedly it could provide for many more deer.

We concluded that these deer killed by wolves were not about to starve, so wolf predation was resulting in fewer deer. Roughly ninety fewer deer. This calculation was based upon an estimated five-day periodicity of deer kills per pack, multiplied by a winter average of six packs in the deer yard for an average of two-thirds of the time between mid-December and late March. To err on the high side, if wolf packs killed deer every four instead of five days, the estimate would be 108 deer.

Inflate these two figures to 110 and 124 to include the scattering of deer killed in the park and that makes up around 6 to 8 per cent of the estimated park herd. An unknown additional number of local non-park deer augment their numbers and lower this percentage.

During the rest of the year, predation apportioned among the three species of prey may account for another 10 or 12 per cent of the park deer. The combined total is a significant but not excessive kill compared to deer recruitment estimates in Ontario of about 35 per cent each year.

When we graphed changes in wolf numbers over the years, they showed no relation to changes in deer numbers. This may be due to differences in the percentages of other prey species taken.

But whatever the reason, clearly something besides predation was influencing deer numbers.

Examining our data further, we discovered that the earlier the deer migrated, the lower their numbers would be the following summer. We would see fewer deer per kilometre driven in the park. Having ruled out malnutrition, that left only hunting by humans, and there was an obvious relationship. When the deer migrated early they were subjected to both a rifle season followed by an archery season that extended right up to a few days before Christmas. Both rifle hunters and archers are plentiful. Their pickup trucks are parked everywhere, especially close to the park. Platforms are built in trees along all the major runways, and hay is spread below or commercial buck scent hung nearby. The earlier the deer migrated, the more were killed.

We thought our information would interest the MNR, particularly because by 1997 deer and hunting success had declined enough to alarm hunters and cause the MNR to establish a citizen's advisory committee in the Round Lake area. Instead, from both the Pembroke and Algonquin Park district offices, the response was: That's good because we have been trying to reduce the size of the deer population for years.

We were amazed. Deliberately reduce the size of the Algonquin Park deer population? All this time we had been trying to figure out what was preventing a further increase in deer – measuring annual browse and the condition of carcasses and factors causing migration and spacing in the yard.

MNR biologist Norm Quinn explained that the food supply was inadequate for the number of deer using the Round Lake yard, a perception he shared with some other managers. However, no recent data supported that belief. Almost forty years previously, in the winter of 1958–59, there had been a record snowfall and Doug Pimlott had found deer starving in significant numbers, but nothing similar has been recorded since then. And our data showed that deer were not suffering from any nutritional stress.

It was a mistake in deer management, easy to make given the MNR's lack of data, but more difficult to understand considering ours. Rarely had the MNR run a deer-checking station in the area to provide an estimate of the number killed by humans. The ministry had no recent estimate of population numbers, and we had not been consulted. The major control on deer numbers had been a far too generous human hunt. Local managers recognized it, and so did the deer committee, so that in 1997–98 the hunting quota was dropped on their advice from six hundred antler-less deer (females and fawns) to one hundred, plus as many bucks as there were licences. Wolf control, of course, was recommended too – it always is. Given the winter ban, the committee proposed incentives to encourage wolf killing before and after. We can only hope the MNR will not act on that one.

Reflecting on our initial questions, the uniqueness of the migratory wolf population following and concentrating with the deer is the result of an amalgam of conditions. These include: the absence of fully territorial wolves in the deer yard resulting in poorly defended or undefended land; the extensiveness of the deer migration across the territories of many packs; the concentration of deer not into several small yards, as once occurred, but into one very central one; and the possible influence of past artificial feeding compounded by deer tradition.

In the deer yard, the migratory wolves, with plenty of food and no land to defend, use simple avoidance instead of territoriality and aggression as a spacing mechanism. Individual deer, intent on finding good shelter and food, reduce the risk of being killed by yarding, but in doing so, expose the population to greater predation. More significant to changes in numbers is the price both deer and wolves pay to humans.

This seems like a maladaptive system. While individual deer and wolves may be maximizing their fitness by migrating, the populations of both species are smaller as a result. By leaving the park, both populations are drawn down by human killing, and predation rates may be greater too.

This conundrum can be interpreted in more than one way. It

may be one among other examples of a conflict between individual and population welfare. Dominant territory holders of some species, such as ptarmigan, stake large blocks of land and expel others, thereby looking after themselves but causing the population to decline.

Or maybe the conundrum is a human artifact of deer feeding, deer and wolf killing, half-protected park populations, and slow evolutionary adjustment.

Maybe the system has gone through a "phase shift" from what it was like in Doug Pimlott's days to arrive at a different set of static conditions from which it cannot easily escape. With disproportionately heavy predation on the few deer that winter in the park, deer may be stalemated into migration at whatever cost.

What will happen next? As always with ecosystem studies, it is impossible to know. But ecosystems are never static for long; some environmental condition will change. Possibly with fewer deer killed by humans, the deer population will rise, leaving larger pockets of deer in the park that live to reproduce. If these deer are at a selective advantage over migrant deer, the wholesale deer migration will end. But it is just as likely that deer recovery will take the long time necessary for the regeneration of better winter cover, if, indeed, the logged-over hemlock and pine stands can recover and do not revert permanently to hardwoods.

Or, with less canid killing in the Round Lake area, true wolf packs may become established that defend the land and repel migrant wolves. Or fur prices may escalate, or climates continue to warm, or . . .

The beauty of natural systems lies buried deep in their adaptive potential, their hidden storehouse of possibilities that hide the future.

NEW ADAPTATIONS, NEW SPECIES

ALL SPECIES swirl into the present out of a long and turbulent past, leaving evidence in their wake of their evolutionary odyssey. Like the tail of a comet, the evidence becomes less distinct with the passage of time. Only scattered bones in tar pits and sedimentary deposits tell us that they lived.

Bones in the southern United States bear witness that about one million years ago a wolf or its immediate ancestor, *Canis edwardii*, first appeared. It diverged either from the coyote or a common ancestor of both wolves and coyotes, *Canis lepophagus*. Later, wolf and coyote were joined by the larger and more robust dire wolf of possible but unconfirmed South American origin. They formed a canid trio that hunted the smallest to the largest land mammals of the Pleistocene Epoch.

They were only the newest model of a very old and successful dog-like design. Wolf-sized animals called "dog-faced cynodonts" first appeared in the fossil record in early Mesozoic times more than 200 million years ago. Cynodonts were part of a megadynasty of "protomammals" that lived before the dinosaurs. They handed on the mainstream evolutionary torch to the precursors of the dinosaurs named Thecodonts, which also included wolf-like predators.

Cynodonts then hunkered down as small forms to survive the age of dinosaurs and re-emerge as our own mammalian ancestors.

Over the last 65 million years, the Age of Mammals, many wolf-like species have come and gone: Dissacus, a member of an extinct mammalian order that lived 40 million years ago, with amazingly wolf-like teeth but sporting hooves; Miacines, early members of the familiar Order Carnivora that differentiated 35 million years ago into dog-like animals of direct wolf-coyote lineage; Mesocyon, with shearing carnassial teeth and a massive skull that lived and died between about 25 and 20 million years ago; Tomarctus, known from fossil beds in Oregon and Nebraska, dating from the Miocene between 25 and 10 million years ago, that is considered to be in the direct wolf-coyote line by some biologists, despite its hyaena-like form. There were cat-like dogs, hyaena-like dogs, bear-like dogs; they all had their day and became extinct before anybody could radio-collar them. Last to bow out, about ten thousand years ago, was the dire wolf. Only the wolf and coyote are left.

Forged in a Pleistocene world of competition and climate change, wolves and coyotes were not well adapted to get along with modern man. Nonetheless, despite human pressure, the coyote has managed to succeed, although millions have been killed over the years by predator control in the United States. Under the same pressure, the wolf succumbed over much of its former wide range.

There are reasons for this difference in persistence, including the coyote's earlier breeding age and the lack of social restriction on the number of breeding females. Wolf and coyote – physically, physiologically, behaviourally, and ecologically – are different species. But not completely.

The first time Mary and I saw the Vireo wolf, he was just a pile of fur partially hidden under October leaves. We had tracked him and heard his howl but never seen him. His completely bare skull, the canine teeth worn to stubs, lay on its side at the foot of a majestic old hemlock. By scraping away the leaves we exposed one mandible, a scapula, both femurs, one humerus. His spinal column was intact to the last caudal vertebra, all but the broad atlas, once the support for his large head. Some small animal, maybe a pine marten, had dragged it a few metres away, then abandoned it. His radio-collar lay on top of his fur, broadcasting its rapid, high-pitched signal to an unlistening and uncaring world, except for us.

He had chosen to die alone in the heart of his territory at the foot of a big hemlock that towered above the hardwoods like a monument. His identity would become etched into its needles as the tree took up his atoms. Five metres away, an iron-stained creek plunged over mossy boulders on its way down through the trees. Its water must have played a requiem, easing the dying wolf's last mortal minutes. Like other wolves, he had died near an active beaver pond. Had the leaves been off the hardwoods, he would have glimpsed the broad sweep of lowland cradling Wilkins and Robitaille lakes to the south – the land that had supported his life, supplied all his needs, rung to his howls, took the impressions of his big feet across its snow-covered lakes.

His had not been a typical life, at least not in his later years when we had come to know him. He had given us a thick file of data, enough that three months earlier we had even predicted his death. His behaviour had become wolfishly unacceptable. Sure enough, in mid-October while flying over his territory, John Pisapio heard his signal on mortality mode.

The Vireo wolf had chosen a remote place to die. We booked a float plane, but low cloud and wind forced us to cancel. Two weeks later we aborted a trip from Waterloo to get him because of high winds and rain. The following week we tried again, driving logging roads to within five kilometres of John's mark on the map. We portaged canoes down a steep trail to Vireo Lake and set out – John and his brother in one, Mary, Michelle, and I in the other.

The previous week's snow had melted, but a scattering of large flakes raced us down the lake. Lacy hemlock crowns along the shore bent in the wind, and the ranks of hardwoods swayed on the hills. A flock of common mergansers, daring winter, lifted off the water ahead, and the occasional wind-tossed raven hurtled by. Otherwise, Vireo Lake was stripped of life, ready for winter.

At the end of the lake we hauled up our canoes, took out the map, and plotted a bearing to the carcass about one and two-thirds kilometres away. The wolf's signal came in from a hilltop when we were halfway there. At his carcass we examined the scene of death, picked up the collar to be refurbished, and packed up his remains into a plastic bag. So ended the record of an unusual wolf life.

According to the capture report filed by Joy Cook on June 1, 1993, almost two and a half years previously, he was an adult male weighing thirty-six kilograms (eighty pounds). She named him Jocko 6, believing him to be a member of the Jocko Lake pack, because the capture site fell three kilometres inside that pack's southern boundary.

Throughout the summer he was located only five times, all but the last fix in the same general area, but always the two radio-collared Jocko Lake wolves were off to the north. His last fix of the summer fell south of the Bonnechere River, where the Jocko Lake pack never goes. So even before that first winter we suspected he was not really a Jocko Lake wolf.

Not until a blustery January night did Mary and I first make contact with him. Earlier that day, Joy had picked up his signal from the air over the Round Lake deer yard. Having left the park only three days earlier, he may have been following the last of the migrating deer.

Five kilometres north of him, the Jocko Lake pack was feeding on a deer out on the ice on Beaverdam Lake. That evening when Mary and I went out to monitor, the Jocko Lake wolves had gone, but to our surprise Jocko 6 (the Vireo wolf) was on the kill. He must have bided his time, waiting in the trees for the pack to depart. For a cross-bearing, we drove to the far shore and, with our headlights off, slowly approached to within 250 metres. We could picture him out there in the dark, wind ruffling the fur along his back as he tugged at the remains of the deer.

Repeatedly our evidence showed that he was a lone wolf. A few days after the Beaverdam Lake incident, we tracked him to a single bedding site in a snowy marsh beside the Bonnechere River.

He ran off just before we got there, a disappointment to Wayne Cunningham, a photographer from the *Ottawa Citizen* who accompanied us. Then another time we put him off a sunny knoll in a south-facing aspen stand where he had been curled up in the snow, basking in microclimate warmth.

He seemed to have an aptitude for finding other packs' kills, which may have been crucial to his survival as a lone wolf. Only four days after taking advantage of the Jocko Lake pack's kill, he was inseparable from the air from a Jack Pine wolf at another deer carcass. At least twice that winter, however, he appeared to have made his own kills. Although old, he was a big, strong wolf.

In the comments section of the data file that winter are repeated remarks about his extensive travels. Four times he returned to the park, often to the vicinity of Robitaille Lake twenty to twenty-five kilometres west of the deer yard. He did not follow a straight line in these travels, on one occasion roaming deep into the Basin Depot pack's territory ten kilometres to the north. Once he stayed in the park only two days before returning to the deer yard. After February 6, however, he remained out of the park, roaming extensively throughout the Round Lake area until early March. Then, one week before he returned to the park for the summer, Joy saw him from the air with another wolf. Had he found a mate down in the singles bar?

Not until the last day of July 1994 did we learn the answer. The Vireo wolf spent that early summer in the same remote area of the park where he had made his winter excursions, defining his territory to include Robitaille, Wilkins, and Vireo lakes. He was around Vireo Lake often enough that we added a new pack name to his identity, and he became Jocko 6 Vireo or, more succinctly, the Vireo wolf. He stayed south far enough to avoid trespassing on the Jocko Lake pack's land as he had the previous summer. Finally we confirmed that he and his mate had at least two pups in a marshy rendezvous site. They stayed there, howling for us on occasion, until mid-August, the end of the summer records.

Sometime between December 15 and 28, 1994, during the height of the deer migration, the Vireo wolf again travelled out to the farmlands around Round Lake. Often that winter we confirmed the existence of a pack of four. The big male was always one of them. Ninety per cent of their fixes fell within a small area covering no more than four square kilometres. Deer were plentiful there, but no more so than throughout much of the deer yard as shown by our track transects. Strangely, the pack's territory was more coyote-sized than wolf-sized.

Also strange was that this winter, the Vireo wolf, now with his new pack, stayed in the farmlands without any return trips to the park. His was the only pack that did. A few pockets of deer remained in the park that winter, enticing a few packs to stay on territory all winter and others to travel back and forth at least once.

The land chosen by the four wolves consisted of some pine-poplar hills strung together by marshes and a large cedar swamp. With all its variety, it was good wolf and deer habitat, but it posed a problem for us. Most of it was private property. The person who owned a central portion of it had little use for wolves, or for us.

Our first encounter with him was along a snowy, one-lane concession road that ended about two kilometres from his farmhouse. One January day, accompanied by a film crew from TVO (Television Ontario), we tracked the Vireo wolf and his pack along the road to an icy overflow where they had cut into the bush. The land on that side of the road was not posted, so we followed their tracks along a creek to an alder tangle where the wolves crossed on thin ice. Normally we would have jumped the creek, but the cameraman and soundman were attached by a two-metre-long cable. To make it across, they would have had to jump in unison. Both men weighed well over two hundred pounds and carried expensive equipment that added even more. We returned to the main road.

The landowner had seen our tracks and yelled at us out his truck window to stay off his land. Our attempts to explain that it was not posted seemed to anger him more.

Our second meeting a few days later did little to enhance our reputation. We had found a road-killed deer and were sure the Vireo wolf, always nearby, would find it too. That was the break the TV crew wanted. To improve their chances, producer Loren Miller phoned the Petawawa Military Base not far from Pembroke and asked for some tank camouflage. The next morning, with the camouflage draped over our truck, we proceeded slowly along the concession road towards the dead deer. Through the tiny holes across the windshield, suddenly on the narrow road ahead, we saw the same man's truck. He stopped dead, probably thinking he was caught in a military manoeuvre. We reached him and Loren got out and tried to explain. When he realized that no tanks were about to appear and he was not in danger, he gave her the same curt warning to stay off his land.

Before daybreak for three mornings we drove out to the carcass. The ravens would arrive as first light washed over the snowy scene. They paid little attention to the camouflaged truck, but we had to sit perfectly still or they would detect our movement and fly off. The Vireo wolf had indeed found the carcass and was close by each morning, especially the last morning when his signal placed him in the trees right behind the carcass. Probably he had eaten his fill and was sleeping it off. Once, the ravens all went squawking up from the carcass, and we could see – and filmed – the Vireo wolf's legs approaching from behind a big spruce. He stopped just short of the carcass, then retreated into the trees. To have lived so long in such dangerous surroundings required great stealth. Many people have glimpsed his legs in the film subsequently shown repeatedly on both TVO and the Discovery Channel.

That winter, 1994–95, back in the Vireo territory in the park, another pair of wolves capitalized on the pack's absence and moved in. We had known about the trespassers since late January. One was Pretty 7, a young female collared the preceding May, who had wandered all summer in the northcentral part of the park near the Petawawa River and once outside the park almost to the Ottawa River. In early January, after travelling to the edge of the deer yard, she took up residence along the Bonnechere River in the north portion of the Vireo summer territory. We discovered one snowy afternoon in mid-March that she had a mate. Mary and I watched them run across a marsh less than 150 metres from the Vireo pack's previous rendezvous site. We wondered what would happen when the Vireo pack returned.

To our surprise, it didn't return. In early May 1995, long after all the other park wolves had gone back to the park, the Vireo wolf was still in the farmlands. Anxious to find out if he was alone again, Mary and I drove up a muddy road to his pack's usual place. The calls of spring peepers cut the night air. His signal was loud when we got out of the truck to howl. A yippy wolf answered us, followed by long, deep howls on the same bearing as the signal. Then off to the right, about sixty metres from the Vireo wolf and partner, came distinctly coyote-like, nasal, treble yap-howls, accompanied by a lower-pitched, yippy voice. Four animals, as expected, but could the big Vireo wolf be mated to a coyote? Could the pack consist of both species?

We targeted the pack for capture, and over the next few weeks John Pisapio and assistants Alan Ramanus and Nadelle Flynn collared the three other pack members: a twenty-kilogram (forty-four-pound) lactating female, a slightly larger yearling female, and a more typical twenty-nine-kilogram (sixty-four-pound) young adult male. Like the howls we had heard, these weights suggested a mixed wolf-coyote pack.

The young adult male surprised us too. If our earlier interpretation had been correct and this Vireo pack had formed only the previous summer, that wolf should have been no older than a yearling. The explanation came a year later: genetics results confirmed that the young adult was not the big Vireo wolf's son, nor was the yearling female his daughter. So, this could not be his pack of the previous summer.

What had happened? In the fall of 1994, he must have lost his new mate and two pups and again become a lone wolf. Then travelling to the farmlands as he had before, he must have joined this resident farmland pack. We called the farmland pack the Byers Creek pack, despite the big Vireo wolf's presence in it.

In late May 1995, the Vireo wolf adopted a strangely ambivalent pattern of movement. Repeatedly, one day he was with his farmland family, and a day or two later was back on his territory in the park. Each time he made the switch, he had to travel through another pack's territory. He seemed torn between his new pack and his old lands.

We wondered if he could be a member of two packs. He always travelled back to the mid- and southern section of his lands near Vireo, Robitaille, or Wilkins lakes, a difficult area for us to access. However, we managed to get close enough to howl at him a few times and confirmed with howling and tracks that he was alone.

Meanwhile, trespassing Pretty 7 and her mate denned in an old clearing beside the Bonnechere River, the northern part of the Vireo territory. They used a sandy embankment that had been excavated more than a century before to form the cellar of a roadhouse. Mary and I kept signal-watch on this fledgling pack. Rarely was Pretty 7 more than a hundred metres from her den. In early July she moved her pups two kilometres west across the Bonnechere River.

One hot July evening, wanting to check on her, we hiked the north shore of the river. Mosquitoes carried us along. After a while Mary turned on the receiver and, to our consternation, Pretty 7's signal came in on mortality mode. What could have happened? Could the Vireo male have come back into this northern sector of his territory? We changed channels and, sure enough, for the first time that summer he was up there.

It was dark by the time we managed to ford the river at a rapids. By flashlight we followed a game trail along the south shore, but soon a complex of beaver ponds blocked us. After groping around in the alders awhile, we were forced to return to the truck and camp for the night.

The next morning we set off early, this time working our way around the ponds and following the signal to the Pretty wolf's rendezvous site. It was at a recently drained beaver pond with new grasses and sedges just starting up. We tracked the signal to a high-and-dry beaver lodge and for a while could not find the collar. Finally, Mary bent over, looked inside the old lodge through a tunnel entrance and saw it lying on the central platform within. Only the collar was there, still bolted up. No blood was on it, no matted hair, but a pair of chip marks along its edges showed where wolf teeth had clamped down on it.

There were no signs of a struggle around the lodge. Fresh pup and adult tracks plastered the mud, but nothing more. For hours we combed the area, searching in increasingly larger circles from the lodge, finding only scats and bones of beaver and deer.

The collar could have come off in a fight, or even in play, but if it were that loose she would have lost it within the first few days after collaring. All other times we retrieved wolfless collars worn for more than a few days, we were able to confirm that the wolf had died. Pretty 7 had worn her's for fourteen months. She was alive when found from the air nine days earlier. If she had been killed just after that, enough time would have elapsed in the summer heat for decay organisms and scavengers to separate her head from her body. How her collar got into the beaver lodge, a large enough entrance for a pup to carry it in, or a fisher or fox, but not an adult wolf, remains a mystery.

The Vireo wolf became the prime suspect. After all, Pretty 7 and her mate had been trespassing, even trying to raise pups on his land. Also implicating him was a change in his pattern of movements. After that, never again did he go back to his farmland family, the Byers Creek pack. He simply deserted them and stayed on his old territory, now using this northern sector that he had not used previously. He even pushed beyond his boundaries, first to the east to within a few hundred metres of the Basin Depot wolves, then a few days later to the west, where he was equally close to a male in the Redpole Lake pack. Perhaps he was looking for scavenging opportunities again.

In August we laid on a few extra flights, anticipating that he would get killed by an adjacent pack, or even possibly by the Pretty female's mate if he was still there. Back in the farmlands, John occasionally heard the Byers Creek pack howl and suspected it consisted of six animals, not just the remaining three. Had the big Vireo wolf been ousted?

He must have died in early September, judging by the leaves partially covering his skeleton. Scavenger beetles, bacteria, and flies had completely cleaned his skull. We had an incisor tooth aged by its annular rings. He had lived ten years, making him the second oldest wolf in our study.

His large skull now sits on the window shelf in my office, grimacing down at me, the mystery of his life gone from the empty braincase. At times I look at it and think about wolf social order. On a genealogy chart drawn by geneticists Sonya Grewal and Paul Wilson is the near-irrefutable evidence that the denning Pretty Lake female, the one that all our circumstantial evidence suggests was killed by the big Vireo wolf, was his daughter.

Reinterpreting, Pretty 7, daughter of the Vireo wolf, had been caught and collared on a dispersal foray looking for a mate, which explains her extensive movements that summer. Eventually she returned to her natal territory with her new mate, found it empty, for reasons unknown, and settled down.

Maybe the Vireo wolf attacked her mate and she joined in. Or perhaps she attacked her father and lost, or her mate attacked him and she was forced to choose which wolf to be loyal to, father or mate – we will never know. The event remains a secret locked up in the forest.

Hybridization is treated largely as a biological mistake in ecology texts. We learn about the immutability of species, about barriers that exist to prevent closely related species from interbreeding, and that hybridization normally results in biological failure. Most often, hybrids have little vigour, or are sterile, or produce sterile offspring.

Yet, recent research is emphasizing that across the span of evolution, hybridization has been a major source of genetic variation contributing in a major way to the diversity of life on Earth. It is one important way that species innovate, fabricate, adapt.

Our experience with the Vireo wolf and the Byers Creek pack made us ask to what extent coyote genes may be infiltrating into the Algonquin Park wolf population. Not only was that question important, it led to some exciting and unexpected discoveries, to no less than a redefinition of the species we were studying.

Genetics research done in Robert Wayne's Californian lab laid the necessary foundation. He and co-workers found that wolves in eastern North America showed a preponderance of coyote-like DNA in their mitochondria. Mitochondria are tiny bodies important in cellular metabolism found in cells of the body, and they contain DNA. Unlike other DNA found in the nucleus of cells, however, this mitochondrial DNA is cloned by the mother and passed to her offspring. The mitochondrial DNA in the father is not inherited. So by finding coyote-like mitochondrial DNA in wolves, the Californian research group concluded that female coyotes were mating with male wolves. The reverse – male coyotes mating with female wolves – was not happening or not detectable. Perhaps a female wolf would be less likely to choose a small, coyote-like animal for a mate.

The Californian group published the frequency of alleles at a certain group of gene loci, or locations on the chromosome, in both wolves and coyotes from a wide variety of places in North America. Alleles are different forms of a gene, and at the loci studied, any one of up to ten different alleles are possible. Obviously, wolves and coyotes share most of their genetic material; after all, humans and chimpanzees share 98 per cent of theirs. However, the frequencies with which various alleles show up in populations of even the same species differ and there also will be some species-specific alleles.

We established a partnership with geneticist Brad White and colleagues at McMaster University in Hamilton, Ontario, to examine our stockpile of blood taken from each wolf when we collared it, and muscle tissue collected when wolves were autopsied at the University of Guelph. Paul Wilson and Sonya Grewal, with the help of a few others, spent long hours in the lab extracting the DNA from blood or tissue of Algonquin wolves, then amplifying and teasing it out to allow identification of the alleles present at sixteen loci.

The results surprised us, even though we were forewarned by the Californian work. Thirteen per cent of the Algonquin Park wolves carried at least one coyote-specific allele, that is, an allele found only in coyote and not in any wolf populations surveyed in North America. Twenty per cent carried wolf-specific alleles. The Algonquin wolf population, then, has experienced hybridization.

Brad does not like to rest genetic evidence on species-specific alleles alone, because if he were to test more populations, they may turn out not to be unique. Geneticists have a way of illustrating similarities among populations called a "genetic tree," based upon comparing the frequencies of all the alleles they sample. The length of the lines between populations, or the limbs of the tree, show how closely populations or species are related. Such a tree, even more than the unique alleles, allows them to show evolutionary lineages forged over the millennia.

The genetic tree Paul and Sonya worked out included the placement of other wolf and coyote populations studied in Wayne's lab, and showed three distinct groupings: wolf, coyote, and hybridizing wolf populations. The Algonquin Park wolf fell into the latter grouping, with southern Quebec wolves and the southeastern United States red wolf. The red wolf (*Canis rufus*), considered a different species, was most similar genetically to Algonquin Park wolves. All three of these populations were closely grouped and distinctly different from other wolves and coyotes.

Notwithstanding the presence of coyote alleles, the Algonquin canids we have been studying are clearly more similar to wolves than coyotes. Like wolves, they eat almost exclusively large mammals rather than mice and hares. Like wolves, they kill beaver, which are almost completely ignored or too difficult for coyotes. The body weights of the Algonquin canids are, on average, much too large for coyotes, though some fall within a range of overlap. The territories of the Algonquin canids are like typical wolves, six or more times larger than those of coyotes. Pack sizes are more wolf-sized than coyote-sized in those that escaped exploitation long enough – twelve to fourteen animals in two cases. We recorded no yearling breeding, which often occurs among coyotes. Algonquin howls resonate from deep wolf chests and are not yippy and nasal like those of coyotes.

Clearly, the introgression of coyote alleles in general has not made the Algonquin population intermediate between wolf and coyote either physically or ecologically. Not yet, anyway. The loci studied, while indicative of hybridization, are largely from non-functional parts of the chromosome, conveying no specific traits.

However, one physical and two behavioural features of Algonquin wolves nagged at us as possibly influenced by recent coyote hybridization. The high degree of social acceptance without aggression between non-pack members is more coyote-like than wolf-like, though more likely it is a result of prey abundance, as discussed in the previous chapter. Also more typical of coyote behaviour is the unusually common split-pack hunting rather than whole packs hunting together, but this trait shows up in red wolves too, making interpretation difficult. Brad thinks that the degree of hybridization found genetically in the Algonquin Park wolves is not sufficient to be the cause of these behavioural characteristics.

More substantive evidence of possible coyote influence was found from skull measurements of Algonquin Park wolves made by student Sarah Stewart. She used a standard set of ten measurements and compared them with published measurements of skulls from Algonquin and vicinity all collected at least thirty years previously. The skulls in our collection turned out to be statistically smaller – not much, but smaller.

Could recent coyote gene swamping be changing the characteristics of the Algonquin wolf? There is no other apparent reason for these smaller skulls. Undoubtedly the invasion of coyote genes into Algonquin Park is influenced by opportunity. Immediately adjacent to the east and south sides of Algonquin Park during much of the breeding season, park wolves, including packless singles, encounter coyote-like animals in the resident packs. Any interbreeding with these animals carries additional coyote genes into the park.

There may be another, equally threatening way that coyote genes get into Algonquin Park wolves. Coyote-like animals may invade.

McDonald 2 Wilno, a young male captured in the summer of 1993, may have been predominantly a coyote. He weighed only twenty kilograms (forty-four pounds). Because he was caught well inside the park, initially we assigned him the name McDonald after the pack that had lived there, even though it had been annihilated down in the farmlands the previous winter. At that time we were still looking for survivors.

After a while it became apparent that he was not a McDonald Creek wolf; he was a farmland animal and had been captured on a dispersal foray. Two weeks later he settled down in mixed forest-farmland south of the town of Wilno. Over the next four years, summer and winter, we tracked him behind estate housing, at the back of farmers' fields, along busy Highway 60, and east to open lands around the "German Settlement." Once, just beyond the last house, he came up the road to our howls, crossed the ditch, circled us through a dark field, and continued along the road almost to the streetlights. Another time he was on the very edge of the bustling town of Barry's Bay.

His territory was long and thin, and only thirty-four square kilometres in area, more coyote size than wolf size. Mostly he was alone, occasionally with a mate. Their howls both sounded coyote-like. John Pisapio found their den one year, but we never confirmed pups.

Then there was Mathews 9, a tiny, fourteen-kilogram (thirty-one-pound) lactating female collared in 1994. She was caught in the interstice between two newly formed packs: Hardwood Lake to the west and Military to the east, in an area still undergoing wolf reshuffling after the loss of the Mathews pack one and a half years earlier. Her life fit no pattern. We could pinpoint no den; she must have lost her pups. In the winter she travelled widely in the Round Lake deer yard, mostly with one other animal, often trespassing in the resident Byers Creek pack's territory. Once, she shared a deer carcass with two wolves from the Hardwood Lake pack. Twice, she made forays back into the park, both times into the Hardwood Lake territory. Strangely, both times, McDonald 1 Hardwood made the trip back too, but separately. They were not found closer than 1.5 kilometres. Both times she returned to the farmlands within a day, but he stayed on.

Even stranger was that on the second of these forays, she was with McDonald 2 Wilno. Two of the smallest animals were travelling together. They met on March 5 when both were trespassing on Byers Creek land. Ten days later they were still together, thirty-five kilometres inside the park, and two days later were back in the Byers Creek territory where they stayed for four days. Then the Wilno wolf left her and returned to his own land.

That May she began to define a new territory partly in and partly out of the extreme southeast corner of the park. A few weeks later she died of unknown causes; John retrieved her decomposed carcass.

There were other small animals, and, scanning their computer files, I have looked for a pattern in their lives. Second smallest was Jack Pine 4, a three-year-old male, sixteen kilograms (thirty-five pounds). Over the one year and nine months we knew him, he seemed normal, always with other members of the Jack Pine pack. Pretty 4, a yearling female, eighteen kilograms (forty pounds), also seemed to live a normal life as part of the Pretty Lake pack. Basin 13, an adult female, 18.1 kilograms (40 pounds), lost her collar at the capture site so we know little about her except that she was an immigrant, unrelated to other Basin Depot wolves. She was travelling with the large alpha-male of the Basin Depot pack when caught.

One striking fact about the eight smallest park wolves is the short time they lived. They averaged one year and two months after collaring. Even this is an inflated value because one of the eight lived four years. Excluding that one, the average longevity after collaring was only nine months.

Another striking fact is a lack of breeding by small animals. Based upon body length, more than twice as many large females were breeders in the Algonquin population as expected from their ratio in the population as a whole. Among fourteen known alpha-females, only two were classed as "small," one being the Byers Creek female living in the farmlands outside the park. Only two other breeding females were classed as small-medium, animals still very close to coyote size. This lack of small breeders could be predicted; if coyotes get into wolf packs, rarely may they attain the necessary dominant social position to become breeders because large size is such an important prerequisite. They might breed, however, if pack structure has broken down.

Three of these small, coyote-like animals that invaded or lived in Algonquin Park were caught where wolf packs had been shattered and the land was either vacant or just being reoccupied. Others lived in packs that had suffered unusually heavy losses. Less than half of them seemed normal.

The clincher to our concern over these small animals came from a phone call from Sonya Grewal just before this book went to press. This set of small animals, all caught in the park, grouped genetically more closely with coyotes than do Algonquin wolves.

Why haven't more coyotes invaded Algonquin Park? Mice, voles, and snowshoe hares, their usual food, seem plentiful enough. In recent decades, coyotes have expanded into closed forest environments similar to those that make up Algonquin Park in New England and the Maritime provinces, even Newfoundland.

The most likely explanation is repulsion by wolves. That guess is strengthened by the observations of Dave Mech, who told me that among his unpublished data is evidence that when the Minnesota population he studies dropped below roughly one wolf per thirty-nine square kilometres, coyotes from surrounding lands invaded. Our estimated Algonquin Park average density is one wolf per thirty-eight square kilometres, right on that danger threshold, crossing it in various years. When the Minnesota wolf population recovered, coyotes disappeared, but with unknown genetic impact while they were there.

Coyote expansion has taken place in eastern North America where wolves have declined. Generally this is believed to be a result of an absence of wolf aggression. Only in the early 1900s after wolves were extirpated did coyotes enter southern Ontario, then wolfless New England, and the Maritime provinces.

As red wolves declined in the southeastern United States between 1920 and 1940, coyotes invaded from the west, or in some cases were deliberately released. According to references cited by

Gerry Parker in his book *Eastern Coyote*, hybridization took place throughout these overlapping ranges in Texas, Louisiana, Arkansas, Alabama, and other nearby states. The body weights of the last wild red wolves measured between 1968 and 1972, just before they became extinct in the wild, were considerably smaller than animals weighed before 1930. Gary Henry, current team leader of U.S. Fish and Wildlife Service's red wolf recovery program, believes, like many others, that the shrinkage in size can be attributed to hybridization with coyotes.

What happened to the red wolf should be a warning for what can happen to wolves in the southern part of Ontario and Quebec. Perhaps the warning is already too late. Graduate student Hilary Sears has collected carcasses south and east of Algonquin Park from commercial trappers who were going to kill them anyway. Weights are similar to those of the last red wolves, intermediate between wolf and coyote. Genetic analysis has confirmed their distinctiveness as more coyote-like than Algonquin Park wolves. Surprisingly, some of these animals come from continuously forested regions just like Algonquin Park.

Despite the appearance of the landscape there as favourable for wolves, logging roads open to public hunting crisscross the land, and there are no controls on wolf killing. Under such unregulated pressure from humans, wolf populations typically decline, while coyotes persist. Outside Algonquin Park we seem to be replaying the last days of the red wolf before extirpation by fragmenting wolf populations and so inviting coyotes in to hybridize and genetically swamp out the wolf. Neither of the possible barriers to interbreeding we have suggested – small body size of coyotes so social inferiority, nor short life spans – apparently have been sufficient. Maybe they will not be sufficient in Algonquin Park either, with continued wolf killing and time. How much time? We will not have any evidence to answer that question until it is too late.

Putting the evidence together, Algonquin Park is a fortress held by wolves, under siege by coyotes. The supply lines for reinforcements have been at least partially severed. Using covert infiltration, the invaders have partially broken down the defences. Given time, might they stage a successful coup? It is a serious threat.

There is more to the hybridization story, and it begins long before coyotes first entered Ontario one hundred years ago. Ron Nowak of the U.S. Fish and Wildlife Service is the acknowledged expert on canid taxonomy. His skull measurements indicate that there are two wolf species alive today. One is the gray wolf, *Canis lupus*. It formerly lived throughout North America and parts of Europe, Asia, and the Middle East, and is sometimes called the timber wolf, arctic wolf, and tundra wolf, which all are the same species. The other species is the red wolf, *Canis rufus*, which lives only in the southeastern United States. In North America, the gray wolf is further subdivided into five subspecies.

Algonquin Park wolves are listed as members of the subspecies lycaon. Not much lycaon is left in the wild. It is gone from all its former eastern United States range, which used to extend down to the Carolinas, gone from the Maritime provinces, and lives today only in southern Quebec and Ontario south of the French and Mattawa rivers.

A plausible evolutionary history supports this classification of the gray wolf into five subspecies. According to Nowak, the red wolf, or a small precursor very much like it, differentiated from the coyote about one million years ago and spread throughout North America. Sometime between 800,000 and 600,000 years ago, some animals crossed the Bering land bridge to populate Europe and Asia. There the species altered to become the gray wolf, forming several subspecies. One of them returned when the land bridge was again above water, about 300,000 years ago. That one, slightly altered, is the subspecies nubilis, alive today and inhabiting most of the remaining North American wolf range.

Subspecies nubilis is larger and greyer than its originating North American red wolf stock, having had the opportunity to change over a few hundred thousand years in Europe and Asia. Possibly it also had the opportunity to interbreed with a long-present wolf-like animal abundant in Europe and Asia called the Etruscan wolf.

After returning to North America, the gray wolf, subspecies nubilis, spawned off the other three gray wolf subspecies. Two became arctic subspecies isolated for a time in unglaciated lands there, and the third became the Mexican wolf isolated by desert in the south.

The gray wolf subspecies that is missing in this story is lycaon. Because of its similarity to the red wolf, Nowak believes it appeared early in the wolf's evolution, but describes no place for it to have lived in isolation long enough for subspeciation to occur. It just does not fit.

The answer to the question of when and where subspecies lycaon arose seems obvious now. Lycaon and the red wolf are just too similar to be separate species. Their skulls are very similar both in size and shape. Both species are smaller than other North American wolf subspecies. Both hybridize with coyotes, whereas only subspecies nubilis in Minnesota (possibly misidentified?) does so to a limited extent, and there may be some evidence for it in the Mexican wolf, which is extinct in the wild but about to be reintroduced from captive stock. In all other places, such as the Rocky Mountains, nubilis and coyotes live side by side but do not interbreed. Red wolf and gray wolf lycaon look so similar that every time Mary or I show slides of Algonquin wolves at wolf conferences, the biologists studying red wolves are amazed. The body weights of red wolves released in the wild, chosen from captives because of their larger size, are identical to those of Algonquin Park wolves. All the other gray wolf subspecies, on the other hand, look very different – bigger and either greyer, whiter, or blacker.

The genetic evidence from Brad White's lab shows that red wolf and lycaon are similar not just because both hybridize with coyotes, but despite hybridization. Strip away the coyote component and the two wolves group even more closely together, further illustrating their unity as a species.

Brad, Paul, and Sonya speculate that hybridization may have occurred at least periodically throughout the red wolf-lycaon evolutionary history, maybe right back to its origins from coyotes or a similar animal. It probably occurred then – and now, because they look so similar – with the wolf just larger, and having disproportionately larger head, broader muzzle, deeper chest, and bigger feet. These differences were not always enough to prevent interbreeding. Through periods of changing habitats as glaciers came and went in the north, often wolf and coyote must have lived in the same places. It is illogical to think that hybridization has occurred only in the past few decades.

With a long history of hybridization, when are genes from parent species validly reassigned as bona fide characteristics of their descendant hybrid species? There is no easy way to find out which genes are relatively new and which have had a long history as part of red wolf-lycaon wolf, but the geneticist team is working on that. We can only describe the genes that are there today. So, instead of using wolf-specific or coyote-specific genes to estimate the degree of hybridization in red wolf-lycaon wolf, it is fully justifiable to interpret the genes and their frequencies, regardless of origin, as characteristic of the red wolf-lycaon wolf species living today.

If wolves were being reclassified anew, and there is no reason not to, there is a strong case to call the lycaon wolf of southern Ontario and southern Quebec and the red wolf the same species. With this new genetic evidence, the present classification of lycaon as a subspecies of gray wolf appears to be unjustified.

Which name should prevail? On a genetic tree, the Algonquin population of lycaon lies closest to the root of wolves, less influenced by coyote hybridization than either the red wolf or southern Quebec wolf. As well, the Algonquin Park lycaon has one unique gene found in one-quarter of the population that has been lost, possibly through hybridization, in southern Quebec lycaon and the red wolf.

So, reclassified, *Canis lupus lycaon* and the red wolf, *Canis rufus*, would both become *Canis lycaon*. A logical common name would be the "lycaon wolf," or "eastern wolf," or the "eastern timber wolf."

Canis lycaon, ironically, is exactly the first name given North American wolves in 1775 by the European naturalist Johann Schreber. He provided that name for a wolf described a few years earlier by French naturalist Georges Louis Leclerc Buffon. This wolf, captured somewhere in New France, was brought back alive to France by military officers. In volume twelve of Buffon's forty-four volume natural history of North America is a picture of this black animal, with detailed measurements of every part of its anatomy including internal organs.

Would reclassification matter? The red wolf became extinct in the wild in the mid-1900s, but captive stock has been reintroduced since 1988 into North Carolina and Tennessee. A vigorous and seemingly successful recovery program is taking place under the United States Endangered Species Act. Recognizing lycaon as the Canadian counterpart of the United States red wolf, which has been the subject of intensive restoration efforts, adds significantly to the case for more adequate protection. So does recognizing its distinctiveness from other gray wolves, whether full species status is accepted or not. In its very limited remaining range, where packs are continually being fractured by human killing, and where it lives in close juxtaposition with coyotes, it may be under unusually intensive genetic siege.

We have no endangered species act in Canada. In this respect, we lag behind the United States by decades. We do, however, list over 275 species, subspecies, and regional populations in various categories of endangerment and have developed recovery plans for some. The governing body is called COSEWIC – Committee on the Status of Endangered Wildlife in Canada – with federal, provincial, and non-governmental representatives.

In a 1997 status report commissioned by the committee, sub-species lycaon was proposed for listing even before this genetics story unfolded. A representative of the MNR opposed it, and the decision was deferred for two years. Now, full species or not, its genetic uniqueness makes acceptance even more indisputable. The MNR has little choice but to comply, then give it greater protection. Politics should not confound taxonomic classification.

We have begun additional research because of these findings. One component is to determine if lycaon hybridizes with nubilis to the north. Another is to find out if any relatively pure Algonquin lycaon wolves exist anywhere outside Algonquin Park, such as in the vicinity of the Magnetawan River to the west or anywhere we have not yet looked in the Madawaska Highlands to the south, the only two large blocks of wildlands left in the subspecies' range. If we do not find healthy, unfragmented populations of lycaon anywhere else, and smaller, more coyote-like animals predominate wherever populations are heavily exploited, which is everywhere outside Algonquin Park, then we will be even more concerned. Algonquin Park may be the last refuge of the purest remaining lycaon wolf.

WILDNESS

Beyond the conspicuous – a moose grazing water lilies, a wolf trotting across a frozen lake, the ranks of Algonquin hills – is a quality, a character, a complexion in nature that comes from something fundamental. It buttresses ecosystems; it provides a foundation. Forged from eons of evolution, built from the intimate intermingling of living things, independent of crushing human dominance, is "wildness" – ecosystems and species shaped through millennia by nature.

Wildness is not easy to find any more. We control nature, directly or indirectly, even in wilderness parks. In the glare of human endeavour, wildness shrinks. Nonetheless, hidden deep in a stand of old-growth pine, strung through the damp lowlands, cresting a distant ridge, are fundamental patterns and basic interrelationships – the rules of life. They are worth finding, necessary for comparison with all the made-over rest.

A hierarchy of scale is the principal design feature of nature, the first diagnostic character that some celestial designer would describe if asked about life on Earth. In all wild places, small animals make a living exploiting small resources in small areas scaling up to large animals exploiting large resources across large areas. Body size sets energy needs, metabolic rates, life spans, territory sizes, and allows ecosystems to provide life support for many living things simultaneously. Every species is structured to live in this hierarchy.

Understanding the wolf, or any species, means understanding its hierarchical place. The wolf's large body, well over the mammalian global average of a mere one hundred grams, means that it has an excessive energy demand per individual, must get its food in large packages, and cover a lot of ground to obtain it. A minimum viable wolf population, able in the long run to maintain its genetic diversity and overcome environmental contingencies, needs a lot of room. Such a population has been estimated at 150 animals using the internationally accepted criteria of at least 50 randomly mating breeders, inflated by immatures and social subordinates. The figure is unrealistically low, because the condition of random mating is not met in wolves due to their pack structure. But the land requirements for only 150, roughly the pre-breeding season Algonquin Park population, is the entire park.

At this scale of a few thousand square kilometres, the wolf has the ability to both stabilize or destabilize ecosystems, dampening prey eruptions or limiting the size of prey populations when it drives system change (top down), easing off its impacts to insignificance when it rides the system (bottom up). In Algonquin, we conclude that the wolf is largely riding more fundamental changes made by logging and wildlife exploitation. The wolf is in response-mode. Too many other events are occurring, park notwithstanding, for it to play a major role, by itself, in changing prey numbers. As well, both Algonquin wolves and their ungulate prey are on, or near, their range-edges, where, like most species, environmental conditions are more variable and significant than species interrelationships.

It might be different in a more stable, range-central environment, one with less human impacts, one perturbed on a frequency of every hundred years or so by natural fire rather than by a twenty- or forty-year logging rotation, not to mention erratic fur prices, changing hunting quotas, and shifting forest-product economies. There, wolves might commandeer a greater influence on ecosystems.

However, what wolf-prey-vegetation-soil relations would be like in more stable environments remains speculative. No wolf studies have been done where human impacts are insignificant (excluding Isle Royale National Park, an island with little possibility of wolf or prey dispersal or immigration). Few large, unstaked, unhunted, and unlicensed places exist, and where they do, wolves are sparse and research costs high. Draw on a map a two-hundred-kilometre radius around every arctic and subarctic settlement: that is the one- or two-day range of a snowmobile and represents hunted and trapped lands. Then map all the exploration and logging roads, and the fly-in hunting camps. Wolves are legally protected on less than 2 per cent of wolf range in Canada, and, even there, protection is inadequate in parks that are too small.

Moreover, wolf and prey populations operate at an even larger, "metapopulation" scale, with even broader landscape relationships. The Burwash caribou herd we studied in the years just before our current Algonquin research moved seasonally in and out of Kluane National Park in the southwest Yukon, periodically exchanging members with the adjacent Aishihik herd. Similarly, a huge Steese-Fortymile herd in Alaska numbering in the tens of thousands shrunk so dramatically that during my Ph.D. years we saw only about a dozen caribou on the northern sector of its range. Just a few years later, a picture in the Fairbanks newspaper showed an estimated ten thousand animals grazing there. They had come back.

There is only one caribou herd in northwestern North America if you accept a proper ecological time-space scale. It ebbs and flows across the land – eddies here, disperses there, declines here, and fills in there. Similarly, there is only one wolf population, the caribou's constant companion, tracking its fate, responding to it both locally and regionally through adjusting densities.

That is how nature works on the large scale. Because of local immigration and emigration, population sizes and boundaries are ever-adjusting, kaleidoscopic, temporary. We know it now, with plenty of evidence, but can we adjust?

Onto this shifting mosaic of nature we have established a small set of disconnected parks and reserves, hoping they will protect the species within. They will, the smaller, less space-demanding species, providing patches of suitable habitat with opportunities for populations to move between them. Red squirrels and river otters are served well by a park such as Algonquin. But not wolves.

For wolves to be protected, first they need an adequate core. It is a fact of geometry that fully 50 per cent of Algonquin Park lies within only ten kilometres of a park boundary. With wolf-pack diameters averaging fifteen to twenty kilometres, only packs living in the centre of the park do not range routinely outside the park. That represents about sixteen to eighteen packs, or perhaps seventy-five animals in late winter. The other half of the population is unprotected part of the time, especially vulnerable to shattered social systems and coyote-gene invasion.

Put only a ten-kilometre-wide protection zone around the park, and wolf protection immediately doubles. Vacant lands where canoeists won't hear wolves will be less common. Coyotes will be held a little more at bay.

But that is not enough. Also necessary are extensive linkages to other parks or wildlands, to provide for metapopulation flow, buffer the vagaries of nature that can lead to local population decline, and reduce both genetic isolation and coyote influence. Such a provision would require broad no-kill zones linking Algonquin with Killarney Park on Georgian Bay to the west, Temagami to the north, La Verendrye and Laurentide parks in Quebec to the east, and the Madawaska Highlands to the south. Call these broad bands "designated wolf protection zones," a term coined by Monte Hummel, and redress to some extent the enormous imbalance that would still exist between wolf protection and exploitation in Ontario and eastern Canada.

The Foys Lake pack, stringing thirteen sets of footprints across frozen bogs, dividing home-chores at its rendezvous sites, forcing its boundaries against the Redpole pack to the west and the McDonald Creek pack to the east, made us rethink the concept of group selection and its implications for wildness. Although group selection is still not widely accepted, we join a growing number of biologists who argue its validity. Why should natural selection operate at only one level, the level of the individual? Better to see it in a nested, hierarchical way, like the very structure of nature it forges. Not only does the best-fit wolf survive to leave the most offspring, but so does the best-fit pack.

Survival of the best-fit group has been so obvious in our own evolutionary history that it should come as no surprise. We, like wolves, were a cooperative group-living animal exhibiting division of labour, competing with neighbouring tribes. Technological advances repeatedly gave one society after another the upper hand.

One form of group selection is more acceptable among biologists: "kin selection" occurs when individuals in the group are closely related. Then cooperation, even altruism, makes the most sense, because members of the group share the same genes – parents, offspring, grandparents, siblings, aunts, uncles, nephews, nieces. Among Algonquin wolves though, what we are seeing is not just kin selection, because the packs are not simply kin groups. We find too much dispersal for that. We had too many instances of adoption resulting in almost as much genetic relatedness between packs as within them.

In the Foys Lake pack, with its extensive, resource-rich territory, were two large adult males and one smaller one, at least two of them breeders according to genetic evidence. The pack must have been formidable to other packs who knew them around their boundaries, and dominant down in the farmlands where packs congregated each winter. But despite its strength, the pack did not survive.

It died largely because the group fitness it represented was for surviving in nature, not for surviving the onslaught of humans. In the end, it did not matter that the Foys Lake wolves were good at making a living, at cooperatively finding and dispatching prey, caring for and teaching their young, and actively or passively defending their boundaries.

What mattered more, but they were not adequately selected for, was avoiding humans: neck snares, bullets, and traps, and staying in the ditch when a vehicle approached instead of running out in front of it. Those are the things that really matter now, under the new world order.

It *is* a new world order, one where humans have taken over as a predominant selective force operating on most species on Earth, and we may not be aware of its frightening significance. It means that the species around us are incrementally, insidiously becoming "made by humans" instead of "made by nature."

The quality of wildness inherent in nature is neither subtle nor obscure; it can be defined, even measured. A wild individual, pack, population, even ecosystem is simply one that is predominantly being continually shaped by natural selection, not by human selection.

A wolf pack with a rendezvous site in an alfalfa field near the Minnesota–North Dakota border, as biologist Eric Gese described to me, is not a wild, shaped-by-nature wolf pack. It is a conservation success but no replacement for truly wild wolves. That it can live there, that wolves have expanded in Minnesota and into northern Michigan and Wisconsin, and in Spain, Italy, Germany, Romania, and other European countries, is due to legal protection. Wolves can live almost anywhere, even in human-dominated landscapes, if there is prey, as long as they are not persecuted.

Contrary to the suggestion I made at the end of my book *Wolves and Wilderness* in 1975, wolves and wilderness are not inseparable. In light of this range expansion, I have reconsidered. Accepting the dose of reality that humans have and will continue to change and control much near-wild land, and that many human influences, such as the spread of contaminants, are so subtle, there is room for conservation policy to maintain wolf populations in places where humans impact them and select for new adaptive traits.

But real, wild wolf populations under the influence of natural selection are different, and they are inseparable from wilderness. To keep nature-forged wolves in parks and surrounding lands, we must maintain their wild, evolutionary crucibles predominantly under nature's control. The wolf – highly social, group selected, cooperative – is not just numerically, but also qualitatively, sensitive to the effects of exploitation, more so than many other species. Social systems are fragile things, dependent as they are upon subtle interrelationships and the passing down of tradition. They can be easily broken.

Wild wolves, not made-by-human wolves, wild grizzlies, wolverines, cougars, great spotted cats, large primates, and all their dependants should be the goal of all large "protected" areas wherever these species are found and, in supportive ways, their surrounding lands. Having such places is a matter of humility.

Under this definition of "wild," the Algonquin Park wolf population fails to qualify. The population declined by 43 per cent between 1989 and 1993, then increased for three years to within 9 per cent of its previous high, then declined again by 28 per cent in 1997, and has stayed equally low into 1998. These changes in numbers have been driven predominantly by mortality of yearlings and adults, with highs of 61, 55, and 36 per cent in various years. Human killing has been the major cause of death, mainly snaring and shooting, and exceeds all other causes combined. It exerts the predominant selective force on wolves over one year old. The killing has resulted in many territory vacancies that have taken up to three years to refill.

Recruitment of pups to yearling age failed to offset losses in years of the heaviest killing. Recruitment has been roughly steady at 20 to 25 per cent, despite exploitation, meaning that the population cannot withstand combined annual mortality of more than that without declining. This level is low compared with other studies, indicating that the Algonquin Park population is particularly sensitive to exploitation. Causes of low yearling recruitment are unknown. Speculatively, canine parvovirus may be killing pups, or they may have low viability due to possible inbreeding depression (suggested by an unexpectedly low genetic variability), or parental care may be inadequate because of a predominance of young parents in the population due to exploitation. Average longevity of yearlings is only 3.6 years, and since wolves normally do not breed until they are two, or sometimes three, years of age, parental experience is limited.

The killing, besides causing numerical drawdown, has influenced social structure. It has resulted in small late-winter pack sizes averaging only between 3.5 and 4 animals. Vacant lands have driven dispersion to high levels (with consequent high genetic mixing within the park and possible increased interspecific pack tolerance). We have found less than expected coordinated pack hunting, less traditional use of den and rendezvous sites, less stable pack boundaries, and more lone wolves, especially adults.

This is an exploited, not a protected, population, a population predominantly under human-selection pressure. Only a handful of packs in the centre of the park live predominantly under nature's influence. They represent less than half the park population, less than one hundred animals, too few to maintain the characteristics of their species in the long run. This constitutes a failure in park management. It rests with the MNR to change that by completing a zone of protection around the park.

We did not expect to find the group-tolerance system of land division that was just as obvious as the standard, defended territories normally described for wolves. Trespass rarely evoked active aggression. Nor did we expect the wolf migration and concentration, the biggest surprise of the study, and a dramatic example of behavioural plasticity and adaptability. In the deer yard each winter, packs showed an even greater level of tolerance by simple, short-range avoidance, and we concluded that this tolerance was largely due to the abundance of food.

But, paradoxically, this concentration resulted each winter, and still does, in population loss: while individuals maximize their own fitness by following their food supply, the population declines due to human killing. Similarly, the deer migration, while adaptive for the individual, exposes the population to greater human hunting pressure, often lowering its numbers too.

These examples show that maximum individual fitness does not necessarily translate, as you might expect, into maximum population fitness. This is especially evident when humans alter the system as they have in and around Algonquin Park. Natural selection, operating on individuals and packs, may not always bail out populations faced with environmental hazards. The broad consequence is that we cannot expect species to adjust automatically to a made-over human world. Species reach an evolutionary accord between individual, group, and population welfare. When environments and selection pressures change, we may break that accord. It is part of life's vulnerability.

With great care we transported vials of wolf blood to the Pembroke Animal Hospital after wolf captures, but we had no idea that they would turn out as significant to wolf conservation as they have. We did not expect to raise the question of whether the wolves we were studying are an entirely different species. Nor did we suspect the possibility that the Algonquin Park population would turn out to be its last extensive stronghold. After a decade of research, a new avenue of inquiry suddenly emerged. We hope, research funds willing, to pursue a scientifically based conservation strategy for remaining lycaon range. With new interest we look at the red wolf recovery program in the eastern United States because we may be studying the same species, with many of the same pressures.

In the interests of not living in a biologically impoverished world, it matters if Algonquin wolves are distinctive from other gray wolves. Much of the case for preserving biodiversity rests at the level of genes. Subspecies have different percentages of genes, and species are even more different. Algonquin wolves trail their own evolutionary history. They may have their own unique ways of dealing with the contingencies of life in eastern forests.

We know that too much association with coyotes can result in gene swamping – the loss of wolf appearance and traits – such as was happening with red wolves just before they were extirpated. We also know that fragmentation of the wolf population by over-exploitation invites coyotes to invade wolf lands. It shocked us to find wolf-coyote hybrids that are distinctively different from wolves on wild lands where we thought there were wolves to the south and east of Algonquin Park. Possibly, gene swamping has happened almost everywhere else in the former Algonquin wolf's range beyond the immediate vicinity of the park.

Will we do nothing, just let it happen, lose the Algonquin wolf, just when we have discovered its uniqueness?

Three prey species provide the Algonquin wolves with food. Of the three, white-tailed deer is by far the most influential, probably because it is easily caught and comes in optimum-sized packets of energy. Wolves show their preference for deer by following their migration and by selectively hunting any that remain on their territories.

The deer population began a slow recovery in the early years of our study, then fluctuated and declined. We estimate recent deer numbers to have ranged between 0.5 and 0.75 per square kilometre over our study area on the eastern side of the park. This figure is low by eastern North American standards, and even for Algonquin Park in the early 1960s when the population was at 5.8 per square kilometre.

These deer, spread out across 2,700 square kilometres in summer, migrate each winter into just a few hundred square kilometres outside the park. This is a large drainage area for a deer yard. Thirty-five years ago, when deer were more plentiful, other yards inside the park were used as well. Timing and completeness of the migration depend upon snowfall, temperature, and acorn abundance in various combinations.

While wolf predation is a significant cause of deer mortality, it is not limiting by itself. Deer make up only one-third of the wolf diet. We found that changes in deer numbers related primarily to human killing, and that has been important in preventing the deer population from increasing. Contributing to its lack of increase, as well, may be reduced cover due to the particular shelterwood system of pine and hemlock logging in the park.

Beaver is the unstudied component in the system, something we hope to rectify because they are important forest architects. We know from scat analysis that beaver is a seasonal food, most important when they are on land in early spring, late summer, and fall. We also know that beaver hair shows up surprisingly frequently in winter scats, and while wolves cannot dig into frozen beaver lodges, they always swing over to check them out. During mild spells, beaver emerge to restock their food supply. Sometimes they are vulnerable to wolves, travelling a hundred metres or more from a hole in the ice.

Moose are at a high density of about 0.5 per square kilometre. Partway through our study, the moose population fell when native people were allowed to hunt inside Algonquin Park for the first time since its establishment. However, after two years, the population recovered, possibly due to the counter-effect of logging that replaced extensive pine forests in the Bonnechere Valley, and to a lesser extent in the Petawawa drainage to the north, with plentiful red maple and poplar saplings, prime moose foods.

We found that wolves kill yearling or adult moose year-round, but scavenging is particularly common in late winter on animals that have died of the effects of winter tick. Moose calves make up a mere 15 per cent of the summer diet. Partly because of this low figure, and the scavenging, we conclude that wolf predation poses a relatively minor constraint on the moose population. More important are range conditions. Evidence of nutritional stress was shown by low twinning rates and, in some years, noticeably small yearlings in the population.

For wolves to be more significant in limiting the populations of either deer or moose, its population would need to be allowed to adjust upwards, rising to a level set by the availability of food. But the Algonquin Park wolf population is limited by heavy human killing and low recruitment.

In a natural system, forest conditions set ungulate densities, which set wolf densities, or wolf densities set ungulate densities, which influence forest conditions. The difference may relate to the frequency of large-scale events such as forest fires, ice storms, severe winters, or wildlife diseases. Both of these systems represent variants on how nature works, and should be allowed to operate in a park.

In or around Algonquin, however, human hunting influences the deer population, human killing influences the wolf population, and logging influences both. Behind the no-cut fringe of trees around lakes and portages is an ecosystem under human control.

Throughout our study, we have searched for a fundamental, sustainable relationship between humans, wolves, and things wild and free. We have wondered, particularly, if science can identify such a relationship and, through ecology, spin out guidelines. If we can go to Mars and build all sorts of elaborate technological mousetraps, we should be able to manage nature in a sustainable way.

Reflecting on our years of study, we realize that we cannot. The complexity of ecosystems places them beyond comprehension. All the interactions between soils, maples, pines, hemlock, moose, deer, spruce budworm, winter tick, brainworm, snow, acorns, logging, hunting, snaring, coyote alleles, gene selection, cooperation, competition, co-evolution – and wolves.

Not through computer models that calculate the yields of deer, moose, trees, or codfish will we reach an accord with nature. Too many models are full of tenuous assumptions, or plain wrong. Nor can we look to a generation of highly trained ecologists conducting studies that fill the scientific journals, although, properly used as a means and not an end, their findings are vital to good conservation.

But our failure to understand the way nature operates can, at the same time, provide the opportunity for our success. Nature's complexity can be, if we so choose, the fount of a deep respect. Trying to understand at least some of the interrelated pieces brings immeasurable satisfaction. It allows us to ask better questions and provides a platform for wonder. Wonder breeds caring. It is simple caring that leads to a cautious sustainable, harmonious relationship with wild things, caring even for the wolf – litmus of our environmental sincerity.

One late-August evening in 1997, we pulled our canoe up in the cattails and leatherleaf that lined the shore of McDonald Creek. We pitched our tent and ate dinner. We were there to find the McDonald Creek pack. The previous winter, all aerial locations on the two radio-collared adults showed them alone. We wanted to find out if they were the only adults, and if they had denned successfully.

With the mist rising, at dusk we set out, tracing the bends in the creek from the shadows piled up along its grassy shores. The dark water slipped under the bow and out behind. We talked in whispers, embraced by the silence of that late-summer night.

Periodically Mary raised the antenna and rotated it slowly through 360 degrees, but neither wolf's signal came in; the wolves were somewhere else. Paddling slowly to avoid hidden rocks, we got back to camp shortly after midnight.

Then, at 3:15 A.M., the wolves found us, their howls gradually impressing themselves on our awareness. I climbed out of the tent for a bearing. A waning moon hung just above the mist still lying over the marsh. Silvery dewdrops clung to the tips of pine needles outlined with clarity in the moonlight. Both collared wolves were there, out along the creek where we had been. They howled on and on, long after I returned to the tent. We lay still and listened.

APPENDIX: The Status of Wolf Management in Ontario, the Case for Wolf Protection Beyond Algonquin Park Boundaries, and the Government's Position

ONTARIO HAS the most exploitive wolf-management policies of any jurisdiction in Canada. Wolves are managed more like vermin than a species with some value. They can be killed without any requirement to report by landowners and by anyone holding a small game licence anytime during the year in southern Ontario, or between September and June in northern Ontario, without limit. Trappers have no quota for wolves as they do for other furbearers. In contrast, other jurisdictions in Canada manage them like other valued game or furbearer species, some provinces with area-specific harvest limits.

In Ontario, wolves are protected only within Algonquin Provincial Park, Lake Superior Provincial Park, the Nipissing Crown Game Preserve, and the Chapleau Crown Game Preserve. These areas cover less than 2 per cent of Ontario's wolf range. Wolves can be killed (depending upon the ethnic origin of the hunter or trapper) inside all other parks, both national and provincial.

Less than half of Algonquin Park's estimated thirty-four to thirty-eight wolf packs have territories that fall primarily within the park. Outside the park, wolves are open to killing just as they are elsewhere in the province, except for the ban applied seasonally (December 15 to March 31) in three townships – Hagarty, Richards, and Burns – that run along less than 4 per cent of the park's boundary. Twenty-four townships abut Algonquin Park.

Algonquin Park wolves warrant special attention because of the park's high usage by the public and the opportunity it provides to hear wolves howl.

Algonquin Park wolves warrant special attention because of their uniqueness. They are either: red wolves, until now thought to be extirpated (and recently reintroduced from captive stock) in the eastern United States, their only known range; or a unique species of wolf (additional to the other two species in the world: gray wolf and red wolf) with its remaining range restricted to southern Ontario and southern Quebec; or a distinctive sub-species of the gray wolf called lycaon that has the same restricted range. More research will determine which of these possibilities is correct.

Whatever its taxonomic status, the Algonquin Park wolf population may be the last remnant of its kind. Hybridization with coyotes has changed the nature of the wolf genetically, physically, and ecologically throughout all equally heavily forested lands south and east of the park. If exploitation is the cause, as appears most likely from our data, then we cannot expect populations of the Algonquin wolf to persist free from significant hybridization anywhere else in its range.

Threatening to Algonquin Park wolves is the same gene swamping with coyotes that has occurred outside the park. (All park wolves carry coyote genes now, although not enough or not the right ones to change their physical or ecological nature.) Coyote genes can invade Algonquin Park wolves in three ways: when park wolves meet coyote-like animals outside the park on parts of their territories, or when park wolves follow migratory deer in winter, or when coyote-like animals invade the park. The presence of coyote-like animals both near and within Algonquin Park appears to be the result of wolf killing.

The following demographic facts make the Algonquin Park wolves vulnerable to human exploitation:
- Population changes between years are driven primarily by annual mortality.
- Recruitment of new animals to yearling age has been steady over the years at 20 to 25 per cent. This level of recruitment is low compared with most other wolf studies and makes the Algonquin population particularly vulnerable.
- The primary cause of low recruitment appears to be a low number of pups by the end of the summer. Among speculative explanations is low parenting success due to inexperience because of the heavy exploitation, the effects of canine parvovirus on pups, and lack of genetic diversity.

Between 1989 and 1993, the population declined by 43 per cent, followed by three years of increase, then a 28 per cent decline in 1997, and a stable low population early in 1998. Mortality rates, estimated from the deaths of yearling and adult radio-collared wolves, have been up to 61, 55, and 36 per cent in various years. These figures are low because they do not include wolves killed and collars smashed without our knowledge.

Human killing exceeds all other causes of death combined. All of this killing occurs when wolves are outside the park. Less than half has taken place within the three-township wolf-protection zone, mostly before the seasonal wolf-killing ban was implemented in 1993; more than half has occurred in other townships adjacent to the park – an underestimate because of our lack of work in recent years on the west side of the park.

Neck snaring is the major cause of death, followed by shooting. Commercial trappers take a minority; more wolves are killed by people who kill them because they don't like them.

This heavy level of exploitation has affected the integrity and fitness of the population in the following ways:

• Whole packs, or enough members to damage the social structure of the pack, commonly have been killed.

• Vacant territories have taken from one to three years to refill.

• Dispersal rates from packs is very high, typical of an exploited population.

• Wandering yearlings and adults are unusually common.

• Dens and rendezvous sites are rarely reused, and territory boundaries alter more than they would if the population was not so heavily exploited.

• Packs commonly split up when hunting, even in winter, showing less cohesion than expected.

**Proposed
Protection Zone**

Legend
☐ Park Core
▨ Internal 10-K perimeter
■ Proposed 10-K protection zone
— Park boundary

0   50km

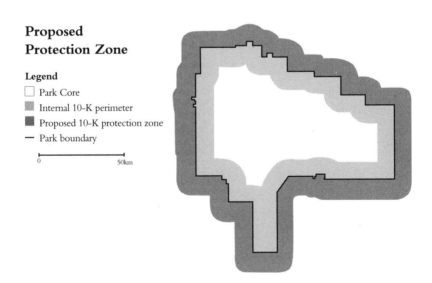

It is the position of World Wildlife Fund Canada, The Wildlands League (with parent organization the Canadian Parks and Wilderness Society), and the Federation of Ontario Naturalists that a ten-kilometre-wide protection zone be established around Algonquin Park. This zone would extend protection to all packs that have most of their territory within the park. This distance is approximated by all townships bordering Algonquin Park. (Exceptions should occur only where livestock losses are verified and cannot be controlled in other ways, and then be government supervised and local.) Furthermore, Algonquin Park should be situated as the core of a linked system of "designated wolf protection zones."

Over the past year, MNR policy respecting the future of Algonquin wolves has been both perplexing and ambiguous. In the summer of 1997, it published a review of our research in the park publication *The Raven* that minimized, ignored, or distorted most of our findings described in this book. The review was based upon no research by the ministry, nor was it written or reviewed internally by any practising wolf ecologist – the MNR has none. Its authors wrote: ". . . wolves die. We are only seeing something that, one way or another, must and does happen all the time. On balance, we [the MNR] don't believe there is any evidence to think, under the present conditions, that the Park wolf population is at risk through vulnerability to human killing outside the Park – or even any compelling reason to expect that it would be."

Our request for an opportunity to publish a rebuttal, common courtesy in most print media, was denied.

Ten months later, in May 1998, as this book went to press, the Minister of Natural Resources recognized the conservation problem our research identified by announcing his intention to establish an all-stakeholder – hunters, trappers, environmentalists, local citizens, scientists – "advisory committee to assist in the development of a conservation strategy for the gray wolf in and around Algonquin Park."

Can such a committee recommend the needed protection for Algonquin Park wolves? Or will it simply camouflage continuing government inertia?

We have made our case. Never in Canada has so much scientific research been made available upon which to base a wolf-management decision. How many more years of evidence, and how many more wolf deaths will it take?

As I write, two more Algonquin Park wolves are on mortality mode, found on this morning's telemetry flight. One of them died outside the park. Their carcasses await pickup.

ACKNOWLEDGEMENTS

WORLD WILDLIFE FUND CANADA'S scientific research program has supplied most of the funding for this research. Its ability to do so is due to the faith that some individuals put in us. We owe a great debt of gratitude to Bill Menzel of Toronto, who supports us both out of his personal concern and in memory of his wife, Oivi. Without his support, our research would not be possible. Others have made major contributions through WWF, particularly Rosamond Ivey-Thom and the McCutcheon family. In recent years, the Wildlands League has supported us through the generous contribution of Glen Davis, who we thank also for editorial comment on this manuscript. Other people made substantial contributions through charitable donations via the University of Waterloo, including Bob Bateman, Harold Cusden, and Kingsley Ward. We thank them all. Both Bill and Glen have had a few good experiences with us in Algonquin Park.

Initial funding was supplied by the National Science and Engineering Council of Canada, and for three years the Ontario Government's Renewable Resource Research program. For a few years, at a crucial time, the International Fund for Animal Welfare threw its support behind us, and we thank Brian Davies. Throughout the study we have received student summer employment grants either provincially or federally.

Recent work to identify the type of canid, its habitat affiliations, and related genetic and disease components have been made possible by a substantial grant from the Max Bell Foundation, and we thank Virginia Froman. Subsidiary funds were granted from Wildlife Habitat Canada.

Over the years, Friends of Algonquin Park, a non-profit organization, has sold our publications and donated full proceeds to us. Wolf Awareness Inc. provided us with some radio-collars in the earlier years of the research, and for a time president Hank Halliday flew telemetry surveys as a volunteer. The Algonquin Forest Authority provided a small grant in our initial years, as did Murray Brothers Lumber Company of Madawaska.

Three outfitters have provided financial help: Mountain Equipment Co-op in Toronto, Trailhead in Ottawa, and Adventure Guide in Waterloo.

Some schools and Scout groups have bought a radio-collar and in that way adopted a wolf. Many of the children in those programs learned about wolf mortality the hard way.

We, and the wolves of Algonquin, owe much to former MNR area manager John Johnson (now working in Peterborough, Ontario) and Pembroke district manager Ray Bonenberg for their courageous stand against the killing of park wolves and support for the three-township ban. John had a lively interest in the details of our work, and we enjoyed many discussions about wolves and deer with him.

Other MNR people quietly supported us from behind the scenes in our efforts to get their employer to resolve problems of Algonquin Park wolf and forest management. We appreciate their assistance.

On a scientific level, District Biologist Mike Wilton was always generous with the moose data he collected and with his time for discussions. In the field, a number of conservation officers have been most helpful: Blake Simpson, and in the early years Pat Sloan, whose patrol areas include the Round Lake deer yard, Charley Bilmer and assistant Larry Cobb, who handle the eastern part of the park, and Ed Hovinga and Art Gamble, who provide student crews with training in bear handling. Park superintendents Ernie Martelle and John Winters have approved our research for annual permits. Dan Strickland provided accommodation at the park museum staff house on occasion.

Many students have cut their teeth on wildlife work with us and contributed through seasonal employment or volunteer positions. We particularly acknowledge the people who earned degrees, especially Graham Forbes (who earned two). We shared much enjoyment and frustration. Other graduate students who have had the satisfaction of making original contributions are Lee Swanson, Joy Cook, Doerte Poszig, John Pisapio, Hilary Sears, Jenny Theberge, and Michelle Theberge. Some students wrote up aspects of the field work into senior honours theses: Lisa Atwell, Mark Hebblewhite, Ryan Norris, Harry Vogel, Sarah Stewart, and Peter Wamberra, the former four working also as summer field assistants. Other students who have worked as field assistants include: Eric Barr, Sarah Bauer, James Bay, Stephan Beauregard, Carolyn Callaghan, Lou Chora, Rod Duncan, Cam Douglas, Carvell Fenton, Nadelle Flynn, April Haig, Andrew Hawke, Willy Hollett, Leslie Hunt, Jennifer Neate, Alison Neilson, Kerri Pauls, Alan Ramanus, Ken Reiche, Hilary Rollinson, Sheryl Ross, Judith Schwartz, Cathy Shuppli, Diane Slye, and Shannon Walshe. Providing lab assistance were Irene Domingoes, Julie Duroo, and Lowell Grieb.

Volunteers from other countries who worked at least three months with us include Katrine Tchanen (Switzerland), Debbie Smith (California), Sophie Alexandre (Portugal), Luis daFonesca Moreira (Portugal), Christina Wolfe (Austria), Marguerite Trocma (Switzerland), and Paul Mosiman (Switzerland).

A few husband-and-wife teams have helped us collect data at various times: Fred and Diane Gregory, Hank Halliday and Val Quant, Craig and Elaine Hurst, Bill and Carrie Steer, and Steve and Alison Woodley.

It has been stimulating to have research colleagues to share the excitement of discovery. Dr. Ian Barker and Dr. Doug Campbell, and in the earlier years Dr. Trent Bollinger, autopsied far too many wolves, but we learned about the accidents and injuries wolves sustain, and their diseases. Ian runs the Cooperative Wildlife Disease Centre at the Ontario Veterinary College, University of Guelph. He acts as an adviser on our drugging and handling techniques. To his students, laboratory technicians, and the staff of the post-mortem room, we appreciate your help.

In the early years we benefited from the genetics work of graduate student Debbie Smith and her supervisor, Dr. Robert Wayne, at the University of California. Sending blood that far proved to be impractical, so we switched to a laboratory closer to home, to Dr. Brad White at McMaster University, whose interpretations of laboratory results opened up our research in new directions. He and forensic technician Paul Wilson and graduate student Sonya Grewal teamed up with us in a continuing partnership to determine what species we have been studying.

Debbie Freeman of the Wildlands League has worked tirelessly to advise the public of the situation Algonquin Park wolves are in, and she does so with the support of Executive Director Tim Gray. Chris Lompart has represented the Federation of Ontario Naturalists. In recent years, Pete Ewins of WWF has taken a management role over our research relationships with WWF. Lynn Gran, and formerly Mary Deacon, oversee WWF donations earmarked for us.

The veterinarians at the Pembroke Animal Hospital willingly answered late-night and weekend telephone calls and went to the clinic to receive our wolf blood, so essential to get spun and keep refrigerated for disease and genetics work: Drs. Stu Mark, Richard Hobart, and Guylaine Charette.

Media people – hosts and producers – have given our work excellent TV exposure and showed a particular interest in our research: Dr. David Suzuki and Caroline Underwood of the CBC's "The Nature of Things," Loren Miller then of TV Ontario, Peter Trueman on contract for TVO, and Janet Smith and Wayne Rostad of CBC's "On the Road Again."

At the University of Waterloo a number of administrators in the Office of Research have managed financial and business affairs, and we thank especially Liz Vinnicombe, Joan Hadley, and Colleen Richardson. Linda Youngblut, Mary Jane Bauer, and Vera Reeve in the School of Planning have provided years of assistance.

In the field, Jim and June Maika, who run Lakeside Variety Store in Bonnechere, extended a great deal of logistic help both to us and our students, from vehicle assistance to message reception. On the Achray road, Gerhardt Schinke and his family, who run Algonquin Portage Store, have played a similar role. On field excursions, Colin Fabian of Bonnechere and Tom Stephenson of Pembroke are always ready to go, and their skills in the bush have been most helpful, especially when the wolves took us to remote places in winter. Other people in the Round Lake area have befriended and helped us or our students, and we thank Delmar and Janet Royce, Ben Burchat, Barry Keetch, and Phil Davies.

We cannot name all the pilots who have flown for us, but want to acknowledge Pem Air as a company – pilots, mechanics, administrators. Officials of the company know our financial constraints and have flown at rates that really represent a donation to our research, and we thank owner Del O'Brien.

We thank Jenny and Michelle Theberge and Mark Lindstrom for comments on parts of the manuscript. Jonathan Webb, senior editor at McClelland & Stewart, provided many constructive suggestions and editorial comments that improved the manuscript.

Finally, Monte Hummel has stuck with us, pledging WWF financial support, furnishing moral support, and insisting in meetings with the MNR that our results be translated into conservation gains. Monte once taught at the University of Toronto with Doug Pimlott. Like Mary and me, he had his life rearranged by Doug's passionate regard for nature, his intolerance of government malaise, and his expectations of us. We hope, between the three of us, that Doug would approve.

BIBLIOGRAPHY

Included in this bibliography are some of the sources to which reference is made in the text. Our study of Algonquin Park has also given rise to a considerable body of published research, including articles, addresses to scientific meetings, and dissertations. These are listed as well.

General

Bakker, R. L. 1993. *The Dinosaur Heresies.* New York: Zebra Books, Kensington Publishing Corp.

Errington, P. L. 1967. *Of Predation and Life.* Ames, Iowa: Iowa State University Press.

Heinrich, B. 1989. *Ravens in Winter.* New York: Summit Books.

Theberge, J. B. 1989. "The future of the wolf: biology or bioethics?" *Seasons,* 29(1):15–20.

Theberge, J. B. 1992. "Wolves, Algonquin Park and the hierarchy of ecology." In *Island of Hope.* L. Labatt and B. Littlejohn (eds.). Willowdale, Ontario: Firefly Books, 247–256.

Theberge, J. B. 1994. "Why Fear the Wolf." *Equinox,* 73:4251.

Theberge, J. B., and M. T. Theberge. 1991. "Wolves and wolf research in Algonquin Park." Wolf Research Publication Series No. 1. Faculty of Environmental Studies, University of Waterloo, Waterloo, Ontario.

Theberge, J. B., and M. T. Theberge. 1993. "Adventures with Algonquin Wolves." Wolf Research Publication Series No. 2. Faculty of Environmental Studies, University of Waterloo, Waterloo, Ontario. 11 pp.

Wilson, E. O. 1975. *Sociobiology*. Cambridge, Massachusetts: Belnap Press.

Wynne-Edwards, V. C. 1962. *Animal Dispersion in Relation to Social Behaviour*. Edinburgh: Oliver and Boyd.

Scientific Articles

Baier, P., and D. R. McCullough. 1990. "Factors influencing white-tailed deer activity patterns and habitat use." *Wildlife Monographs*, 109:1–51.

Ballard, W. B., J. S. Whitman, and C. L. Gardner. 1987. "Ecology of an exploited wolf population in southcentral Alaska." *Wildlife Monographs*, 98:1–54.

Ballard, W. B., L. A. Ayers, S. G. Fancy, D. J. Reed, and M. A. Spindler. 1990. "Demography and movements of wolves in relation to the western arctic caribou herd of northwest Alaska." Alaska Department of Fish and Game, Research Report.

Barker, I. K., J. B. Theberge, P. S. Carman, and A. I. Wandeler. 1996. "Prevalence of antibody to canine parvovirus-2, infectious canine hepatitis, canine distemper and rabies in gray wolves (*Canis lupus*) from Algonquin Park, Ontario." Abstract. 45th Annual Conference of the Wildlife Disease Association, Fairbanks, Alaska.

Brown, W. K., and J. B. Theberge. 1990. "The effects of extreme snow-cover on feeding site selection by woodland caribou." *Journal of Wildlife Management*, 54:161–168.

Carbyn, L. N. 1982. "Coyote population fluctuations and spatial distribution in relation to wolf territories in Riding Mountain National Park, Manitoba." *The Canadian Field-Naturalist*, 96:176–183.

Carbyn, L. N., S. M. Oosenbrug, and D. W. Anions. 1993. "Wolves, bison, and the dynamics related to the Peace-Athabasca Delta in Canada's Wood Buffalo National Park." Circumpolar Research Series Number 4, Edmonton, Alberta.

Delgiudice, G. D., R. O. Peterson, and W. M. Samuel. 1997. "Trends of winter nutritional restriction of ticks and numbers of moose on Isle Royale." *Journal of Wildlife Management*, 61:895–903.

Forbes, G. J., and J. B. Theberge. 1992. "Importance of scavenging on moose by wolves in Algonquin Park, Ontario." *Alces*, 28:235–241.

Forbes, G. J., and J. B. Theberge. 1993. "Multiple landscape scales and winter distribution of moose, *Alces alces*, in a forest ecotone." *The Canadian Field-Naturalist*, 107:201–207.

Forbes, G. J., and J. B. Theberge. 1996. "Response by wolves to prey variation in central Ontario." *Canadian Journal of Zoology*, 74:1511–1520.

Forbes, G. J., and J. B. Theberge. 1996. "Cross-boundary management of Algonquin Park wolves." *Conservation Biology*, 10:1091–1097.

Forbes, G. J., and J. B. Theberge. 1996. "Influences of a migratory deer herd on wolf movements and mortality, in and near Algonquin Park, Ontario." In *Ecology and Conservation of Wolves in a Changing World*. Canadian Circumpolar Institute, Occasional Publication 35, Edmonton, Alberta, L. N. Carbyn, S. H. Fritts, and D. R. Seip (eds.). 303–314.

Fritts, S. H., and L. D. Mech. 1981. "Dynamics, movements, and feeding ecology of a newly protected wolf population in northwestern Minnesota." *Wildlife Monographs*, 80:1–79.

Gasaway, W. C., R. O. Stephenson, J. L. Davis, P. K. Shepherd, and O. E. Burns. 1983. "Interrelationships of wolves, prey and man in interior Alaska." *Wildlife Monographs*, 84:1–50.

Gauthier, D. A., and J. B. Theberge. 1987. "Wolf predation." In *Wild Furbearer Management and Conservation in North America*. M. Novak, J. A. Baker, M. E. Obbard, and B. Malloch (eds.). Ontario Ministry of Natural Resources, Toronto. 119–127.

Gese, E. M., and L. D. Mech. 1991. "Dispersal of wolves (*Canis lupus*) in northeastern Minnesota, 1969–1989." *Canadian Journal of Zoology*, 69:2946–2955.

Keith, L. B. 1983. "Population dynamics of wolves." In *Wolves in Canada and Alaska*. L. N. Carbyn (ed.). Canadian Wildlife Service Report Series 45, Ottawa, Ontario. 66–77.

Mech, L. D. 1977. "Productivity, mortality and population trends of wolves in northeastern Minnesota." *Journal of Mammalogy*, 58:559–574.

Mech, L. D., L. D. Frenzel, Jr., and P. Karns. 1971. "The effects of snow conditions on the vulnerability of white-tailed deer to wolf predation." In *Ecological Studies of the Timber Wolf in Northeastern Minnesota*. L. D. Mech and L. D. Frenzel (eds.). United States Department of Agriculture, Forest Service Research Paper NC-52. St. Paul, Minnesota. 35–51.

Messier, F. 1985. "Social organization, spatial distribution, and population density of wolves in relation to moose density." *Canadian Journal of Zoology*, 63:1068–1077.

Nelson, M. E., and L. D. Mech. 1981. "Deer social organization and wolf predation in northeastern Minnesota." *Wildlife Monographs*, 77:1–53.

Nelson, M. E., and L. D. Mech. 1986. "Relationship between snow depth and gray wolf predation on white-tailed deer." *Journal of Wildlife Management*, 50:471–474.

Nowak, R. M. 1995. "Another look at wolf taxonomy." In *Ecology and Conservation of Wolves in a Changing World*. L. N. Carbyn, S. H. Fritts, and D. R. Seip (eds.). Canadian Circumpolar Institute, Occasional Publication 35. Edmonton, Alberta. 375–397.

Parker, G. R. 1973. "Distribution and densities of wolves within barren-ground caribou range in northern mainland Canada." *Journal of Mammalogy*, 54:341–348.

Peterson, R. O., J. D. Woolington, and T. N. Bailey. 1984. "Wolves of the Kenai Peninsula, Alaska." *Wildlife Monographs*, 88:1–52.

Peterson, R. O., and R. E. Page. 1988. "The rise and fall of Isle Royale wolves, 1975-1986." *Journal of Mammalogy*, 69:89–99.

Pimlott, D. H., J. A. Shannon, and G. B. Kolenosky. 1969. "Ecology of the timber wolf in Algonquin Provincial Park." Ontario Department of Lands and Forests, Research Report 87. Toronto, Ontario.

Potvin, F. 1988. "Wolf movements and population dynamics in Papineau-Labelle reserve, Quebec." *Canadian Journal of Zoology*, 66:1266–1273.

Stephenson, R. O. and D. James. 1982. "Wolf movements and food habits in northwest Alaska." In *Wolves of the World: Perspectives of Behavior, Ecology, and Conservation*. F. H. Harrington and P. C. Paquet (eds.). Park Ridge, New Jersey: Noyes Data Corporation. 26–42.

Theberge, J. B. 1969. "Observations of wolves at a rendezvous site in Algonquin Park." *The Canadian Field-Naturalist*, 83:122–128.

Theberge. J. B. 1989. "Guidelines to drawing ecologically sound boundaries for national parks and nature reserves." *Environmental Management*, 13:695–702.

Theberge, J. B. 1990. "Potentials for misinterpreting impacts of wolf predation through prey:predator ratios." *Wildlife Society Bulletin,* 18:188–192.

Theberge, J. B. 1991. "Ecological classification, status, and management of the gray wolf, *Canis lupus,* in Canada." *The Canadian Field-Naturalist,* 105(4):459–463.

Theberge, J. B. 1992. "Concepts of conservation biology and boundary delineation in parks." In *Ecosystem Management of National Parks, Western Region.* Canadian Parks Service: Seminar Proceedings. J. D. Henry and B. Lieff (eds.). Faculty of Environmental Design, University of Calgary.

Theberge, J. B. 1993. "Ecology, conservation and protected areas in Canada." In *Parks and Protected Areas in Canada, Planning and Management.* P. Dearden and R. Rollins (eds.). Toronto: Oxford University Press, 137–153.

Theberge, J. B. 1993. "Parks – isolated patch or regional matrix." In *Ecosystem Management for Managers.* Canadian Parks Service National Workshop. S. Woodley (ed.). Heritage Resources Centre, University of Waterloo.

Theberge, J. B. 1995. "A faunal species approach to landscape linkages." Presented Second International Symposium on Science and the Management of Protected Areas, Halifax, Nova Scotia. May 1994. In *Ecosystem Monitoring and Protected Areas.* T. B. Herman, S. Bondrup-Nielsen, J. H. M. Willison, and N. W. P. Munro (eds.). Science and Protected Areas Association, Acadia University, Wolfville, Nova Scotia.

Theberge, J. B., and J. B. Falls. 1967. "Howling as a means of communication in timber wolves." *American Zoologist,* 7:331–338.

Theberge, J. B., S. Oosenbrug, and D. H. Pimlott. 1978. "Site and seasonal variation in the food of wolves in Algonquin Park, Ontario." *The Canadian Field-Naturalist,* 92:91–94.

Theberge, J. B., and D. A. Gauthier. 1985. "Models of wolf-ungulate relationships: when is wolf control justified." *Wildlife Society Bulletin,* 13:449–458.

Theberge, J. B., G. J. Forbes, I. K. Barker, and T. Bollinger. 1994. "Rabies in wolves of the Great Lakes Region." *Journal of Wildlife Diseases,* 30:563–566.

Theberge, J. B., M. T. Theberge, and G. Forbes. 1996. "What Algonquin Park wolf research has to instruct about recovery in the northeastern United States." In Wolves of America Conference Proceedings. Albany, New York, November 1996. Defenders of Wildlife, Washington, D.C., 34–40.

Theberge, M. T., J. B. Theberge, G. Forbes, and S. Stewart. 1996. "Is the Algonquin canid a wolf or a coyote?" In Wolves of America Conference Proceedings. Albany, New York, November 1996. Defenders of Wildlife, Washington, D.C., 208–211.

Wilson, P. J., S. Grewal, A. Sipek, J. B. Theberge, M. T. Theberge, and B. N. White. 1996. "A molecular-genetic estimate of the extent of wolf-coyote hybridization in the wolf population of Algonquin Park, Ontario." In Wolves of America Conference Proceedings. Albany, New York, November 1996. Defenders of Wildlife, Washington, D.C., 204–207.

Unpublished Conference Proceedings

Theberge, J. B., G. J. Forbes, M. T. Theberge, and S. J. Cook. 1995. "Does a 7500 km² park protect a wolf population?" Algonquin Research 1987 to present. Presented at Wolves and Humans Conference, Duluth, Minnesota.

Graduate Theses

Cook, S. J. 1996. Behaviour and conservation of winter populations of migratory wolves within and adjacent to Algonquin Provincial Park, Ontario. M.A. thesis, Faculty of Environmental Studies, University of Waterloo, Waterloo, Ontario.

Forbes, G. J. 1990. Moose winter habitat, and habitat disturbance in Algonquin Provincial Park. M.A. thesis, Faculty of Environmental Studies, University of Waterloo.

Forbes, G. J. 1994. Wolf-ungulate relationships in Algonquin Park, Ontario. Ph.D. thesis, Department of Geography, University of Waterloo.

Swanson, L. 1993. Migratory behaviour and management of a white-tailed deer herd in Algonquin Region, central Ontario. M.A. thesis, Faculty of Environmental Studies, University of Waterloo.

Undergraduate Theses

Atwell, L. 1996. Seasonal changes in the summer diet of wolves (*Canis lupus*) in Algonquin Park, Ontario. Department of Biology, University of Waterloo.

Grancock, A. 1998. Microsattelite analysis of two Laurentian Highland canid populations outside of Algonquin Provincial Park. Department of Biology, McMaster University.

Grewal, S. 1996. Genetic assessment of the wolf population in Algonquin Park. Department of Biology, McMaster University.

Hebblewhite, M. 1995. Habitat separation of white-tailed deer and moose, and the refuge hypothesis of *P. tenuis*, Algonquin Park, Ontario. Department of Biology, University of Guelph.

Norris, R. 1997. Spatial dynamics of a winter migratory wolf population: eastern Algonquin Provincial Park, 1990–1993. Department of Geography, University of Waterloo.

Poszig, D. 1998. Gray wolf responses to shifts of white-tailed deer adjacent to Algonquin Provincial Park, Ontario, Canada. University of Waterloo and Philipps-University of Marburg, Germany.

Stewart, S. 1996. Tooth and skull analysis of wolves (*Canis lupus*) from Algonquin Park, Ontario. Department of Geography, University of Waterloo.

Swanson, L. 1993. Differences in diet among wolf packs in Algonquin Park, Ontario. Department of Biology, University of Waterloo.

Vogel, H. 1990. Changes in numbers of white-tailed deer, Algonquin Park, Ontario. Department of Biology, University of Waterloo.

Wamberra, P. 1996. Correlates of body size in wolves (*Canis lupus*) in Algonquin Park, Ontario. Department of Geography, University of Waterloo.

INDEX